P9-DDR-400

AN AMERICAN SOCIAL WORKER IN ITALY

AN AMERICAN SOCIAL WORKER IN

by JEAN CHARNLEY

University of Minnesota Press, Minneapolis

Printed in the United States of America at the North Central Publishing Company, St. Paul

Library of Congress Catalog Card Number: 61-7941

PUBLISHED IN GREAT BRITAIN, INDIA, AND PAKISTAN BY THE OXFORD UNIVERSITY PRESS, LONDON, BOMBAY, AND KARACHI AND IN CANADA BY THOMAS ALLEN, LTD., TORONTO

TO MARY JO

IN EVER-SO-PARTIAL PAYMENT

Acknowledgments

TO EACH OF THESE PEOPLE I am grateful for their part in this book:

To Silvano Garofalo, known as "Guido" in the book, graduate student in Romance languages at the University of Minnesota, who was heroic in leading a none-too-apt student into "questa bella lingua."

To my family, Debby, Blair, and Mitch, who did the thousand generous things a family does to help a book-writing "lady of the house."

To Mary Jo Grathwol, supervisor at Children's Service, Inc., St. Paul, Minnesota, for seeing so surely in the carbon copies of the diary the book-to-be and for her careful and loving criticism as it was developing.

To C. Wilson Anderson, then executive secretary of Family and Children's Service in Minneapolis, Minnesota, for giving me leave to go to Italy, for struggling through my carbons and seeing something in them, and encouraging me with still more leave . . . this time to write one day a week while working for his agency.

To Paul M. Thompson, supervisor of the Children's Unit at Family and Children's Service, who for more than two years shouldered a part of my job so that I could write.

To Grace C. Mayberg, supervisor of the Consultation and Referral Unit at Family and Children's Service, for criticism par excellence.

Finally, to all my dear and anonymous friends and co-workers in Italy, who listened so intuitively with a third ear, who taught the teacher so patiently, and who showed flexibility and generosity far beyond the call of politeness or international amity.

JEAN CHARNLEY

AN AMERICAN SOCIAL WORKER IN ITALY

The Beginning

Now it is all over and past. I have been back at work at my agency for three months. The trunks have arrived and all the beautiful things we purchased in Italy are given away as gifts, hung on our walls or in our closets, or lovingly placed in jewelry boxes and desk drawers. The Italian adventure is over, but a hundred things keep it alive for me: the plunging ceramic horses over our fireplace . . . my co-worker of Italian descent who sometimes greets me in Italian in the morning so that that beautiful language comes to me like a nostalgic phrase from Respighi.

I am glad to be where I am, sitting at my desk in the Children's Unit of Family and Children's Service in Minneapolis, and I don't wish myself back in Rome. Not really. Perhaps occasionally for fleeting moments. But only as I might wistfully wish momentarily to be back in any other happy experience. Just for a moment. Until with a sudden flash I remember that no one can really have an experience twice. But when I am lonesome for the color of Rome, or the fragrance of Rome, or those odd, frightening, and sometimes comical experiences I had when I first began to practice my profession in a foreign tongue, I find it satisfying to retell my story. And I think it is a story Americans would like to hear — not just because of its "message" (though there is validity in that) but also because it is a remarkable and engrossing kind of adventure with the romance of a foreign setting, the baffling challenge of an impossible assignment, and the suspense of wondering what fantasy tomorrow will bring. The story has all this — all the color and comedy and tragedy that somehow became interwoven into a six months' assignment as a Fulbright grantee to practice social work in Rome.

The story properly began in 1952–1953 when my husband was a Fulbright lecturer on American journalism at the University of Florence. Our whole family was there and we quickly and happily attached ourselves to that unique city where history had been frozen in the Renaissance and where even a brand-new Florentine soon knows the charm of merging into an ancient setting. At first I felt I would never have enough of walking the streets and drinking in the beauty of the city. But after a while, as I walked, I began to be painfully aware of the beggars who held out their hands at every block – the faded, tired young woman who always clutched a pallid sleeping child in her arms, the man who begged me to buy his violets, for "if you do not, signora, what will my children eat on the morning of the birth of Christ?" I remember him so well perhaps because his was the first full Italian sentence that got through immediately. For so unprofessional a reason as this, I, a social worker, had bought his violets.

I thought about the beggars, the poverty, the little boys who were always on the streets doing jobs during weekday mornings. Why weren't they in school? The social worker within me began to wake up. I was working a few hours each day, writing a book on foster home placement of American children. But it was nearing the end of our stay before I really began to look at the squalor and beauty and warmth and tears of Italy with the questioning eyes of my profession.

Was the two-year-old who slept all day in her mother's arms really drugged? To whom could I, or an Italian citizen, protest? What of the children of the man who moved me to buy his violets? How did I feel about having learned later that under the violets he carried black market cigarettes? And what of those endless, ubiquitous lines of little boys and girls who walked down the streets two by two in their smocks . . . the boys in black sateen with stiff white collars and a flowing splash of red or blue ribbon at the chin, the girls in checked gingham, sometimes red, sometimes blue? Always the boys and girls separate, never mixed together, never laughing or noisy or naughty. Always a nun or two at beginning and end of the solemn little processions.

Were they orphans, as my maid had explained, or did Italians use the word "orphans" loosely, as do many Americans, to describe children whose living parents were unable to make a home for them? What did it do to them, this marching when they should be playing, this living with nuns instead of parents, this knowing only an institution for food and study and school and prayer? Some of the experts of my profession had written that this is the kind of life that makes schizophrenes; others said sociopaths; still others that it did different kinds of damage to different children. All agreed that this kind of living would produce emotionally damaged adults. So I looked closely at the marching children. "That tiny little girl with sad eyes," I said to myself. "What is happening to her right now? What will she become? Is her future as black as I think?"

I looked at the softly curling brown hair, the full rosy cheeks, and the eyes that watched her own brown sandals and never raised up to the blue Italian skies above her, never lifted high enough to glance at Michelangelo's mighty David that dominated the beautiful squares through which she walked. "How is it with you, little girl?" I asked myself. "Are you destined to become a sick adult? What can I, an American social worker, do for you, and for the little blonde who walks behind you, and for the tall, stooped girl who wears a patch over one eye?"

"Buon giorno," I said when she became aware of my eyes on her. She returned my greeting quickly and embarrassedly. It was a stupid thing to have done, greeting one child in a group of thirty. I had wanted to talk with her and so my greeting had popped out. But if I could have drawn her away from the group and taken her home to play in our garden with my children and fed her and put her to bed, I still could not have asked her what I wanted to know. You do not lightly ask a six-year-old how it feels not to remember her mother; or what it's like to sleep on a cot in a room with twenty other motherless girls; or what she thinks when she sees other little girls in ruffled dresses skipping down the street tugging at their fathers' hands, and their mothers there too, holding a little brother's hand. No, even in English I do not ask these questions of children with whom I work (though often they find ways to tell me with words or actions). But how could I help even one Italian child in the few weeks that we had left in Italy? And what could I do with or for or about them when I could speak so little of their language? Best to go back to your villetta now and write some more on your book about how to help the American children who don't have adequate parents. This is something you can do. And this I did do, until the very end of our Florence year. But at last I let some of the pain, some of the wanting to understand seep back into me, and I arranged for an interpreter and an appointment to visit an institution for children.

My interpreter had chosen an institution for delinquent boys. Only blurred memories of this visit come back now. First I saw the thirteenth-century monastery, with its massive vaulted ceilings, its vast stone steps that led up to the dormitories and down to the kitchen, and I felt the coldness and dampness that pervades all these magnificent, austere old palaces. The coldness in the unheated palaces and museums of Italy creates a depressing shiveringness that the American accustomed to central heating cannot imagine. I wore my boots and my Minnesota winter coat was buttoned up, and even so I was numb with cold as I walked through these rooms in which the boys studied, ate, and slept.

Sometimes I thought that Americans are soft and that Italians do not feel the cold as much as we. But I remember the infirmary where ten boys lay in their beds and a doctor wearing his white jacket and stethoscope over his overcoat bared the chest of a boy with a racking cough. The director said to the translator that the problem of colds and flu was bad. It was not, he assured us, entirely impossible to care for a sick boy adequately. But his staff was out with colds so much of the time, and there were so few adults for so many children . . .

I discovered by asking that all of these delinquents were being held for exactly one "crime": stealing food! A difficult problem for the administration was to get them to leave after a few years and go out to face again the uncertainty of how they would eat. I learned that there was just one room for parents to visit on Sunday afternoons — a very small room for what looked like about fifty boys. When I asked whether parents used the visiting privilege, the director did not know; but after he had inquired from several staff members he came back with the answer: "Yes, a few do, the first few years." I saw the shop where boys could learn to be printers. The equipment was good and the samples of the boys' work seemed excellent. I saw the play yard within the walled garden where fifty boys had to take all their outdoor recreation and I wanted to cry. All those big boys had less outdoor play space than our own two children had behind our garden wall on the other side of the city.

I saw these things and many more. But what good did it do me to know about what went on behind the walls of this lovely cold old monastery if I could not talk about it, or raise a voice in protest? I scolded myself for having gone to look, and I tried to push the thing out of my mind and lose myself again in the charm and beauty of life in Florence. I believe it is wrong for anyone to go behind closed doors to peer at human misery unless it is for the purpose of finding a way to do something about it. I had no business just looking into the lives of these unhappy children if I had no intention of trying to help them.

The weeks ahead went by quickly with school closing for our eight- and ten-year-olds, who learned to bow and curtsey to their teacher each morning almost automatically. My husband by now was as comfortable with the title "professore" as he used to be with "mister." And I could communicate in my ungrammatical way with the maid, the gardener, the shoemaker, and a policeman.

On our last night in Florence, our children came downstairs in robes and slippers ten minutes after we had put them to bed to beg us for one more drive through Florence. We yielded quickly — we too were having a little trouble saying good-by. Then our younger redhead, who had spent a good bit of his time mourning over lost hours at Camp Warren in northern Minnesota and his gang on Carroll Avenue in St. Paul, surprised us by saying, "It seems like a bad dream that we are leaving our beautiful little city forever tomorrow."

His father began to talk to him about how long forever is, and told him that if, years from now, he still valued this memory enough, he'd surely come back. And I added to this a favorite remark of my grandfather's: "Be careful what you want with all your heart and soul, because you're sure to get it!"

After we had put the children to bed for the second time, Mitch and I sat on the front steps enjoying the perfume of our garden and the soft Italian night. Our gardener, Gino, walked past and called out, "Felice notte!" Mitch had to translate for me: "Happy night." It was happy and sad all mixed up together.

We talked about Blair's remark and I asked, "I wonder when we can come back?" I had said "when" and not "if." Mitch said that in five years he would be able to ask for a sabbatical leave, and then . . . He imitated the Italian shrug we knew so well which always ends, "Chi sa?" (Who knows?)

I hoped aloud that it would be no longer than that. Maybe I knew then that if it happened again in five years it would not be enough just to live in Italy—that the next time I would have to try to do something for Italy's children. Or perhaps, looking back, I inserted this idea later.

Of one thing I'm sure. That is that between our leaving and our coming back again in January of 1958, I frequently found myself thinking about what one American social worker might be able to do to help Italy's children even a little.

II

It was September of 1956. The Fulbright application blank lay there on the table before me. The time had come to mold the dream of helping Italian children into a sound professional plan that a committee in Washington, and later another in Italy, would accept.

To apply for a grant to work abroad was a curious experience for me. There was a little of the sensation of sending in a two-rhyme jingle praising soap or soup or kitchen cleanser. It would take such exceptional good luck to win. The prize would be the chance to work in Italy. The feat would be finding a way to offer my professional services meaningfully. Almost at once, the similarity to a contest fell away and the solemnity of the task took over. I brought back to my mind the picture of the marching children in their identical smocks; I saw the boys in their institutional beds and heard again their racking coughs; I remembered once more my strange sensation at giving lire to a woman who begged for food for her drugged baby.

How could I, Jean Charnley, do something in a six months' period that could help these children even a little? First, I had really to believe that I could help. Otherwise, it would be wrong to fill out the sheet and sign my name. And then, the "how." How could I marshal what I had learned and used for the welfare of my American clients into a plan that would help Italian children? I remembered wryly that our consulting psychiatrist had once said that people in the helping professions had rescue complexes. I didn't deny it. My rescue complex was right on top as I struggled mentally for days with the problem of making the complex into what would sound like a reasonable program of professional activity to the Fulbright Commission.

I began with the fact that I had only six months in which to work if my application should be accepted. Mitch and I had come to the conclusion that we shouldn't be away from our jobs in Minneapolis for more than seven months, and so I had chosen to apply for a short-term Fulbright. For several days after I read the forms, I thought of and discarded courses of action until the night when, at my typewriter, I found one had taken shape in my mind. My proposal was based partly on humility. Because I was afraid that I would never learn enough Italian to teach or work directly with social workers, I asked for a research grant. I felt certain that I could trust my senses and my knowledge of children if I were to study them in their institutional settings. In the end I would write a book or a research report that would combine what I had seen in Italy with what I knew of separation anguish for children in America. Someone in Italy, I hoped, would translate my ideas so that they would reach the people there who were responsible for planning for the upbringing of parentless children.

Satisfied with my plan, I wrote it. And rewrote it. And rewrote it again until I thought it was as good as I could make it. And when my draft on yellow paper was as good as I could make it, I brought it to Mitch, who read it through carefully and liked it. (He liked everything about it except my spelling of "responsibility" and "accommodate." But this professor of journalism, in twenty years of marriage, had worked out a way of living with a social worker whose list of words she couldn't spell seemed never to disappear.)

We sealed it in the envelope, stamped it, and drove downtown to mail it at the post office. Things always seemed more completely mailed in that box in front of the post office. This mattered a lot to us as a family. We knew that Mitch could probably get his sabbatical leave, and he had a job he wanted to do in Italy. But for all four of us to go again, it took this grant for me.

As the mailbox clanged shut, the letter had ceased to be my carefully thought-out professional application, and turned into the rhyming jingle with which I might, with the most outrageous luck, win a coveted prize.

It was mailed, and Mitch and I slipped back into our jobs. We both remembered how we had waited for many months after his application five years earlier. We agreed that it was not good to expect to be accepted.

The first letter from the Fulbright office was not the wonderful kind that had come to Mitch: "We are pleased to inform you that you have been awarded . . ." I shall always remember how he met me that night at the door with a martini in each hand, saying, "Jeanie, drink to a year in Italy!"

My letter began with regrets that there were no suitable research grants available. "However . . ." "However" is a double-edged word. After something good, it usually dilutes the goodness. After something bad, it inserts hope. This "however" indicated that there were grants available for lecturers and if I would list the subjects that I felt I could teach in social work, my application would be given serious consideration.

That night at home Mitch and I reread the Fulbright catalog. I really would have to lecture in Italian. (I would have been more than a little challenged by the thought of teaching social work in English.) "I'm a practicing social worker, not a teacher," I protested. Mitch said that teaching was not something done only in a school. Supervision in social work was teaching, as was leading institutes at conferences of social workers.

"But in Italian!" I reminded him that in high school and college I had never dared go beyond the second year of any of the three languages I had tried to learn because I always felt flunks coming on. The thought that I should lecture in Italian was as frightening as contemplating lecturing in a medical school on metabolism.

"Sit down and take off your shoes," Mitch said. (It's always easier to get me to agree to anything with my shoes off.) Then he began to play the role that he had always played so well in our marriage. It's the "you can too do it" role. Twenty-one years before, he had been my major adviser when I was a student in the school of journalism. And through the years from time to time this comes back to both of us and in the end I almost hear myself saying, "All right, if you think I can, Mr. Charnley!" I don't want to give the impression that he says this lightly. For example, if I say, "I think I could learn to make homemade bread," or "type with all ten fingers," or "paint the bathroom," he's quite firmly negative.

So I was faced with another application blank, and this one had none of the charming challenge of the first, in which I tailored a dream into professional language. I listed the subjects in which I felt reasonably at home: casework with children, supervision of caseworkers and students, psychological and social development of the child, advanced casework. I described my intuitive approach to the Italian language, but followed with a promise that if I received a grant I would begin to study right away.

This second application I mailed in an ordinary box three blocks from home.

Within a short time a long-distance call from Mr. Francis A. Young, executive secretary of the Committee on International Exchange of Persons, reached me at my office. My application had been accepted in Washington and correspondence with Italy indicated that I should be receiving formal acceptance from there in a day or two. There were posts available in Milan, Bologna, and Rome. Did I have a preference?

Such magical names with such marvelous associations! In a flash, I pictured the Milan cathedral — that incredible monument in pure Gothic lace, and only a few miles away Lake Como. Commuting distance? Perhaps we could even live in one of those pastel villas that cling so precariously to a mountainside swooping down into the black-green lake. Oh, surely Milan would be wonderful. Bologna? This I knew less well, but wanted to know it better. I thought of its great university. I remembered its funny leaning towers, and the blocks and blocks of arcades so that you could walk forever outdoors in the rain and never get wet. I thought too that the phrase "alla Bolognese" after the name of anything to eat — spaghetti, veal, a dessert — was a guarantee of excellence. Certainly Bologna with the hills pressing in on the city limits would be marvelous.

But I heard myself saying, almost without hesitation, "Rome." Rome — that sprawling metropolis where ancient ruins and modern buildings are so perfectly wedded. Rome, the eternal city, city of flowers, fountains, music, and color. This was for us.

"Yes, Mr. Young," I heard myself saying, "We should prefer Rome."

Later I was professionally happy that I had chosen Rome because of the warmth and generosity of the people with whom I was to work. I suppose their equal could be found in other Italian cities, but I came to think of the good will of the Romans as an essential part of my success with a hard job.

The grant was to begin sometime shortly after the first of January. Now we were faced with getting ready.

Getting ready involved many things. The first was to tell the children. Debby, our fourteen-year-old, was overcome — for a few days her feet scarcely touched the floor. I remember how she took to singing an Italian song, once popular in America, that she hadn't sung for months: "Le scarpine che ballare, ballare . . ." (Shoes that set my feet a-dancing, dancing . . .).

Our twelve-year-old son, Blair, had quite an opposite response.

We had taken him to Italy five years before just at the age when nothing seems as important as your own gang, the newly formed Cub Scout troop, the first summer at camp. He had learned to write in Italy, too, and when he returned to America, his teacher had taken a jaundiced view of his "fine Italian hand" with the neatly crossed sevens. Though we remembered many things he had loved, and the "beautiful little city" he had wanted to see again, he tended to sum up Italy as a place with too many castles and museums. He greeted the news of our plan to go back dourly and told his father that he wished he were a milkman or a grocer or someone else who stayed put in a good city once he found it.

Mitch and I plunged into a flurry of getting ready to leave our jobs, renting our house, figuring and re-figuring the family budget. We had nine months. That really was enough for almost everything except my most important preparatory job — learning Italian.

The Fulbright Commission sent me the names of three of my predecessors in Italy. I was breathless, yet some of my anxiety lessened. Of the three names, only one was Italian, so it seemed likely that two American social workers had learned a way to use the language. Included were their addresses in America with the suggestion that I write and ask questions.

Those addresses were precious to me. They seemed a lifeline to reality as I worried, "What's it going to be like?"

III

I made a lot of waste motions trying to prepare for the challenging and none-too-clearly understood job ahead. It seemed to me that if I were to teach, I should begin gathering books, pamphlets, and outlines for courses as they are taught in schools of social work in America. I spent several pleasant but impractical evenings with my backdoor neighbor, a teacher of social work, drawing up a list of books for easy reference and poring over her outline of courses. Another kind of waste motion, I found, was the night school course on supervision I registered for.

Actually, I had had many years' experience as a supervisor of students and caseworkers and had developed enough firm opinions so that I had recently begun to plan a book on the subject. But somehow I had been unable to believe that teaching could be anything but standing up in a college classroom and following a careful outline on which students later are quizzed.

I had no way of knowing then, as I do now, that you can't take an American textbook or an outline for a course in casework, translate it into Italian, and use it in Italy. The words will translate well enough, even though I was later to struggle long and hard to find the appropriate Italian phrasing for as simple a term as "foster home." But if words can be forced, stretched, and bullied into translation, cultures cannot. So my efforts to learn how teachers do it in America were of little value to me when I began to work in Italy.

One thing I did was truly helpful. I found Guido Farnalla and began to have conversations with him.

Speaking Italian with Guido, an Italian-born graduate student at the University, began to build in me some sense of security that I could at least communicate once I found myself in Italy. He said at our last meeting, "I think they may find your verb forms a little unusual, but you can always make yourself understood." His prediction was accurate on both counts.

IV

There remained correspondence with former Fulbright grantees and with my astonishing future boss, Father F. Xavier de la Roche, to help me understand what was ahead.

First to arrive were photostatic copies of reports by two former grantees describing their accomplishments. I read the reports with a horrible fascination. They described Herculean assignments marked "accomplished." My question was whether they would have been assigned fewer than three full-time social workers in America.

The reports added a weighty straw to my burden of anxiety, and I had an impulse to call the whole thing off. Instead, I wrote to each of the ex-Fulbrighters, saying: "I'm scared. I do want to do it, but it seems impossible."

Within a few days their answers arrived — such full, generous answers that I felt safe in signing to arrive in Rome soon after January first to begin my six months' assignment.

Having signed the acceptance statement, I began to receive other materials from the State Department — instructions about passports and travel allowance, a welcome letter from the Fulbright Commission in Rome with instructions that I write the head of the New Roman School of Social Work, Father de la Roche. The name — surely not Italian — seemed to epitomize the foreignness of my assignment.

On June 4, I mailed a letter to Father de la Roche describing my limitations and my capacities and raising questions about the areas in which I could be expected to lecture — child welfare, supervision, or human development. I was assuming that I would write the lectures out, have them translated when I got to Italy, and learn to give them in Italian. I estimated that three one-hour lectures a week during a six months' period would be the equivalent of a fairly fat book. I was willing to try, but now I wanted to get a running start by writing some of the lectures while I was still in America.

Early in July, I found Father de la Roche's answer in the mail. It arrived when I was home alone; Mitch and the children were vacationing. I remember how eager and excited I was as I drew out three single-spaced typewritten pages, and then my astonished disappointment to find them in Italian. "You clever social worker," I thought angrily, knowing that Father knew English perfectly, "how you bring me face to face with my reality!"

With Mitch and Guido both out of town I had the choice of living with my curiosity until I saw Mitch or attempting to decipher the letter myself. I settled down alone that night with our big Italian-English dictionary and worked until long after midnight. I struggled with words I had known and used five years before. The fact that I couldn't recognize written words that I knew when they were spoken frightened me anew.

Sometimes I couldn't believe that Father's letter was really saying what it clearly said. For example, his plan seemed to be to have me teach a seminar in October. Didn't he know that my grant would end on August first? I finally abandoned it and went to bed.

But the next day I looked again at the letter and the string of words penciled between its lines, and I found that as rested eyes strung the beads of words together, they described an exciting program to which I could look forward.

I was to be assigned to three different agencies in Rome, all of which dealt with problems of needy children. All the agencies offered institutional care, and none had access to what, Father said, I had called "home helfers." (Homemakers, probably, but why did he use a word like "helfers"? If he was going to throw a third language into our correspondence, this was really going to be impossible!)

He suggested to my great delight that I should spend time in these agencies and at their institutions familiarizing myself with social workers and their work. After I felt sufficiently acquainted with them, I could begin, at a pace that seemed comfortable to me, to criticize, teach, and act as consultant.

Toward the middle of my stay, he hoped, I would be able, with my own knowledge of student supervision, to help social workers in the three agencies who were supervising students. (My American knowledge was to have been enriched by experimental supervision of several Italian students.)

The assignment went on and on . . . all good, solid, sensible uses of the time of a visiting "expert." I respected the intelligence of the man who had outlined the program. His plan seemed feasible, even though it was caught in a six months' time limit. I felt I could have comfortably and happily followed this program in English. But what I could do with it in Italian — chi sa?

I remembered wistfully that this was a far cry from my original wish to go back to Italy and do something about all those children growing up in institutions. But on the heels of this thought came the second — that there could be no more effective way to help the children than through working with agency heads, supervisors, and teachers in a school of social work. Almost all casework in

Italy must be entangled in the problems of the institutionalized child, I guessed.

If I needed further reassurance that this could truly be a way to help the children, it came soon in the form of a letter from the Fulbright office in Rome. The office had seen my first request to do research, as well as my second application for a lectureship. It would be entirely possible, they assured me, to do some of each and I must not feel as though I had been permanently forced to abandon my hope of getting to the children in institutions in Italy. There would be an opportunity for this too.

The assignment was a good and appropriate one. I was happy with it. All that remained was to follow the last paragraph of Father de la Roche's letter.

"Mi raccomando, cara signora, di imparare il più rapidamente possibile e il meglio possibile, l'italiano, perchè tutti i Suoi rapporti saranno con persone che non conoscono l'inglese e non potranno, vista la loro natura, essere fatti con l'interprete."

("I recommend, dear signora, that you learn Italian as rapidly and as well as possible, because all your relationships will be with persons who do not know English and because, given the nature of the relationships, it would be impossible to work with an interpreter.")

Now I had had it – all I was to know until I arrived in Rome. Now there remained only getting there.

V

The packing and the house leaving were quite easy. But there was a hard part. That was saying good-by to Blair. Blair's dislike of trading his eighth year at grade school for "a lot of crummy old castles" never wavered.

He was grumpy and his grumpiness zoomed when he heard the three of us practicing our Italian around the house. Close friends who had loved him since he was born solved the problem: He could live with them, finish the school year, and, on June 1, fly to Rome to join us. He snatched at the suggestion and from then on he too began to hum "Le scarpine che ballare . . ."

It was a rugged decision for his parents. How do you go about saying a four-and-a-half-month good-by to a thirteen-year-old son? And how do you push your heart down from your throat every time you think of a spindly redhead flying from Minnesota to Italy completely on his own?

We managed it. I guess Mitch and I could accept it because of the obvious good sense of the plan. I was reminded of the pain I have seen in parents when they have chosen foster home placement for their children. In the end they can bear it when it is right.

The day came when Blair and our friends stood on the ground and our plane soared away from the Minneapolis airport. The sunlight danced in Debby's red hair — exactly the color of Blair's. She wrinkled her nose. "Arrivederci, Minneapolis," she said. "Ciao, Roma!"

VI

From the date of our flight until I reported for work at the Fulbright Commission in Rome on February 5, less than three weeks passed. They were full weeks — crossing the Atlantic, stopping at Tangier and the Canary Islands, and docking at Naples to pick up our Volkswagen Microbus, the delightful eight-seater, which we had already paid for in Chicago.

By the second afternoon in Italy we were established in a pensione looking down on Via Veneto, Rome's fashionable international street. We telescoped our preparations for living in Rome into as short a period as possible and in ten days I felt ready to begin work.

We chose an apartment in a new building in the suburban Monte Sacro district. Climbing the eighty-one steps to get to our floor was rough, but a family council decided that the view was worth it. And we thought the rooftop terrace that ran the full length of the living room and dining room, level with the top boughs of the great Roman pines, was itself worth the 80,000 lire ($130) a month.

Acquaintances who lived four blocks from us in Minneapolis and who were to become our close friends in Rome had word of a miracle-working maid named Maria. We and Maria had our interview, liked each other, and began a happy relationship. For

Debby we found a tutor—a most attractive and cultured American Negro, Phi Beta Kappa, graduate of Haverford. Mr. Moses, who was studying ancient art in Rome, was willing to work six hours a week with Debby. Within a few days Debby was well into what was to be the most enriching educational experience of her life. Soon the unfamiliar language of the classroom floated through the apartment. Sometimes it was talk of isosceles triangles, sometimes molecules, but the part Mitch and I enjoyed most was hearing them read Shakespeare together. "I am Caesar!" Mr. Moses would proclaim in his rich baritone voice: Debby's high soprano responded, "I am Brutus!"

Settling in Rome was easy and comfortable. Five years before in Florence, it had seemed much harder. Now the two months' deposit of rent in advance (prescribed by Italian law) and the minute household inventory, counting every ashtray and coat hanger, were old stuff. And we got a special break. Our delightful landlady had worked for General Mark Clark during the war and spoke fluent English with what Debby called a Bronx accent. She did more than just help us get settled. She taught me where to shop, what to pay, what bus to take, what glove shop to use. She is the kind of Italian who expects people to be courteous and fair because they are American. She and her husband had so strong a preference for Americans that when we left Rome six months later they refused to interview some very solid sounding Britishers.

We had disembarked at Naples on January 28. By February 7, I had had two professional appointments to acquaint me with my work. Then meetings and the rush of names, places, facts, figures, and philosophies came at me at an overwhelming rate. After two confusing weeks I decided to sort out my thinking and my scattered notes in the way most typical of a social worker on a case. I began to make a progress record of my experiences—a case history of a job in Italy.

My background as a journalist led me to keep a carbon, and this I sent to my closest friend, Blair's "foster mother," who is a social worker in St. Paul. Partly this was to save me from letter writing.

She would want to know about my job and this was the easiest way to do it.

Writing the "diary," as Debby dubbed it, gave me a way of studying and integrating what I was learning. And it started this book. My friend in St. Paul wrote, "Jean, for goodness' sake, keep on with the diary. I have loaned it to Phil [her husband], two social workers, and my cleaning woman. They are all complaining bitterly that you are late with the third installment."

That letter planted the idea, though it was a long time germinating. But little by little, as the charm and pain so closely intermingled in my job in Italy kept finding expression, I knew that I was keeping a diary for a third purpose. This was an experience that I wanted to share with other Americans. And, almost a full year after I started it, I began the job in Minneapolis of going through the case history to rewrite it as a story.

A problem that made me stand still for several months had to do with my friends and co-workers in Italy. My feeling about most of them is one of deep affection, admiration, and respect. One can't watch them struggling against enormous odds in their planning for thousands of children, caught in the binding, ancient, unyielding structure of their own culture, without appreciating that these are heroic people.

But to tell the whole story as I saw it, I must now and then criticize both the culture and my friends, for no one can depict a culture or a person honestly without all the colorations. However unwillingly, I faced the risk of hurting some of those who reached out with generous hands to help me.

To soften this hurt, I have disguised people, schools, institutions, and organizations. I have Americanized or altered names. I have taken time, places, and people, cut them up like a jigsaw puzzle, and reassembled the pieces. Brought back together, I think, so that they form a true picture — as true as I can make it — of what happened during these six rich months in Italy.

THE DIARY

February 5

I HAD RECEIVED a call from the Fulbright Commission office asking whether I could keep an appointment with Signorina Scalzo, assistant to the executive director of the commission.

It was a golden day—one of those shining days of February's false spring that fortifies one for what Italians call "crazy March." The sun was streaming down and the city was alive with people going about with their coats wide open. I walked from the bus stop down Via 20 Settembre, past the flower stands. I passed the fountain with languid lions whose supercilious, simpering lips spew sedate little streams of water. (Travel writers often refer to the beautiful fountains of Rome. Sometime I'd like to read a travel article that describes the works of art that misfire.)

Because I was a few minutes early, I stopped at a shopwindow next door to the building in which the commission was housed. I stopped to look in at the outrageously beautiful crimson lingerie lavishly frosted in black lace and wondered who would wear it. A little girl of about eleven brushed past me staggering under her heavy burden of carnations. Their spicy fragrance filled the air I breathed. A wave of infatuation with Rome choked me.

I went inside, found the elevator, and discovered to my dismay that it was operated with a key. As I was ruefully looking at the long flight of stairs, a man approached with a bow and a key and let me into the elevator. He asked me what floor I wanted and when I said "quattro," he gently corrected me, "quarto," so that next time I would know enough to say "fourth" instead of "four." This episode seemed to exemplify the method by which a foreigner learns a new language. The Italians, almost without exception, are skillful and gracious language teachers. Their warmth in correcting never makes their foreign students feel stupid.

The Fulbright office buzzed with a duet of two languages — a secretary in one office was speaking English to an American while her co-worker beside her talked on the phone in fluid Italian. I stopped at the mailbox to pick up letters from friends, social work magazines to which I had subscribed, and, at the bottom, the first and greatly yearned for letter from Blair.

Just as I tore it open, I was told that Signorina Scalzo would see me. Past experience had taught me that Blair's letters were never more than three sentences long so I scanned it quickly as I walked down the hall. Because I was reading instead of looking where I was going, I walked straight into a man carrying stacks of papers. "Mi scusi, signore," I said. A bright moment — my automatic response had been in Italian, not English!

Signorina Scalzo was a handsome woman. She represented a type of elegant Italian that has no counterpart in America. Her grooming and selection of clothes produced an effect that had a little of the stylized, unreal, but stunning impact of a Vogue model photographed in an improbable pose. Many American women, I'm sure, strive hard to look like this. But, to my knowledge, only a little group of Italian women ever achieve it.

This meticulously wrought appearance, while it suggests a lack of warmth, doesn't mean that warmth doesn't exist. But it always made me feel as though my slip were showing, my fingernails dirty, my hat crooked. With women like Signorina Scalzo in Italy, I found that I had to discipline myself to fight off a feeling of dowdiness and to move out from concern about myself to seek the human warmth that usually lay beneath the precise exterior.

Our appointment lasted almost three hours — fairly typical, I was to learn, for appointments in Italy — and was interrupted in the Italian manner for tea which a little man in shirt sleeves and white apron brought on a tray from a nearby caffè. These coffee- and tea-serving men and boys appeared during virtually every business meeting in Italy. They always puzzled me because I was never certain whether it would be polite for me to offer to pay for my own tea.

Signorina Scalzo's orderly mind went to work deftly and surely on my problems. Housing, transportation, and an Italian tutor were our beginning.

As a Fulbright lecturer I would receive a maintenance allowance of 458,333 lire on the first of each month. My mathematical weakness made it impossible for me to turn this into the dollar equivalent, but Signorina Scalzo told me that this would be about $740. In addition, I was to receive a total of 156,250 lire ($250) for "incidental allowance" for the six months. This was to cover such additional expenses as necessary travel to other cities, rent of a typewriter, hiring of a tutor. In other fields, I noticed, the allowance might be used for laboratory equipment, microfilming, art supplies, or renting a "concert-type piano."

Signorina Scalzo told me next about others in Italy who had grants in social work. I was bothered by the fact that among the students there were none who had master's degrees in social work from American schools. This meant to me that students direct from college with no training in social work would be coming to Italy to learn how to do their first social work in Italian graduate schools and in an Italian culture. It seemed all wrong. It was as though an Englishman had decided to begin learning to write poetry in French. Possible, I suppose, but very odd.

I questioned Signorina Scalzo about why students were chosen who didn't know social work in America and she explained that the Fulbright Commission in America preferred to have vacancies filled by students rather than by lecturers because a student could live for so much less. Therefore, Italy had more than twice as many opportunities for students as for lecturers. Once a social worker had his master's degree in America, he no longer considered himself a student. It seemed to me that this system short-changed both the student and Italy. But, aware of my newness, I said no more about it at this time.

There was just one other American professional social worker on a Fulbright in Italy in 1958. She was lecturing in Milan. I never did meet her, although I longed to in the months when I tried to understand the Italian scene with my American eyes. I should have liked to profit from her experience, four months older than mine.

After a quick description of the current program, Signorina Scalzo began to share her knowledge of social work education in Italy. When I realized that it was her job to do this for people with dozens of different professional orientations, I became aware how skillfully she handled her challenging job.

These were the Italian schools of social work which she described:

The New Roman School of Social Work. This is the school of social work headed by Father de la Roche. Though Catholic in its thinking and orientation, it is not Vatican-dominated. Signorina Scalzo explained to me that I would need to get a sense of the fact that schools and agencies may call themselves Catholic when they are in no way related to the church. She described this school as a fine one. (Good news, for this was to be my school.)

The Italian School of Social Work. An excellent school of social work with headquarters in Milan. It is non-Catholic, non-political. It has many branches, but none in Rome.

The Bianchi School of Social Work. This school stands alone in another city without other branches. It had a curious history. Several years ago it asked the Fulbright Commission to provide it with an experienced teacher of casework from America because it wanted to set up an Italian school that would follow as exactly as possible the American pattern. A brilliant American woman named Mary Rollins came and spent two years doing exactly this. She and the Bianchi faculty produced what may have been the best school of social work in Italy. Then came intrigue which resulted in Miss Rollins' return to America feeling deeply embittered. Forces which Signorina Scalzo said she did not understand—sometimes called Communist, sometimes socialist, sometimes religious—were said to have infiltrated effectively, flushing out the best of the school's faculty, including Miss Rollins. Now, rumor had it, the Bianchi School was an inadequate school indeed. It no longer asked the commission for Fulbrighters. Fascinated, I asked more questions. Signorina Scalzo said, "To really know and understand, to sort rumor and prejudice from truth in situations like these in Italy, would become a life's work. All we really know is that things are different and no one is asking our help. We have so much more to do than we can that we leave it at that."

The School of the Holy Spirit. This is the church-dominated school that blends the philosophy of Vatican thinking and social work practice. It is exceedingly poor as a school and is held in very low esteem by agencies and other schools of social work in Italy. Even most of the clergy reject its graduates. In expressing these attitudes, Signorina Scalzo illustrated an aspect of Italian Catholic thinking that is baffling to most Americans. Intelligent, "good" Catholics in Italy are perfectly comfortable condemning many activities that stem from the Vatican. They love and revere "il papa," as they call the pope. In Signorina Scalzo, it seemed to me, I was listening to a dutiful daughter speak of her beloved father warmly but in words that clearly admitted: "Father is growing a little old and crotchety. We mustn't let him upset us with his quaint ideas."

The League School of Social Work. This, said Signoria Scalzo, is the best school of all. Its main office is in Rome but it has several branch schools throughout Italy. It is non-Catholic and non-political, and seems to have achieved the solidest faculty of any school in Italy. There is more status and job security for League graduates than for graduates of other schools.

As I heard of the many schools and their branches I asked how many schools of social work there were in Italy and learned to my astonishment that there were fifty-three. (The last time I heard, there were fifty-two in the United States.)

"Why so many?" I asked.

Signorina Scalzo told me that formal education for social work was just twelve years old in Italy. Italian women saw the work as challenging, interesting, and socially acceptable. There weren't many economic opportunities for educated women.

"But aren't they producing more graduates than the field can use?" I asked.

She agreed that they were. It was a very serious problem. Rumor had it that fewer than a fifth of the graduates of the past year had found work.

Signorina Scalzo changed the subject to tell me some ingratiating anecdotes about Father de la Roche, who would be responsible for setting up the program I was to follow.

With great delicacy and discretion she prepared me for the man I was to meet in a few days. Descriptive adjectives that I extracted from her conversation were these: brilliant, urbane, sophisticated, iconoclastic, scholarly, bombastic.

I commented that a former Fulbrighter had told me that though Father impresses one as hard and even frightening, he has the capacity to be a very good friend. Signorina Scalzo agreed.

She called Father de la Roche on the phone and arranged an appointment for me two days later. She spoke to him in lively Italian, and though I listened hard, I caught only a phrase here and there.

February 7

AT SEVEN FIFTEEN this evening Mitch drove me to my appointment and let me off with plans to meet me at a caffè in two hours. The address was in a section of old Rome where the buildings were majestic, cold, and labyrinthine. I entered a great stone doorway and found myself in the typical ground-floor indoor court with two sets of stairs leading upwards. Five minutes of searching yielded no sign of a school of social work, so I walked to the far end of the court to the portiere's quarters. The window of his kitchen looked out onto the inner court and though I could see a steaming kettle on the stove, there seemed to be no one around. I knocked on the door, but no one came.

I had a moment of panic. It wasn't enough that I had to go present myself to this eccentric priest, I couldn't even find him. I would be late if I found him at all. As a social worker he would put psychological implications on my tardiness. I felt deserted, baffled, and frightened.

Finally a dark little man wheeled his bicycle into the court and leaned it near the portiere's door. I pulled my courage together and tried to explain my problem to him. Shades of Guido! He would not have been proud of his pupil. How do you say "wrong address"? I finally got the idea across, though the man's manner suggested that he was listening to a gibbering idiot. Yes, he was giving me a new address, but the words came to me in a meaningless jumble. I took out a paper and pencil and said, "Lo scriva, per favore." He wrote the new address down.

I went out into the street and held the paper up to the light of a shopwindow. It was written in that funny Italian script that is totally illegible to me. But, I reasoned, though I couldn't read it, an Italian could. I stopped an elderly man, showed him the paper, and asked "Dove?" (Where?)

He spoke lovely clear Italian, slowed up nicely for my inexpert ears. Graciously he walked to a corner and with eloquent gesture showed me that the sign was that on the paper. I had only to walk down to 137B. The warmth of my thanks, I could tell, surprised him! I hurried along the street almost happily. I would be only ten minutes late and surely it would be acceptable to say, "You see, I was given an incorrect address."

At 137B I found again, of course, an old palace. With real confidence, I marched into the open court and straight up to the portiere asking the number of the New Roman School of Social Work. He shook his head. He had never heard of it. Surely the signora had made some mistake?

Yes, I groaned, I had made a mistake. But it was very important that I find the school right away. Could he help me? He scratched his head, paused, and yelled, "Ida!" A stout disheveled woman with a big baby on her hip came out and he explained my problem. She asked me voluble questions I couldn't answer, then went to the foot of the staircase and bellowed "Giorgio!" She must once have been an opera singer of powerful if not dulcet voice, I decided. Giorgio looked twenty-one and seemed to weigh about eighty pounds. The man and woman explained my problem to him as though he would surely have an answer. I glanced worriedly at my watch. Giorgio looked from me to them and back again.

"Scuola," I said hopelessly. "Scuola per gli assistenti sociali."

The light of understanding broke eloquently over his thin face. "Ah, sì, sì, sì, signora!" I was later to realize that the Italians have a special facial expression that means just that one thing: "At last, I understand!"

Giorgio would accompany me. I followed him at a trot down the street. Perhaps he thought it appropriate that I should follow him rather than walk beside him, but I had to walk faster and faster trying to keep up with him. Less than a block down the street he stopped and gestured: "Here it is!" Another palace with another first-floor open court. I was beginning to distrust these places. He read my mind, led me in, pointed to the lovely sign that said "New Roman School of Social Work." The number of the palace had been not 137B but 177A. I started for the elevator but he motioned me toward the stairs, explaining that the lift was broken. I don't know how he knew—maybe he was just playing the odds. Later I was to realize that half the elevators in old Roman palaces are broken.

He pointed up the staircase to a lighted door. "There," he said soothingly, "the school!" I thought I should tip him. But how much would be right? And how would I know one coin from the other in the dusky light? I reached into my purse and grabbed a random collection of little coins which I tried to give him. "Oh no, signora," he said and hurried off into the dark as I called my thanks after him.

By the time I had climbed the stairs and asked the receptionist for Father de la Roche, I felt I had expended as much energy as I usually put into two days of work.

Father de la Roche greeted me warmly in wonderfully clear English. He looked colorfully in keeping with the disquieting personality sketches I had been given. He was a tall, stout man whose brown friar-like robe stretched out over his stomach and fell in folds from it. The fringe of curly hair around his bald pate looked carefully disarranged, as if by a make-up artist. His thick, curly eyebrows, also disarranged, came to funny triangular peaks in the center. He usually held a cigarette in his mouth even while speaking, and ashes cascaded down the front of his cassock.

I remember thinking he looked neither Italian nor French, as his name suggested. He had a sandy coloring accentuated by faded blue eyes. I decided that he looked like my stereotype of an Irish Catholic priest one might meet at home.

Father de la Roche led me down the corridor past many small offices to his own. He chatted warmly and pleasantly and I found his English perfectly clear and nicely spiced with fresh little variations on our idioms that added both charm and flavor to what he was saying.

His office was small, crowded with chairs. His desk was a maze of papers, books, and small ashtrays stuffed to overflowing with cigarette butts. He told me that members of his faculty would be coming in to meet me and would join him in planning a program of activity for me soon, but that he and I could get started right away. He began to describe the agencies in Rome with which I would be working and his sentences were so tightly packed with vital information that I asked whether I might take notes. This pleased him, I think.

I wish I could bring back all the color and vigor of his speech. My notes focused primarily on the facts, which were astonishing enough in themselves. But I remember especially that I found it startling to hear a priest in his clerical robes use "hell" and "damn" almost like punctuation. His lively wit reinforced my feeling that he seemed like an American-Irish priest.

As he talked and I scribbled, five or six members of his faculty came in. Some stayed only a little while, others for an hour or more. All were women between thirty and forty. For the most part, they looked like any group of American social workers—rather good-looking, well-groomed women in tailored clothes. I was introduced to each of them, but most of their names and faces blurred together.

I do remember a woman in her early thirties – fast-speaking, severely handsome – who smoked as much as Father and I. She would talk to him at a violent pace, apparently feeling that communication with me was impossible. Later, he told me that she was brilliant, "his right arm," and that she taught casework almost as well as it was taught in America.

A very attractive woman who approached the sartorial perfection of Signorina Scalzo came in. She spoke a little English. Father told me that she had studied social work in America. When I asked, "Where?" she responded that she had spent six months studying in New York, Cleveland, Boston, Chicago, and "a few other places." It occurred to me that plans for foreigners were stupidly made. She could have learned something had she stayed in one place, but in moving around like that, all she could really do was to look at the veneer of social work.

At one point a short, stout woman came in who spoke to me in careful, musical Italian with the expectation that I would understand, and blissfully I found that I could. When others talked too fast she would call out firmly, "Piano! Piano!" and they would slow down for a few words and then race off again. Father referred to her several times as "signorina" and she patiently and firmly corrected him, "signora." When she was out of the room he told me fondly that she was "his left arm." I made a quick guess that Father had not liked to have his left arm get married. She was the only married woman I met that night, and in the months to come I met no more than three or four signoras in the field of social work. (Perhaps professional women of Italy are not encouraged to marry?)

One more faculty member stands out in my memory. She was a slim, fragile girl who looked about twenty-three. Her face was accented by heavy glasses. I had a feeling that I was seeing an anxiety-ridden woman. When we were alone, Father told me about her – "a lovely woman . . . really exquisite, but so unsure of herself!"

As Father continued his discussion, he switched now and then to Italian, which he spoke slowly with many colorful gestures. I wanted to weep. I could understand so much of the Italian around me, even the machine-gun tempo of "the right arm" at times, but not his. I suspected that I was hearing Italian with a French accent.

I took notes furiously. Surely this was a mental exercise to end all mental exercises . . . taking notes in English about information I was getting in Italian. Father eyed my notes from time to time and said firmly, "When you do not understand me, raise your right hand. Now, don't you lie to me!" Childhood memory of minding priests stirred in me and I found my right hand going up again and again.

Often it was one word that confused me. When I raised my hand, he would give me three or four paragraphs of English. I'm sure this grew boring for his faculty, for one by one they would look at their watches and leave.

The group voted Father down at the point when he happily presented a plan that I should assist the executive secretary of an agency in Rome with her intake screening process. When his whole faculty said firmly that this was not a good idea, he looked like Lionel Barrymore mumbling to himself when his plans were frustrated. I expected him to explode. But after a little squirming and sputtering, he bowed to the majority will.

I began wondering in this meeting — and was to wonder through my future contacts with the New Roman School — just how well these bright women and this eccentric, brilliant man worked out their interrelationships. This instance in which he yielded to them was one of the few I saw. He played his role of executive masterfully and without a speck of ambivalence.

The meeting was interrupted by the inevitable little man taking orders for coffee. It was eight thirty and it took real self-control on my part to fight back the impulse to ask for a large sandwich. My dislike of the vast quantity of sugar that half fills the Italian demitasse emboldened me to ask in Italian for "black coffee without sugar, please."

A murmur of pleasure arose from the group on hearing me speak Italian. I had momentarily overcome a block that was to plague me all my time in Italy. Like many Americans, I felt comfortable speaking Italian to people who knew no English, but I always felt stupid when I used bad Italian in front of someone who understood my language.

Father looked happy. He had wanted me to speak Italian and had urged me to "have courage." That evening and in many future evenings I discovered how hard it was to fight that will of iron.

I continued to scribble and to wonder anxiously whether what I was writing was accurate. I remember being stopped by the world "soldi" and I whispered quickly to the faculty member who had studied in America, "What is 'soldi'?" A look of merriment crossed her face. "Soldi" means money. I knew three other words for money, but not this one, and I thought it unfair for a language to allow so many synonyms.

After the faculty had left, Father told me about his dream of bringing a foster home placement program to Italy. (I had learned that there was none except for some very odd placements of babies with wet nurses in the rural areas.) He had felt that the opening fire from a propaganda gun should be shot at social workers and the Roman community in late October, at the Italian equivalent of the National Conference of Social Workers. He was "distraught" at the thought that I would not be there in October, but he hoped I would lend my "sophisticated imagination" to helping him and the heads of four other schools of social work to plot the strategy.

I told him that nothing would please me more. I had learned to my dismay that evening that ten per cent of all Italian children were predestined to spend the first sixteen or eighteen years of their lives in institutions. It seemed to me that foster home care was the avenue to salvation for these children, and I felt that any help I could give to attack this problem for even a very few children would be a most important contribution.

As I talked he burrowed among his papers and finally triumphantly came up with the one he was seeking. He explained that he believed that no one would pay any attention to the idea of foster family care because they would say that you could never persuade Italians to take in other people's children. So he and a young man whom he referred to as "my most excellent statistician" had made a design for a study. It was a questionnaire which would involve interviewing some eight hundred people in six or eight Italian cities to learn whether, if the Italian laws — which, as they stood, left a foster parent in an alarmingly unprotected legal position should the child be injured or should he damage someone else's property — were changed, and if an agency would pay "a modest stipend," and if, and if, and if . . .

I studied the questionnaire with mounting concern. The wording and planning seemed to me extremely naive, and many questions seemed to beg for negative answers. I asked him whether people whose doorbells were rung could really concern themselves with such a theoretical situation. "But, of course," he said, brushing my protest aside.

The questionnaire seemed to me to distill the essence of my problem in working with Father. It was intellectual, fancy, and perhaps the worst way to find out what he wanted to know. How to explain this?

My direct approach failed. I twisted to another approach. "But how costly to do it this way!"

The frustrated Lionel Barrymore look again. It was comical, appealing, and bumptious all at once. I struggled to steady the corners of my lips. "That's just it," he said. "It will cost a thousand dollars. And where in Italy can I find a thousand dollars? In America, you'd just write a letter to Mr. Ford or Mr. Rockefeller, and presto — five, ten, twenty thousand dollars for research."

He looked even more deprived than when he had spoken of other "handicaps," such as the fact that three or four of his faculty must share an office and I'd just have to find a spot to squeeze in somewhere. "How," he demanded, "is Italian social work to come of age without money for statistical studies to show the way?"

I commented that in America we had usually moved empirically toward social betterment and that the studies often came long after the changes had been achieved. He fidgeted. I was expressing a philosophy he didn't like. "All things are possible in America," he said.

I began to get a sense of Father's problem. He had begun life as a scholar and a series of circumstances had catapulted him into the strange and practical field of social work. Perhaps the scholar didn't warm to the vital, day-by-day steps needed to help troubled people with the basic necessities of life. He would be one who would not like social work to be described as an art. He wanted it to be a science. Poor Father de la Roche! Miniver Cheevy was born too late . . . Father de la Roche had been born too soon to be in a position to make the learned studies he wanted. I suggested that perhaps he would let me take a copy of his questionnaire home so that I could go over it. This pleased him. Perhaps this American woman did not, after all, completely scorn the scientific approach.

We had been alone for a long time now. Poor Mitch, drinking endless cups of caffè nero and probably unable to find the school if he had gone looking for me at the first wrong address! I gathered up the statistical study and my voluminous notes, stood up, and extended my hand.

"Father," I said, "it is late. I've kept you much too long!"

"Not at all," he said, really meaning it. (After all our appointment had lasted only three and a half hours.)

I found Mitch happily poring over a newspaper at the caffè. He had discovered that I had started out at the wrong address, but had felt more serenity than I about my ability to find the right one.

February 8

IT WAS NOT until after breakfast the next day that I felt up to facing the notes I had taken the night before. My funny scrawls reminded me of some baffling notes I had taken years before as a journalism student, when I had tried to "cover" my first speech.

It turned out to be a speech illustrated with slides and I had had to take my notes in the dark.

The comparison seemed apt. I had taken these notes in the double twilight of two languages. But when I began to work with them, the information I needed fell into reasonably good order. They seemed sensible . . . if only I were not mistranslating a vital word here and there.

There were three agencies in Rome in which I was to act as a consultant. All of them were engaged in planning shelter care for children.

The first agency was Italian Children's Service. It seemed to me most closely related to those American agencies that administer federal programs like Aid to Dependent Children. The rules under which it operated were referred to as "Italian law." These laws, drawn up during the Fascist regime, reflected in a positive sense the Fascist philosophy that the physical well-being of a nation's children is a source of power. Italian Children's Service seemed to be financed, like all other agencies, with some tax money, some church money, and some money bequeathed by "the rich."

The functions of ICS, as I shall call it, were many, varied, and confusing. The agency ran a group of "houses of maternity" which were set up in neighborhoods much as are settlement houses in America. (I never did get to visit one. This seems too bad, for I suspect that there are aspects of this kind of planning that America might profit by imitating.) In a house of maternity any woman of the neighborhood can get free obstetrical service, one large, well-balanced meal a day if she is pregnant, and day nursery care for her little children; they, in turn, can get at least one and maybe two hot meals a day. (The day nurseries are called nidi, "nests.")

The nests with their hot lunches provide one of Italy's only real answers to the stark poverty and starvation that is the most common cause for families being split up and children being sent to institutions. With children fed and cared for, the mother can work to help support them.

The houses of maternity by their very function, I was told, housed the essence of life's major experiences for much of the community. It was here that an unmarried girl would learn that she was indeed pregnant. It was here that a gaunt, hungry mother might learn that she was indeed to have another child. And as these women left the obstetrician's office, a social worker stood ready to talk with them at the precise "moment of crisis of their lives." I wondered what a social worker says to the woman who faces her thirteenth unwanted pregnancy in a land where birth control is illegal. What does one say to an unmarried mother who knows that economically it will be impossible for her to keep the child she is to bear and that she has almost no alternative to giving him up? And how does a social worker greet a woman after she has delivered her legitimate baby? "For seven months you have been allowed to eat one good meal a day here. Now that the baby is born, he may eat here, but there is no more food for you. There is no food, no 'relief department' for the hungry parents of Italy. Somehow, you must find a way to manage . . ."

For many years ICS had been run by doctors with various kinds of civil servants assisting, and these women of varying educations and backgrounds came to be called medical social workers. They were, of course, untrained in social work thinking, and they followed submissively the orders of the doctors. Finding a way to get trained social workers into ICS and its houses of maternity was one of the tasks that Italian social work had set for itself. The intrenched, vested interests of the "medical social workers" and their determination to preserve the conservative, medically inspired *status quo* of the agency presented a formidable challenge for young, newly educated social workers. It took a special kind of dedication to stay and propagandize and bore from within. When I asked Father what parts of the program the trained social workers were trying to change, he said that it was the job of social work to bring an awareness of the psychological necessities of parents and babies which at present were almost entirely overlooked.

ICS also had the job of deciding which mothers were adequate to give sound physical care with the financial assistance of the nest and the hot lunch. Those who failed were "persuaded" to send their children to institutions. They would not lose custody of their children and could take them home when they were financially able. But having seven children in seven institutions who get moved around in a large geographical area for a number of years is almost the same as losing custody. Parents literally do not always know where their children are. They can find out by asking, but what does it mean to a poor and hungry parent to have seven addresses of seven institutions scattered throughout a twenty-mile area? What does it mean when you are too poor to afford even a six-cent bus fare, and you haven't seen some of your children in five years? Besides, when you do go and say, "I am your mama, cara," the little ones cry hard and want to go with you and the nuns in charge become angry. What can you say if you do manage to get to one or two of your children on Christmas Day or Easter Sunday? For most parents it seems better to let those children become a cloudy memory. Don't the old women say that sometimes, when these children are grown, they seek out their parents? There are even stories of strong, healthy boys of eighteen who have found jobs and bought presents for their old parents. The Italian sun is warm and full of the fragrance of flowers. When you haven't had much to eat, it is easiest to sit in the sun and dream a pretty dream . . .

Another function of Italian Children's Service was to supervise the institutions. This meant that the social workers visited to bring more children and to plan for each child as he grew from one institution's age group to another. There were institutions where babies stayed from birth to about two and a half. Then it was time to move on to another that would keep children from two and a half to perhaps six. And another where they stayed from six to ten. And so on.

The social workers were busy moving children soon after their birthdays and finding new institutions that had room for one more. This was always hard, for though each Italian town was dotted with children's institutions, the number of children needing their care seemed to grow and grow. Like the nightmarish dream of the sorcerer's apprentice, I thought — except that in this dream, one was flooded by homeless children instead of buckets of water carried by brooms. The only way to stop it would be more jobs for fathers — jobs that would pay enough to feed large families — or birth control to meet the problem at the source. But in Italy one doesn't spend much time dwelling on birth control. Because of course, everybody said, it could never come to Italy!

In between the tragic uprootings and movements of children, the social workers try to catch their breath and find the time to gently educate the sisters who care for the children. "He misses his mother, Sister. Yes, you and I know that she is not a good woman, but Carlo needs to dream and pretend she is. We mustn't take that away from him." Or, "I don't think he's really feeble-minded, Sister. He's so very frightened by all this moving about. He needs to sit on your lap and be cuddled." The nuns are basically kind and gentle women expressing their love of God through caring for His children. But it requires so much patience for one little nun to care for so many children. And these social workers with their modern, fancy ideas . . . "Don't they realize how much energy it takes just to get the children fed and bedded down? Sit on my lap, indeed! When does she think I sit down? You have to sit down to have a lap. And how can I hold one child when twenty are needing it?"

The director of ICS was a warm, clever woman. Father had told me that she was a distinguished graduate of the New Roman School. In fact, as one of the first graduates, she had got her diploma in the early days before the school knew how to teach casework. (What in the world, I asked myself, does a school of social work teach before it knows how to teach casework?) Signorina Maria Mannini, this director of ICS, had written a "really distinguished thesis" on the subject of the damage done to children by the rhythmical moving from one institution to another.

ICS had the basic right to withdraw licenses from institutions whose violations of minimum standards were gross. On one occasion, Signorina Mannini did just that, to the surprise and admiration of the social work community. But, of course, this drastic solution had to arise from really extreme violations. Already in Italy there were institutions so crowded that two children slept in one narrow cot. Under these circumstances, one was slow to close institutions.

According to Father de la Roche, Signorina Mannini had that special gift of diplomacy that made it possible for her to educate the mother superiors to use new ideas of discipline without threatening their sense of autonomy. Real improvements had occurred in some of the ICS institutions because of her efforts. She worked especially hard at maintaining family ties for institutionalized children, and her efforts to help them get home for vacations at Easter and Christmas had resulted in some older children's finding places in their own homes – places which certainly would not have been held for them without the zealous work of Signorina Mannini in teaching the understandably dubious nuns about the values of family ties.

ICS had a third function which interested me greatly. It maintained a group of wet nurses to whom newborns were taken for the advantages of mother's milk. The doctors at the houses of maternity made the decision as to which baby should have mother's milk and which should begin his life in an institution. Babies of tuberculous parents, babies whose parents had had venereal disease, congenitally deformed babies, and premature babies were often chosen for wet nurses. The wet nurses usually lived in little communities about twenty to fifty miles from Rome. They were chosen by the doctors on just three criteria: (1) their milk supply was adequate; (2) they were free from venereal disease; (3) their husbands had not been incarcerated for serious crimes.

Father de la Roche had told me that these were ignorant women in impoverished hillside villages where only the meagerest of existences could be wrested from a dry and rocky soil. The children were absorbed into the brood of the wet nurse's own family; three, four, and even five years after placement a social worker might turn up, claim her agency's child and take him off to an institution. "Let me see," I could almost hear her saying to the wet nurse, "which of these is the Italian Children's Service child?" And then, for the thousandth time, there would occur one of those appalling separations that Italian children experience. The child would leave behind the little house in which he was reared, the woman who had suckled him, the children who had been his brothers and sisters. Sometimes he would be leaving kindness, goodness, and warmth. Other times he would be leaving an impoverished home in which he was "the strange one," so that only the terror of the unknown ahead of him could drive him to cling to this odd family relationship that a doctor in Rome had so casually set up for him. This, I realized, was Italy's only real experience with foster home placement. It was barbaric in its simplicity and naiveté. But it was a beginning, and on such a beginning it might be possible to build.

Father de la Roche had paused to let me feel my way into this strange social problem. He had said, "Perhaps you, as a stranger, could suggest two or three simple diagnostic criteria beyond the three odd ones the doctors have settled on to aid in the selection of these women. The social workers are powerless before the prestige of the medical profession, but if you, as a foreign expert, could hit on just a few things the doctor should inquire about beyond blood tests and milk supply, it would help."

The second agency in which I was to act as consultant was the Society for Assisting Needful Children, SANC. My point of contact at this agency was Italia Lombardo. Signorina Lombardo was also a graduate of the New Roman School, and when her name was mentioned Father de la Roche and his faculty fairly oozed approval. SANC concerned itself mainly with children over five. (I had the impression that ICS began with infants and ended its work at about their twelfth year. SANC seemed to carry through to nineteen or twenty.)

SANC worked hard to elevate its standards. It was trying slowly to replace old political appointees with graduates of schools of social work. It had achieved many good things. All its workers now made regular records of what they did for clients. (Nothing Father could have said would have shown me more graphically how truly social work was in its infancy in Italy.) It had a Child Guidance Clinic to which it could refer children. Father had added, "The Child Guidance Clinic seems to be doing nicely and doesn't need your help." (At last, something that I wasn't to do! It had a refreshing sound.) A brief question about the clinic disclosed that there was a terrifying sameness to its diagnoses. All the children referred to it seemed to be suffering from lack of love.

Father had envisioned my role at SANC as assisting Signorina Lombardo in the intake process. As the cases piled up on her desk she read and assigned them – give a child's parents 250 lire (40 cents) a day to feed him at home, find a new institutional setting for an "incorrigible" child, and so on. Father had seen me helping her make these decisions. As I was struggling with a flooding sense of my own inability to do this in a strange culture, his faculty unanimously vetoed his suggestion. I was grateful.

We had finally decided that I would help Signorina Lombardo with problems in supervision, supervision of both workers and students, and that I should act as a case consultant to make suggestions on especially hard cases.

I was delighted with this plan. Perhaps I really could help with this. I was also to help her with the strategy of "propaganda" to make the agency perform in a more professional manner.

The third agency to which I was assigned was called the Agency for Survivors of Workmen, the ASOW. To me this was the strangest of all. Because I got in so deep with my assignments at ICS and SANC, I never did get to work with ASOW. I describe it here only to illustrate how strange the structure of a foreign agency can be.

This agency was housed in a huge and prosperous heavy industry plant in northern Italy. Salaries of social workers, their offices, and the funds with which they worked were all furnished by the company. The social workers had no supervisor except a plant foreman whose primary interest was making the most convenient and economical plan for children whose fathers had been killed or had died of illness while employed by the company. Usually it was cheaper to pay for their care in an institution than to give the funds to the mothers of the children. So, if any complications arose, his decision was always to institutionalize. The social workers yearned for a supervisor who was a social worker and somehow managed to get a "secret" one, Signorina Sletto. Her existence was unknown to the company. Workers had to sneak their case histories out to her for supervision. Father thought that Signorina Sletto had a very hard job; and in his words, "Sometimes she would like to cry on your breast." My help to her would require several hours of commuting — sometimes by her, sometimes by me. Father also thought she might like me to do an in-service training program for her staff. It would probably take place at her house because I was to join Signorina Sletto in being a secret from ASOW. This suggestion came after three hours of conversation; I wondered with amusement what the National Association of Social Workers would think of two kinds of supervisor who functioned in secret outside an agency. I asked who paid Signorina Sletto's salary; the answer was lost in my notes and my bilingual struggle.

These were to be my three agencies. I was apparently to play multiple roles in each of them. If I had felt in America that I needed to be three people to do the assignments suggested to me, I now felt that I should be at least six.

Besides the descriptions of my three agencies, my notes had other interesting tidbits about social work in Italy:

Adoptions. Almost impossible in Italy because of the legal structure which goes back to early Roman law. The structure is rigid and hard to change. The laws that fight adoption provide that (1) adoptive parents must be fifty years old and childless; (2) even though an unmarried mother signs papers to surrender her child, she may always claim him later. There is no legal way to protect the adoptive parents. For these reasons, though Italy was full of orphans after the war, only about eight hundred could be sent to America. (I suspect they were abandonees.)

Alliances. This relationship, which is not illegal, makes it possible for a family to take in a child which may be adopted when the would-be parents reach their fiftieth birthdays. The child may not legally use their name nor may he inherit from them if they die before they are fifty. In the case of an alliance, natural parents may demand the right to visit and not infrequently have asserted their claim to the child in adolescence. Understandably, only a few very brave people turn to alliance as a method of getting a child.

Foster Family Placement. Except for the use of homes of wet nurses, this kind of work with children is virtually nonexistent in Italy. Father de la Roche and other social workers who have been to America dream of the day it will come. Among forces that conspire against it are laws of responsibility which mean that foster parents can be fined and imprisoned for the destructive actions of the child or for its injury while in their care. Another problem is that deep-seated beliefs about "the heredity of behavior" in the Italian people make them fearful about how someone else's children will turn out. Still another problem is the class society. Italy has its poor and illiterate people (to whom the needy children are born) and its group of rich. Father had said, "Italy is like an army made up of generals and buck privates. There are no sergeants or lieutenants. We'd like to place the privates' children with people higher in rank than other privates, but lower than generals." I questioned this briefly. "Why not with their own class? Why not cross class lines? We do both in America."

His weariness began to show. "In America an office boy can grow up to be president of General Motors!" he said testily.

Another problem in the establishing of a foster home program is that school lasts only four hours a day. In this nation without Scout troops or playgrounds it is wearing to be constantly supervising someone else's child.

Father had made a puzzling statement that I was to hear over and over: "Italians love their own children, but cannot be bothered with other people's."

In this long interview I learned even more things than I was able to get into my notes. What I did get down was challenging, sobering, and no little alarming. But it was not so overwhelming that I questioned my being there. I found myself eager to get started on whatever part of the job I could break off and call my own. I knew that if I could accomplish one-tenth of what Father had suggested that night, I would have done a man-sized job.

February 12

AT TWO O'CLOCK the phone rang and Signorina Quinzi, the handsome faculty member from the New Roman School who spoke a little English, told me that at four thirty I was to meet the executives from my agencies. I shuddered at the lateness of the call—how easily she might have failed to reach me! (During this period of slow development of my work, Mitch, Debby, and I often went off for several hours of sightseeing.)

I had learned something about meetings in Italy. I knew I must eat a hearty snack before leaving home, and I knew enough of the problems of communication to be nervous.

Father de la Roche met me warmly and apologized because he had to catch a plane for Milan that night and therefore could be at the meeting only a few minutes. We met in what I gather was a classroom of the school—a room about thirty by thirty—where we all sat around a big table. On my left was Signorina Quinzi, who seemed to be chairman. On my right was an Italian girl who looked so young that I thought she certainly must be a student. Later, very slowly, I began to understand that the measures by which we judge women under forty in America seem not to apply in Italy. Although this girl looked to be sixteen, I suppose she may have been twenty-six.

As I sat chatting with Signorina Quinzi, the coffee man came and took his order; it was fully twenty minutes after the meeting had been called that its members began to appear. I was introduced to each, we shook hands, and I bravely said my "piacere" (a pleasure).

I recognized some of the members of the faculty whom I had met that first night. There was the firm "right hand," for example, and there was Father's "exquisite one." Where was the short "left arm," the one with the lovely slow, musical Italian? The "right arm," the woman of the machine-gun speech, sat near me and began a careful conversation. Was I liking Rome? Had I visited St. Peter's? She had heard I had lived in the beautiful city of Florence five years ago. Was I sorry not to be there again? Glory be to God for dappled things! I could understand her. I had the feeling that she seemed equally pleased and surprised to be conversing with me. I was working very hard. Father bustled in and out of the room carrying papers and shuffling through them in that funny disorganized manner that seemed to me to characterize his every movement and totally to deny his real personality. He smiled benignly at "the right arm" and me as he heard us speaking Italian.

"Ladies," he said, "do continue your light chatter. I'll join you presently." (Light chatter? My life's blood!)

A charming young girl in pigtails with bows at shoulder length approached me and spoke to me in smooth English. (Whoever invented the stereotype that Italians "speaka, drinka, eata"? I never heard one person in Italy do it.) "I have heard, signora, that you seek a tutor who is well versed in Italian, English, and the language of social work?" I agreed that this was so. "I have a dear friend who will teach you to speak very correctly because she has a degree in literature. She also is very clever about social work talking." I exchanged addresses and telephone numbers with her and learned that Signora Giorgiana Ugonio lived not too far from my house. I also learned that she was "with child" and that she would telephone me soon to let me know whether her husband would approve her becoming my teacher. When the girl left me, I was told that she was a student in the school and there had been a notice on the bulletin board to find a tutor for "l'Americana." And she really was seventeen. (Students tended to be around eighteen when they entered a school of social work. In America, students already have their bachelor's degrees. This was why I always felt as though I were in a high school when I saw the students.)

About forty-five minutes after the meeting was called, it appeared that we were all assembled. I felt at home in the group as I looked around. They really looked and acted much like American social workers — all except in their tardiness. That one resembled the head of Children's Service in St. Paul, and the faculty member beside her looked amazingly like my first teacher of casework. Was there a universal pattern of appearance for women in social work? But perhaps it was my fantasy reaching to make one thing in this situation seem familiar.

Father took his place near the door. I asked the girl on my right to list the names of those present and the agencies they represented. She did so in that mysterious Italian script — so lovely and so illegible to me. But Mitch would be able to read it and I could study it later.

Signorina Quinzi called the meeting to order. She was speaking very slowly and I could understand her. We had come together to meet Signora Charnley, who was a gifted and experienced social worker from America with only one wish — to be helpful to all the agencies present and to the school. They should talk over and decide tonight where I was to go first and how I was to get started.

A stoutish woman of forty-five began to talk in rapid Italian and when the others called out "Piano! Piano!" she merely caught her breath. I gave her that undivided attention that I think I hadn't used since I tried (in vain) to understand geometry. Her words — words I didn't even know — were getting through to me. She was giving me a case history and wanted help with her problem. As I understood paragraph upon paragraph of rapid Italian, I remembered that the Catholics in Italy speak of the miracle of the "gift of tongues" for which the Holy Ghost is especially responsible. It seemed unlikely that He would choose to enlighten a heathen like me, but perhaps in Italy, and for the salvation of Italian children, He might have crossed sectarian lines.

It was Signorina Maria Mannini, the director of Italian Children's Service, who was describing a case history that presented grave problems to her. It was the first case history I had heard in Italy and I listened fascinated to realize that, though parts of the problem were intrinsically Italian, many were as American as peanut butter.

Her client was a poor woman who had come to Rome years before from Sardinia. (Sardinians are often backward, uneducated, and primitive, I had been taught.) She had met an evil man of forty-five who seduced her. When she was pregnant she learned that he had three or four dead wives. After the birth of the baby, the man's twenty-five-year-old son of a former marriage came to visit, and he impregnated her for the second time. So she had one child by her husband and one by her stepson and they all lived on together; who was father of the third baby was anybody's guess.

Things went from bad to worse for "the poor little one" and she had many children placed in many institutions. She became so immoral that some of the children did not seem to belong to either of the men in the household. Some of her children she kept with her. She seemed to like her girl children a little better than her boy children. But there was one exception — a boy named Franco whom she seemed really to love. Franco was twelve and lived in a children's institution near Rome. ICS arranged for him to visit at home always for Christmas and Easter vacations, but his mother's home was so immoral that they decided to have him visit at the home of a nearby aunt. This maternal aunt was also somewhat immoral, but not so immoral as the mother. Franco was a problem child. He was very naughty and drove the nuns crazy because he would not mind even a little. Now, at twelve, he must either go home or move to a new institution. ICS had him studied at the Child Guidance Clinic, where the diagnosis was that "Franco is suffering from lack of love." What, asked Signorina Mannini, is ICS to decide? Should it send him on to another institution where he will continue to suffer from lack of love? Or should it try him at home with his immoral mother, or near to her with her "somewhat immoral" sister? Signorina Mannini repeated firmly that his mother really loved Franco.

I was so elated by understanding the case history and so interested in the problem that I was unaware for a while of the group pattern. Nobody except me was interested in Signorina's problem. The others were chatting together and Father was shuffling his papers, impatiently snuffing out cigarettes in an overflowing ashtray, and in general overplaying the role of impatient male.

Finally, before I could react aloud to the case history, he said irritably, "Signorina Mannini! Signora Charnley is to be with us only six months. She has a great deal to bring to all of us and we must find a way to use her time wisely. We must not take it up with easy situations like this. Even a totally inexperienced student would know that Franco cannot go back to such a home!" This seemed to me a real scolding. But Signorina Mannini was smilingly impervious to Father's remarks, though he did successfully interrupt her story.

Father gathered up his papers, shook hands with me, made his adieux and left. Signorina Quinzi moved back deftly to chairing the meeting as he bustled out the door.

I was having my first puzzling experience in how to respond to a request for help that came at me at the wrong time and place. The problem of Franco was not an easy one. How does one weigh his being exposed for a few years to an immoral mother "who really loved him" against another five years of institutional living which could mean psychological death to this kind of fighting, "naughty" boy? Could one, in Italy, help Franco and his mother, through concerted casework, to live together in a way that would yield Franco the emotional satisfaction he so desperately needed? I had known Francos in America, but in America we could have used the half-way separation of the foster home plan.

I found myself involved in Franco's problem and wanted to talk more with Signorina Mannini about it, but that wasn't the time. After the meeting perhaps . . . but could I find the vocabulary? . . . and wasn't it foolhardy to presume to suggest a casework plan in a foreign culture? No, I could best help Franco by saying nothing until I knew more about the world in which he lived. I did wish, though, that I could get a word or two to Signorina Mannini to tell her that her questions were not naive, as Father had implied, that the best of American social workers would not have found the answers "easy ones suitable for an uneducated student."

I pulled my reluctant imagination away from Franco to focus on the faces around me. Another woman was talking — this one, the list of names told me, was Italia Lombardo, a supervisor at SANC. My first impressions of her remain sharp even though later I was to find her my closest professional friend in Italy.

Italia Lombardo looked very American. What was it that made me feel this? Not her sandy coloring, because I had years before given up the stereotype of Italy as a nation of black-eyed brunettes; not the casual but very attractive way she wore her tweedy skirt and bulky sweater. Probably it was the harassed look I had so often seen on woman executives trying to plan for so many desperate children with so little money available. That was it. Italia Lombardo looked like an anxious, overworked, over-burdened American social worker who was sensitive to the unmet needs of the children for whom she felt responsible.

Signorina Lombardo was outlining the problems she faced, the problems with which she hoped I would help. There was the problem of time and how best to use it. How did you advise a student, for example, how much time to give to parents, to the nuns, to the wet nurses who care for the children, to older brothers and sisters? "It's not simple, this problem of time," I said sympathetically. One faculty member responded with a bit of asperity, "We know it isn't simple, Signora Charnley."

The group joined in developing the problem. When fathers were imprisoned, somebody asked, where would workers find time to determine whether the mothers were fit to live with the children alone? "How much time does a worker have?" I asked and got the puzzling answer, "As little as is humanly possible."

I asked how large a social worker's caseload might be and got the incredible answer, "Two hundred children." I commented with the help of Signorina Quinzi that I was unable to help with the problem, but would they be interested to know that American studies had shown that wives and children of imprisoned men often did quite well together during the time that the husband was gone? American social workers had discovered that it was common for a mother to tell the children that the father had abandoned them rather than admit his imprisonment. Such a falsehood, however, could be destructive to a child.

Signorina Lombardo focused her lovely green eyes on me. This was helpful; this interested her. "Also in Italy," she said, "this is a problem. Some day you will need to explain why it is better to tell the children such a harsh truth." This was her gracious acceptance that we would be working together and that I would have things to tell her.

I realized as I listened that my invariable response was to try to keep children out of institutions. This was prejudice based on ignorance. Before I could really help with any case discussions, I must have a searching firsthand knowledge of what life was like for the institutionalized children of Italy.

Now with only a little help from Signorina Quinzi, I decided to try to express some ideas. (Strange how much easier it was to be brave about the language when Father was out of the room.)

I said that I would be wanting eventually to come to their agencies, to read their records and to help with problems they chose to bring to me. But first I must get better acquainted with their child-clients. I especially needed to know what life in the institutions was like. I could understand this only by observing it at first hand. Would it be possible for them to arrange for me to visit some institutions? I did not want to go like a casual visitor, but would like permission to sit with the children, to see them at their meals, in their classrooms, when they played. After I had visited a number of kinds of institutions — for girls and boys, for all ages of children — perhaps I would feel more secure about trying to apply my American knowledge to their problems with Italian children.

They greeted my request with surprise and, I thought, looks of real approval. My question set off such a hubbub of discussion that I was unable to understand more than phrases. I did catch the idea that the nuns would be threatened . . . it would be hardest to get in to see little illegitimate babies because the nuns are so secretive about them . . . should we show her the very worst, where there are two children in one cot? . . . how would she manage without a translator?

After they had discussed my request backward and forward, I suggested a plan of action. I would give them all my telephone number. I didn't understand Italian on the telephone well, but my husband or our maid could take down appointments and addresses. Perhaps they could tell the nuns that I was a visiting American who worked with children in America and I wanted to see whether groups of Italian children acted like groups of American children. This would not make them feel that I had come to criticize, but really just to learn. They should also tell the nuns I spoke "a brutal Italian" (this is the literal Italian idiom) and would not be talking with the sisters, I'd just be watching the children.

They were pleased with my stratagem, and said they thought visits could be arranged. I said that after I had visited a number of institutions, I could call on them at their agencies and they could decide how they wanted me to work for them.

They asked me when I would like to begin my visits, and I responded, "Tomorrow." They laughed heartily as though I had made quite a good joke—and of course I had in this country where it takes days of plotting to make a plan.

Gradually the group broke up. As each one left, she came up and shook hands with me with a pleasantry. They were happy I was here; they had always found American social workers helpful; my Italian was really much better than I knew. I tried to make polite small responses and wished I had one more hour ahead of me with Guido because anything polite I would try to say, such as "you are very kind," would meet vigorous denial. Much, much later I learned that this is a form of Italian courtesy. The effect on me was to make me feel that I had said something inappropriate.

Signorina Quinzi and I were the last to leave. She said that she felt we had accomplished a great deal. If I ran into problems I should feel free to telephone to her or Father de la Roche. Her English fell on hungry ears. "How lucky I am," I thought, "to know English really well and have the privilege of using it most of my life."

As she left me at the door, she said, "You must not worry about your Italian. Before long, you will be a great master of our language."

February 13

THIS WAS THE FIRST DAY in Italy that I truly felt as though I were going to begin to work. I had had to grow accustomed to three days with a quiet telephone and then a request that I keep an appointment two days later. I had learned five years before from Mitch's experience and the experiences of our many Fulbright friends that this is par for the Italian course. But I remember a feeling of discomfort. I was being paid. There was so much to be done. My puritan conscience heckled me, which was very unfair of it when there was nothing I could do about it.

Today the phone rang and rang. My tutor-to-be, Signora Giorgiana Ugonio, phoned and congratulated me because I spoke "such clear American." Her compliment seemed appropriate. Signora Ugonio was willing to come to our apartment three times a week until I confessed to the awful eighty-one steps. This made us decide that because of her pregnancy I should go to her house.

There were calls from the executives of "my two agencies," Signorina Mannini of ICS and Signorina Lombardo of SANC. Each of them explained that appointments had been set up for me at institutions for children. I understood them quite well despite the hazard of telephone communication. (Six months later talking on the telephone was still hard. I remained dependent on the clues in face and gesture that mark Italian conversation. I had to turn the telephone over to Mitch or Maria for instructions on how to find my way to agencies or children's institutions. I felt bad about this failure until Mitch reminded me with amusement that this was what I always had done at home too. Why should I be able to follow directions in Italian when I couldn't in English?)

The mail brought forms from the Fulbright office to be filled out and returned. I began to look about for an appointment calendar and this suddenly made me realize happily, "At last! I'm in business!"

In the evening some acquaintances from America who had a Fulbright grant in sociology invited us to their home. Among the guests was an elegant elderly woman named Sofia Picciano. Signora Picciano, I learned from my hostess, was a Milanese contessa, a widow, who now lived humbly in Rome and who supplemented her meager income by tutoring Americans.

I sat beside her for several hours and had a real feast asking questions about the Italian culture as it applied to the work I was about to begin. I have recorded this evening's conversation because it is an example of what can happen to anyone in a new culture who is seeking answers. Months later, as I painstakingly and unbelievingly found one thing after another that she had told me to be false, I was still struggling with the idea that surely it must have been I and not Signora Picciano who had been wrong.

Signora Picciano told me that she pitied me if I was to be working with nuns in Italy. They were harsh, unpleasant, sadistic women, very lazy and very proud (false). Many of them had had no more than five years of schooling (true). When I questioned why they should be so harsh when the nuns of America tend to be warm, gentle women, she said it was because most of them had grown up in orphanages and had not experienced the gentling love of their own parents (false). She added that now with times so good in Italy very few non-orphans were choosing the religious life (false). Years ago in Italy, Italians who became nuns or priests were third and fourth children in the family—girls, who, when they failed to marry, became nuns because the life of "just praying" appealed to them more than losing status by seeking a job (I never found out whether historically this was true or false).

Signora continued that I would see some pretty unpleasant behavior in women if I really succeeded in penetrating the convents (rarely true). The mother superiors were "absolute despots" who ruled their convents autocratically; no one, not even the pope, could interfere with them (partly true; apparently none of the Catholic male hierarchy could force a mother superior to change her rules, but the rules imposed were, for the most part, humane rules).

She said that the nuns were so harsh that I would find them unfit to be around children (false). The signora told me a story about some "lovely feminine American woman like yourself" who went into the orphanages trying to bring about certain small reforms. She had been appalled to find all the little children wearing black smocks. Her plea had been "Let the children have a little color in their lives. Let their smocks be pink or blue. Let them have some pretty little trinkets to brighten the rooms in which they sleep!" Signora Picciano reported that the nuns were furious at this frivolous suggestion and would have none of it (probably false; in visiting institutions, I found many children in black sateen smocks, but I found even more dressed in pretty colors.)

Signora told me about a certain institution for abandoned babies in Florence. I remembered the place because I had often walked to it five years before to look inside its open court at the marvelous Della Robbia ceramic wreaths and statuettes of cherubs. The signora told me that in one end of the open court, which is never locked at night, there is a huge wheel that turns under a little swinging door. A mother may slip in at night and in secrecy put her baby on the wheel and gently turn it so that the baby disappears beneath the swinging door. Thus, the nuns never see the mother of the baby they find on the wheel, and the mother never sees her baby again; nor could there be any way that a mother could later claim a specific baby as her own. (This "ghost story" is apparently true; a number of Italians told it to me.)

I asked Signora Picciano about what Father de la Roche had told me of the strange and constricting adoption laws of Italy and the law of penal responsibility that would make temporary foster parents jeopardize their own security if something happened to the child for whom they cared. She agreed that this was accurate. I remember that for perhaps a month I kept repeating questions about these laws to various informed Italians, hoping against hope that I had somehow misunderstood and that there was indeed a loophole that would let adoption really be one way of helping at least a few of these children out of institutional care.

There is no way now to count the hours that I put into working my way through the misconceptions that Signora Picciano had so firmly planted. I often wondered later why she had misinformed me. I have concluded that something in her life experience must have made her hostile toward nuns so that she needed to give me this frightening and inaccurate picture. Or was she hostile to me, or to Americans or Fulbrights, or what?

Many months later I shared my puzzlement with our hostess. She laughed and said, "My husband and I have also found her to be a gold mine of misinformation."

The Contessa Picciano stands in my mind as a kind of symbol of the wrong roads and false trails one may take in struggling to learn and understand the truth about a culture. I should have been more aware of this. I would not have been deeply surprised to hear that some American had totally, and perhaps innocently, misrepresented a part of our culture in trying to explain it to a foreigner. After all, we all suffer from distorted vision caused by the faulty glasses of our prejudices.

February 19

MITCH DROVE ME to Signorina Mannini's agency, Italian Children's Service. This was to be my first view of a social work agency and I was looking forward to it. ICS was located in a handsome new building that was a good example of recent Italian architecture—modern in plan and facilities, but comfortably housing statues, murals, and mosaics in its lobby and along its passages and staircases.

I opened the heavy, ornately carved wooden door and found myself in a long, wide, empty reception hall. I wandered down it looking from one unmarked door to another. Finally a woman who looked like a secretary came along and, when I asked, she led me to Signorina Mannini. We went through a series of unlabeled doors twisting and turning until at last we reached an office that Signorina Mannini was sharing with six other women. I was discovering that in Italy you have to have a fairly high IQ to find the people with whom you have appointments.

My apology for being ten minutes late surprised her. Now I understand why. To be ten minutes late for an appointment is in effect to be twenty minutes early.

Signorina Mannini introduced me to the women in her office and in several adjoining offices. In a spacious and elegant office a young man about thirty shook hands with me, welcomed me to Italy, and said that his agency was at my disposal. After we had left, Signorina told me that he was "the executive" and that he would like an appointment the following week to discuss "conditions of social welfare" with me. I asked her to arrange a time, but it never happened. Perhaps it was just as well, because when I mentioned my expectation of this appointment to Father de la Roche, he said, "The man is a political appointee and a fool. Refuse to waste your time with him!"

Signorina told me that she was going to take me to a children's institution. Since it was such a beautiful day, would I care to walk? I would indeed; and the beauty of that walk along the Tiber, with the awesome Castel Sant'Angelo ahead and the starkly white dome of St. Peter's off to the left, is still alive in my memory. We turned away from the river in a few blocks and, twisting and turning through increasingly narrow streets, found ourselves at the door of what appeared to be an old and dilapidated stone building. Inside, I discovered that we had merely gone through a gate into a garden so highly and firmly walled in ancient stone that I had mistaken the wall for a sturdy building. At the end of the garden was a small, battered house whose windows had been cracked and sealed and whose shutters had long since given up their original color and now hung at crazy angles. The garden in which the little house stood had a faintly neglected look, too. (A neglected garden in Italy—even in the poorest districts—is a rarity.)

Signorina knocked at the door of the little house, pointing out the brass name plate. It read "The Little Shelter of Santa Anita."

We entered the house through a small kitchen — ugly, cramped, and poor; but for all its lack of paint, I got a quick impression of immaculate cleanliness. A gray-haired woman furiously scouring a copper pot greeted Signorina warmly and went to find "la direttoressa."

The direttoressa was a gaunt wisp of a woman whose strangely ugly face was accented by a cast in one eye and an odd twist of a smile. She wore tattered widow's weeds. It was obvious that she and Signorina were very fond of one another, for only after a long affectionate greeting was I introduced. She spoke softly, explaining that since this was Ash Wednesday, the first day of Lent, "the most reverend father was saying the holy Mass and administering the blessed ashes to the children." Signorina looked disconcerted. "Are you Catholic?" she whispered. I responded that I was not but that, since I had been educated by nuns, I had an understanding of Ash Wednesday and other church customs. She looked relieved.

We walked into a room full of little girls. The sight struck me like a blow. I wondered then whether it would haunt me all my life. I don't know. Perhaps other sights I was to see blurred it somewhat, but the memory is still agonizing.

Along each of the four walls of the room was a simple wooden bench. In front of each bench was a large, heavy marble table that served, it seemed to me, almost to pin the twenty little girls on the benches against the walls. There they sat, a roomful of pretty children from two to four. Each child sat still with tiny hands clasped and looked at us with large and only faintly interested eyes. The dreadful part of the picture was the passive way they sat with quiet hands resting on the table and lusterless eyes. They seemed unaware of each other and they were almost completely still. Not a toy was in sight. Three young women in the middle of the room were supervising them—scarcely a job for one woman, I thought, so patient and motionless did they sit.

In a nearby room I could hear that special singsong drone that means in any culture a Catholic priest saying Mass. I was introduced to the women in charge and the children stirred a little. One little girl sneezed and a quick adult hand reached out to wipe her nose.

As the woman and Signorina whispered together, I looked more closely at the children. I remember feeling that they were like big, soft dolls, and very pretty dolls too. I saw many hair styles — carefully made long curls, fat glossy pigtails, and one small head with straight brown hair pulled back in a circular part and topped by a glorious big hair ribbon. Blondes, redheads, plump and skinny children, and only a few of the true brunettes that are the American stereotype of what Italian children look like. Care had been taken with their clothes, too — pretty dresses in pastel colors and not the uniforms I was to come to hate for the institutionalized children of Italy.

No, they weren't dressed all alike, nor did they look alike. But in the way they sat so still, without squirming or turning either to the children beside them or to the adults in the room, was a uniformity that seemed awful to me. A little girl of about four whimpered. Some impulse made me translate the look on her face, rightly or wrongly, to mean "feeble-minded." She looked straight at me. "Mama?" she asked, pointing at me. It was one of the most plaintive questions I had ever heard and my eyes smarted with tears. "Mama?" she repeated. To my shocked disbelief, the women laughed together. "Carola thinks the Americana is her mama!"

I went over to the child and touched a frail blue-white little hand. "No, darling, I am not your mama," I said.

The women turned their attention to me. They understood why I was here. I wanted to see the children and how they were cared for. One of them picked up the beautiful blonde child with the long curls. They brought her to me. I was told that she was "very beautiful and very intelligent. She was a good eater." The woman lifted her starched pink gingham skirt. "See what fine legs she has. Pinch them a little. What good muscle tone! We feed her very good food, signora. Go ahead, pinch her legs to see how healthy she is. So beautiful and healthy — and neither her mama nor her papa want her. Too bad!"

I was numbed with shock. This child was old enough to understand what they were saying. They brought me three or four others, all of whom remained passive while the woman handled them gently and tenderly but with a subtle lack of acknowledgment that they were human beings. I wanted to scream my protests. They brought me from another room a little girl not quite two — the only homely child I had seen. Signorina Mannini exclaimed at her "improvement." Oh, these women were proud of the way in which they had saved this little one. She came to them after a "terrible trauma" and she didn't know how to eat and the doctor had said, "She will, of course, die." But they had taken a spoon and hour after hour had drizzled warm milk down her throat until little by little she had chosen to begin to swallow. And now today for lunch she had eaten soup with pasta, an orange, milk, and cheese. They had worked this miracle in only two months. With unhesitating fingers the woman who held her pushed the baby's lips apart to show me proudly that she was getting new teeth.

I wanted to hold that baby — this little one who had once decided not to survive in a terrifying world. She had been seduced back into living by little trickles of warm milk. And for what was she to live? To be a silent good doll who sat prettily at a table with other children beside her, being stonily quiet because "the reverend father" was saying Mass?

I was afraid to speak. This much emotion interfered with thinking in either English or Italian. I reminded myself that this was my first experience and I had not come to hurt the feelings of well-meaning adults caught in a cultural trap they had not created. Finally I asked, "But why are they so quiet and good? Children of this age need to be noisy and run and jump about." Again they thought I had not understood. They were quiet so as not to disturb "the reverend father."

The women led me down the hall to see so that I would understand better. I looked into the little chapel ablaze with candles and garish with heavy gilt frames and boldly painted plaster statues, all set into a maze of velvet and gold cords and submerged in glorious fresh flowers. Did this besplendored room suggest heaven to the little girls?

The congregation was made up of three nuns, about five teen-agers in blue-checked smocks, and a dozen five-year-olds, "the old girls" of the Little Shelter of Santa Anita who, this year, as they approached their sixth birthdays, would be planned for by ICS.

I guessed that the teen-agers must have been from some nearby institution for adolescent girls who came to Santa Anita's to help. Now they began to lead the little ones up to the altar, where the priest sprinkled little handfuls of ashes on the tops of their heads. Why didn't he do it like an American priest, a neat little blob on the forehead easily washed off? Think of shampooing all those dolls with their long hair! (I hadn't learned then what I know now. That is, that regardless of ashes and such things, in Italy, one brushes hair in the winter but doesn't wash it until spring has surely arrived. Italians aren't foolish about this like the crazy Americans, who seem to beg for pneumonia by washing their hair in winter!)

I was dismayed when a woman made an adolescent give up her kneeling bench to me. I was urged to kneel; so kneel I did to listen to the Latin words meaning "Dust thou art and unto dust thou shall return!"

We went into the dormitories. Cribs were apparently used for all the children. About every sixth one had a wet mattress draped over the side to dry. I commented that I expected they had a problem with wet beds. (The Italian word for bed is "letto.") Though I could say "wet bed," I didn't know how to say "wet the bed." Signorina Mannini taught me that you say "peepee in letto." "Peepee" is an international word!

The word for enuresis (which sounds much like English) came into the conversation and Signorina assured me that until a child is three, he merely "peepees in letto" but after this, he is "enuretic."

I asked whether they had many enuretic children, having

learned that in America enuresis is an acute problem of institutionalized children of all ages. I was told that they had none because enuresis is so easy to cure. As a social worker who had struggled with foster mothers' wails through the years and who had sat through endless psychological and medical conferences that seemed never to yield anything really helpful in combating this problem, I was all ears. It was as though someone had said, "Cancer is so easy to cure." Of course, I quickly asked how.

Most children in Santa Anita's shelter slept dry by the time they were two. But nobody thought anything of it unless they slept wet after their third birthdays. Those who did constituted a very small minority. These children were drawn to the attention of the pediatrician who gave them vitamin B_1 and this, of course, cured them all! The only explanation for this "miracle" that I could think of was the power of positive thinking.

The impact of seeing these tragic children, coupled with the rush of astonishing information that was coming at me, made me uncertain about our closing conversation. This related to what would happen to the children when they reached age six. I think the direttoressa said that they then became Signorina Mannini's problem. Some who were illegitimate would go on to other institutions, some would go back to parents' homes. I had the impression that neglect of babies may have been the factor that had precipitated placement originally, but I couldn't be sure.

We walked back through the room of passive little girls and Signorina Mannini greeted each one with warmth and spontaneity that were real. (The sound of the droning priest was gone and we could now speak in normal voices.) Signorina Mannini had a quick way of greeting these children one by one with a word, a smile, or a gesture that made me think, "She is made of the same stuff as good American child welfare workers."

When we had left the Little Shelter of Santa Anita we walked together out into the brilliant February sunshine, so bright that we had to squint against it. She showed me the garden where the children played and, reading my mind, said, "They are not so good and quiet when they are outdoors playing with their balls and their dolls." She took out her handkerchief, wiped her eyes, and said, "It is very very sad, is it not, all these beautiful little girls who must live like this?"

I agreed fervently. I asked whether the Little Shelter was an example of "a good children's institution." She hesitated, choosing her words slowly. "It is never good that little children should live like this. Santa Anita is fortunate because the women who care for the children really love them and work hard to make them healthy. It suffers from a lack of money and too few adults to care for too many children. But it is rich in human warmth."

I asked about the direttoressa. Was she a social worker? Who paid her salary? She was not, I learned, a social worker. She was "a good woman who is a widow." As for her salary, nobody paid her. I learned that she lived in the Little Shelter and often worked fifteen hours a day, but she did it "to help the little girls."

Puzzled, I asked one more question. Was she some kind of nun? Signorina sighed at the problem of making me understand. "No, she is a widow with grown-up sons and grandchildren. Her work she does out of her own generosity."

Poor Signorina Mannini! What I couldn't tell her was that her Italian was clear enough to me. It was what lay behind it that made me distrust my ears. I had seen dedication in America, but never anything like this.

With the understanding I'd see her again soon, we parted, she to return to her agency, I to take the bus home. I walked heavily, feeling impervious to the sunshine and the beauty around me. They had no power to penetrate the gloom brought on by what I had seen.

I shivered, remembering again the words, "Pinch her little thigh, Signora Charnley, to see how firm the muscle tone is!" And I heard again the plaintive little cry that questioned "Mama?"

Ash Wednesday! The first day of Lent! The beginning of a period of sorrow and penitence. I had heard Catholics in America say, "I've got the Ash Wednesday blues." I wondered whether anyone had ever felt the Ash Wednesday blues as fully as I was feeling them that sunny day in Rome.

February 20

My second institution visit had been arranged by telephone with a Signorina Fortunata. I hadn't the least idea who she was. I had been home alone when she phoned and I thought I had agreed to meet her on a street corner near the Church of Santa Maria at ten o'clock.

The day began bleakly—I had been unable to shake the depression that had grown from yesterday's view of an institution. I didn't think I would recognize Signorina Fortunata, and my sample of her Italian on the telephone had convinced me that I wouldn't understand a word she said. The weather matched my mood with a steady, cold drizzle that soon penetrated my topcoat and gave me a pang of homesickness for a nice honestly cold Minnesota February day. What a fraud the temperature reading was!

Signorina Fortunata did look familiar. She was a softly pretty woman I had met the first evening in Father de la Roche's office. A member of his faculty, probably. She was extremely difficult to understand, and she lacked that sixth sense that let so many Italians understand me. We had a miserable time. I think she was as bothered by this failure as I, for she seemed to work hard at communicating with me. We had a long walk in the rain before she saw and hailed a taxi. I quickly got out my money. (I had learned that college professors' salaries often were as low as $40 a month.) She protested, and demanded to know why I thought I should pay. "Because it is more just," I said lamely, straining more for vocabulary than sense. She laughed spontaneously, and from then on we communicated a little better.

Our taxi drew up at a building very modern in styling that looked like a handsome small American hospital. The similarity continued as we went indoors. It was just that. A hospital for babies. But, and this was a dreadful thing to see, it was a hospital for healthy babies who lived as though they were sick babies. First I was introduced to the direttoressa, a handsome brunette of about forty who was an M.D. She spoke to me in what sounded like excellent French, but I urged her to return to Italian. Her Italian was fairly clear. She had one linguistic trick which was a wonderful help — she knew how to count in English. I always got lost in numbers.

She was most pleasant and gracious, very proud of her hospital, and very patient with my language problem. But in spite of all this, I took a quick, unexplainable dislike to her. The phrase "controlling woman" kept popping into my head, even though I couldn't for the life of me say why.

First she took me into an admitting room which contained the usual equipment of a pediatrician's office. She reached into a file and selected, apparently at random, a child's chart which she allowed me to look at briefly. The first sentence read, "The mother is dead and the father must work." She showed me records in which the child's weekly weight and length, daily bowel movements, food intake, and so on were all neatly charted. There was even a daily temperature chart. She pointed to a slight elevation in temperature for the first three days of the child's placement. She explained that this elevation occurred with nearly every child who came to the hospital. It was the child's response to a "change in environment." (I wondered whether American children showed this response to change in environment. I was glad I didn't know — that it was not in the American pattern to take the temperature of healthy children for years on end.)

Our first stop was at the isolation rooms where there were two recently admitted children in adjacent glass cubicles, each room big enough to house comfortably an immaculate crib, a bathinette, a basin with running water, and a low shelf with handsome, new looking toys on it. The baby in the first cubicle looked to be about eight months old. He was a peaked, solemn little boy who burst into tears when he saw us. The doctor rapped on the window and urged him in a loud, cheery voice not to cry. A door from his room opened into another where a nurse in uniform was diapering a tiny baby. The doctor indicated that we wanted to see this baby better and I expected the nurse to do the natural thing — pick up the baby and bring her to the window. Instead she wheeled the bathinette up to the window.

It was a beautiful, plump baby who looked at us through sleepy eyes. This little girl-child, who had been admitted ninety-six hours before, had at the very least been well fed. Both children were in isolation rooms where they would remain for twelve days to be certain that they were not bringing new germs into the institution. There would be a nurse on duty with them twenty-four hours a day. Usually one nurse would have four or five newcomers to look after. Yes, these two babies had both shown the typical temperature rise on admission.

I looked at the sterile cubicles and ached for these two. Why did I hate isolation for a baby? Babies at this age do not need other children for companions. They were getting amazingly close and, I gathered, expert attention. I eyed the cubicles again. That was it. Those cubicles looked like a place where you would be left for the last half hour on your way to surgery. There was no chair for the nurse to sit in. How could she hold a baby for his bottle, or rock him, or play with him?

There were, I think the doctor said, three nurses who took the twenty-four hour shift. I asked whether the same nurse stayed with a baby; the answer was "not often." Hesitantly I suggested that American doctors believe that it is not good for babies to be cared for by many different people. In the best American hospitals, we try to keep the same nurses in charge. She looked only mildly interested and said, "That would be hard to arrange."

Now in response to the doctor's suggestion, the nurse wheeled the sleepy little girl away and went through the door to the crying boy. He stopped crying when he saw her. "See," the doctor said as though to reassure me, "he was all right. Just lonesome."

I was glad to turn away from the boy and continue the tour. The heavy depression that was a hangover from yesterday's tour was intensifying.

Each room we visited was filled with excellent equipment, such as the best American hospital-schools might have. The laundry's shiny vats, the doctor said proudly, sterilized every garment in scalding steam.

We went into a kitchen where three nuns and some lay women

were preparing pranzo (the noon meal). This day the children would eat a thick meat-and-vegetable soup, bread, fresh apples, and milk – some in bottles with nipples, some in little cups. I was assured that the children ate very well and that the kitchen was managed by a fine dietitian.

Next we went into a classroom where a statue of the Virgin looked down on medical charts, a skeleton of a foetus, a huge celluloid ear, and a collection of anatomical drawings of babies. I saw the light. This was a training school for babies' nurses. They took a three-year course to earn their diplomas. Every student nurse who attended a baby was supervised by a graduate nurse.

We moved on through the upper floor where I saw the nurses' quarters – starkly neat and clean and somehow making me think of a nun's cell. I saw the student nurses, pretty girls in their early twenties, who wore uniforms in pink and white.

On and on we went through this handsome, marvelously equipped building seeing no more babies and not even hearing them cry. Apparently the soundproofing was excellent because on the third floor the doctor opened a heavy door and I found myself unhappily back in a long hall of glassed-in cubicles. Here the children were housed about three or four to a cubicle, assigned strictly according to their ages.

We started with the newborns, who had one student and one graduate nurse for each group of four. In vain I looked for the comfortable chair. I asked whether the babies were held when they had their bottles. The doctor gave me a sharp look, sensing my displeasure at her wonderfully efficient hospital.

"They are," she said, "when the nurses have time."

But I observed in the nurses very little handling of babies. Repeatedly, when we wanted to see babies, their cribs or bathinettes were wheeled to the windows. The cubicles were so glaringly clean that I half expected to see a nurse immerse her hands and arms in an antiseptic solution before touching a baby.

As we moved down the corridor the babies grew group by group a little bigger and older. Now we were approaching babies who had exchanged their white kimonos for checked gingham smocks

— red checks for the boys, blue for the girls. The cubicles were a little bigger too, to make room for excellent play equipment — scooters, playpens, little swings, and rocking horses. Children were being encouraged to support their weight by clinging to the nurses' fingers while they tried to take their first steps. My doctor guide called encouraging "bravos" through the glass compartment at the babies who tried to walk.

I knew that I was being depressed by the cold, sterilized quality of the setting and I kept reminding myself that babies really wouldn't mind this. It was just a silly whim. Or was it? These were joyless children. Something spontaneous and bouncy that bubbles up in most babies of this age was missing.

At one cubicle a nurse had put a baby who looked to be a little over a year old on a bathinette and was carefully and sternly cleaning his nose with cotton fluff. "Ah," I thought, "the rejecting nose wipe." (I used to teach young social workers how, by watching a mother when she wiped her child's nose, to learn a great deal about how the mother felt about both the child and dirt.)

My doctor guide had a disconcerting way of reading my disapproving thoughts. She rapped sharply on the glass window and called sternly, "Softly, when you clean a baby's nose!" (This was a graduate nurse. Three years of study had taught her all about germs — but not how to be gentle.)

On we walked past the cubicles with the handsome equipment and the unbelievably large complement of adults. The doctor proudly pointed out charming little gingham bags for the older children, names beautifully embroidered on them. Each bag contained a clean handkerchief, a tiny toothbrush, a little comb.

Now we were seeing children who were old enough to walk and have haircuts. Boys and girls had the same haircuts, very short and homely Dutch bobs. How un-Italian! (In Italy the hair styling for little girls seemed to me to have been as carefully chosen as that of their mothers.) But how sanitary and easy to shampoo!

I was taken into a glaringly white bathroom and saw the rows of little toilets just the right height for two-year-olds — no wooden or plastic seats, so the little bottoms would rest on the cold but sanitary porcelain. I saw row upon row of basins large enough for children to sit in, with ingenious and easily controlled overhead showers. "The babies are bathed once a day, at the very least," the doctor said. I wondered about showers for little ones. Didn't it frighten them? "They don't like it, at first," she agreed, "but after a while they get used to it." I recognized that I was being negativistic. In America we do not put little children under showers, therefore it is cruel to do it here. Perhaps they came to love it. I was trying to hide my critical responses from the doctor, but she was disconcertingly perceptive. I think she was also deeply puzzled that an American—a member of that nation that loved things nice and efficient and clean—should be critical of her efficient and spotless hospital.

I asked about toilet training and found at last something I could approve. It was begun at around eighteen months and was initiated by the impulse in the child to copy what he saw his little friends doing. Beyond a "bravo!" at a successful performance, no pressure was exerted on the children. It was unnecessary because the children taught each other so well.

We moved on into the playroom for the older children. This room was for the "good walkers." I would guess the children to be between two and a little beyond four. No child looked near the top limit of five.

The astonishingly high ratio of adults to children continued. What a relief, though, to see the children outside their glass cubicles! At one table a group of about five sat watching a little boy who washed a rubber doll in a basin of rich soap suds. He used a brush and scrubbed hard. "Bravo!" said the doctor. "Get your baby good and clean." Other children watched, but not with lively interest. There was no impulse to reach out and grab his equipment. There was no tugging and pulling at each other, no spontaneous smiling, laughing, or crying. A small thumb crept into a small mouth and a quick nurse's hand calmly extracted it. I asked then about thumb sucking, suddenly aware that I hadn't seen it even in the littler babies. I was told that sometimes it occurs before children are two, but "they outgrow it then."

At a table children were playing with bread dough much as American children play with clay. One little girl took a bite and submissively spat it out when a nurse held a hand under her chin.

In the playhouse a blond boy dusted solemnly with a huge feather duster. "Poor lamb," I thought, "where would he ever find dust in this place?" The doctor saw me eyeing the boy and whispered that he had an American father who had left him and returned to a wife and family in America. Every now and then he would write to learn how his son was. I asked whether someday the man would bring his son to America and she responded unmoralistically, "I don't think his American wife would like that."

"And his mother?" I asked.

"Abandoned," she answered.

I walked over to the child who went on with his dusting. I greeted him in Italian and he smiled back at me. I tried a "hi!" He went back to his dusting. It seemed sad to me that here was a little American boy who didn't know what "hi" meant.

We left the sunny, well-equipped playroom with the children who had everything and yet had nothing. A little girl grabbed the doctor around the legs and gave her a string of wooden beads. "Oh, thank you," she said, putting them on. "That's just what I was wanting." Her words were right. Her tone was wrong. She always talked in a very loud voice, perhaps because she so often called to them through glass walls. She seemed to me to have some of the false heartiness of a department store Santa Claus.

The woman puzzled me and I puzzled her. Her passionate attention to what is sanitary and medically sound was as much a religion for her as my belief that children have a basic right to warm, spontaneous, one-to-one relationships with a mother-person was to me. We were both, I decided, passionate women with causes whose causes lead in opposite directions and who get in each other's way.

I was full of questions that outstripped my vocabulary. I wanted especially to know whether these children didn't all become ill when they left the institution for a world that had in it even a normal amount of dust and germs. And I was haunted by a memory of what Margaret Ribble and other distinguished child psychiatrists said – that it had been demonstrated many times in many settings that healthy babies in places like this soon lose their appetites and begin to develop a wasting-away disease called murasmus. The cure for murasmus is to transfer the children to foster homes, where they experience the happy stimulation of being part of a family, germs and all. Before the cause for murasmus had been discovered the incidence of child mortality in these well-run hospital settings had been very high in America. I must learn the answer to this question at least.

The hospital had been in operation for seven years. The average population was just under sixty babies. There had been time for a good bit of turnover since most of the children did not arrive as newborns. "Have you ever had the sad experience of having a baby die while under your care?" I asked.

Just two, she said. Both were babies with congenital malformations that had necessitated surgery. Each child's death had been associated with the surgery. Why, I asked myself, was it different here? I couldn't even speculate about the answer then.

Signorina Fortunata and I left together. At times during the tour she had chatted with the doctor but almost never with me. I think she was puzzling over why the doctor and I could understand each other though she and I could not. Enunciating carefully, she asked me whether I had liked what I had seen. I said that I had not. It seemed wrong to me to keep healthy babies in hospitals and treat them as though they were sick babies. She agreed that "that place" (I had acted out my rejection of it by not learning its name) was "too cold and too sanitary."

"Santa Anita's is better," she said.

With some surprise I found myself agreeing. This sanitary place had wiped out briefly my memory of yesterday's big, passive dolls. That hadn't been good. But it was, as Signorina Fortunata had said, better than this.

February 21

MITCH DROVE ME to my third institution on this morning. The address took us straight out into the country just a few miles from our apartment. The sign at the entrance said, "San Francesco's Little Nest for Children." Mitch was late for an appointment downtown so I sent him on his way and began a block-long walk under a row of umbrella pines that led to what appeared to be a gentleman farmer's suburban home. The vegetable gardens that I passed, the chicken coops, the small barn all seemed done in miniature. The house, large for a family, was small for an institution, I thought. Everything about the grounds was charming despite the creeping neglect and poverty that marked it.

The door to the big house was opened by a tiny nun who listened to my explanation that I was the Americana, the social worker, who had come to observe the children. Apparently puzzled, she ushered me into a stiff, frigid little parlor and seated me on a faded red velvet chair.

The mother superior came in, shook hands pleasantly, and seemed to understand what I was saying. What was there about that brown-eyed, rosy-cheeked, plump face that made me think "peasant"?

She said that the children were about to have school. Would I care to attend? I would indeed.

I was taken into a classroom where twenty-seven little boys sat at desks in a classroom not unlike the classrooms of my childhood. The children, between three and six, were dressed alike in faded, patched, black sateen smocks worn over short trousers and sweaters. They wore short socks and scuffed, run-down-looking brown oxfords. Their little bare legs made me shiver — the usual American response to bare-legged children in winter, though to Italians it was as natural for boys and girls to have bare legs as bare faces.

The differences between these little boys and the children I had seen before came to me joyously. Here were squirmy, mischievous, lively, giggling children.

The tiny nun clapped her hands for attention and suggested

that each child stand beside his desk for the morning prayer. About three-fourths of them did as they were asked; but in the back of the room several remained on the floor and continued high-spiritedly running toy cars into each other. The mother superior and the little nun seemed indifferent to their noise. The children made the sign of the cross and began to say the "Ave Maria." One tiny boy who looked no more than two gazed around puzzledly. A third nun had come into the room. She stood behind the tiny one and guided his little hand in the sign of the cross and then taught him the praying position. The mother superior whispered gently to me that this boy was new yesterday.

Prayers finished, all the boys sat down, except a few wanderers and the noisiest players at the back of the room. The others looked to the little nun with happy alert faces. One little boy with violently crossed eyes began to fight with a larger youngster, trying to take some kind of paper away from him. The big boy pushed the cross-eyed one away. Cross-eyes began to flail hopelessly and angrily. The third nun left her small one, went to the boy, held his arms down, and whispered gently to him. When he relaxed and cried she gathered him into her arms and kissed him. Aware of my eyes on her, she seemed embarrassed, as though she thought perhaps I would disapprove.

The mother superior told the children that Sister Carla would tell them the story of the wine. They looked pleased. Nun number three left her comforted boy, went out and came back with a glass of ruby wine on an elegant little tray. I was given a chair and settled down happily to take in my first classroom lecture in Italy. It comes back to me like a little drama.

SISTER: "What is it that I hold in my hand?"

CHORUS OF CHILDREN: "Sister holds a glass of red wine!"

SISTER: "In the fall of the year the farmer harvests his ripe grapes. What does he use the grapes for?"

CHORUS OF CHILDREN: "To make wine!"

SISTER: "Is wine good?"

CHILDREN: "Wine is very good."

SISTER: "Is wine good for children?"

CHILDREN: "Yes, wine is good for children." (Shades of the W.C.T.U.!)

SISTER: "And how should little children take their wine?"

CHILDREN: "Children should take a little wine in a glass of water."

SISTER: "And what happens to us if we drink too much wine?"

CHILDREN: "It makes pains in our stomachs and our heads."

I thought to myself that this classroom was where I really belonged. This lovely, clear Italian was precisely at my level. Despite the damp chill of the unheated building I felt a glow. I could understand — and I was among happy children.

The lessons went on. Every child got a pretty scrap of colored construction paper to learn how to make little cups. The boys who had been playing on the floor moved to their desks and clamored for their favorite colors. Blue ran a poor second to red.

Some of the boys who had participated in the lesson about the wine looked a little uninterested and decided to get acquainted with me. A sweet-faced blond boy came up to ask me whether I had brought any candy. I told him I was sorry I had not. My accent interested them and they began to sense that I was unusual. One little boy discovered the leather buttons on my coat and he and a companion began to count them. Another child wanted to see how my purse opened and closed. The little nun interrupted her lesson on how to make paper cups long enough to ask, "You give your permission for the children to touch you, signora?" I quickly agreed, admiring her tactful question.

Questions began to spill out of my five new friends. When I couldn't understand them, I said, "Non parlo bene italiano." They looked astonished. An adult who didn't know how to talk very well! But it was more than evident to them that I didn't. In speaking to children in Italian, one uses the personal, informal "tu" form of pronoun and verb. In my struggle with learning the language, I hadn't bothered with this refinement. It seemed to children that I was addressing them as "sir" and "madam."

My five friends left me to go back to paper cups. I continued to watch admiringly the light-to-nonexistent discipline in the room.

Children who wanted to make cups made them. Others did whatever they chose, even if it was so noisy that the little teacher had to work hard to be heard above their voices.

The teacher clapped her hands lightly for attention — we would now go into the playroom, since it was too rainy to play outdoors. She led me to the mother superior, who suggested a tour of the institution. It was just what it had seemed — the somewhat rundown former home of a wealthy family. Its two bathrooms were upstairs and totally inappropriate for little boys — especially for twenty-seven little boys. One was trimmed in very scarred black marble!

I saw the stern little dormitory-like bedrooms and four beds with wet mattresses out to air. (Four wet beds out of twenty-seven . . . not bad.) The mother superior said philosophically that there are always some boys a little slower to learn than others. I looked at the covers. They seemed too light. I asked whether the children would be warm enough in their beds. "Oh yes," she said, "they often throw covers off voluntarily."

As the nun showed me about she said that they were very poor and sometimes worried about having enough to feed the children. The sisters' financial worries were great. The owner of the house wanted to sell it. If he should find a buyer, where would they and the children go?

She asked whether I had come to choose a child to take back to America with me. We had a linguistically puzzling encounter then in which I again described the reason for my visit. She seemed glad to have me, whatever my motivation.

As we moved back toward the stairway she showed me a little room with two beds. One was for a nun and the other for any child who was sick. I asked whether the children were often sick. She said that once they had a great problem when a new child brought in a disease and they all got speckles on their faces. I shuddered. Twenty-seven cases of measles and seven nuns to care for all of them. A "very generous" doctor always came to care for any child who was sick.

We moved back to the playroom. I saw an astonishing sight in what had once been the drawing room of the home. The children were playing a game much like Farmer in the Dell, and all except about three had chosen to join in.

The child who was the Farmer sang a long and complicated verse. I sat down to watch and listen. I heard five different children sing the solo, and every one did it beautifully, singing proudly and freely in clear and accurate voice. Except when I have heard carefully trained boy sopranos, I have never experienced such wonderful singing by children. When I commented, the mother superior denied the compliment in polite Italian fashion. All I could learn was that the nun who had taught the boys to sing had been transferred the preceding month to a branch of the order in another city. "The boys still sing well even though she is gone. Now they teach each other to sing well."

They played their game a long while, and the little teacher nun and her assistant joined hands and played with them. How very tired these women must be when night fell! I asked about the other four nuns, for I had been told there were seven. The mother superior said that they did the cooking and cleaning and helped the gardener. Someone had been very kind and had given them a washing machine to do the laundry, so that wasn't hard any more!

It was time for a new game. The nuns gave every boy a soft rubber ball and set up some portable wooden targets with colored bull's-eyes. The boys made up their own games. Some aimed at the targets; some at each other; and several made up a kind of kick-ball which is the most natural of all games in this soccer-playing nation.

The balls flew in all directions, hitting the children, the nuns, me, the moth-eaten old fern, and a gaudy picture of St. Francis feeding the birds. Nobody minded. The balls were soft.

I had been aware of an abnormal child back in the classroom, but now I had my first quiet chance to observe him. His face was mottled and purplish. His nose streamed steadily and terribly and he wore a plastic bib to catch the drippings. The three nuns were forever wiping his nose—gently and compassionately—and giving him reassuring little pats. He rode a gaily painted tricycle—the only toy in the whole institution that could have cost more than a dollar. He rode it proudly but poorly, constantly running into people, not maliciously, just inexpertly. He would get himself boxed in corners and couldn't figure how to back out. With complete fascination I watched boys no more than three or four years old help him back himself out. No other child apparently considered asking for a turn on the tricycle. All seemed to copy the nuns' gentle help to the boy. I asked the mother superior what was wrong with him; I think she said that he suffered from "retardation of the blood circulation" and that the doctor was trying to think of a way to help him. The doctor checked him every week.

As I sat there, I saw another bit of generosity. A little boy under three stood in the center of the floor crying silently. An older boy asked what was the matter. Hearing the answer, he went and got another ball for the small one.

As the game lost its interest, the children began to turn again to me. The first boy came up and ran his hands lovingly over my face, down my body, down my legs to my ankles. He gave them a little squeeze, and walked away. The hunger for love in that gesture was heartbreaking.

A chubby little boy climbed on my lap with a quick "You permit, signora?" and snuggled back, sitting content for perhaps fifteen minutes while he watched the boys play. Then, without ceremony, he slipped off and left me.

The children patted my hair, tugged lightly at the buttons on my coat, ran chubby hands down my nylons, and treated me almost as though I were a new big doll. The mother superior watched my face to see whether it was all right.

One little boy stood behind me with a hand on my shoulder and sucked his thumb. I asked the mother superior in sign language whether she had many thumb suckers. "Just that one right now," she said. "Usually he does it only when he hears music. It is all right for little children to suck their thumbs if the thumb is clean." Then she seemed to remember that I was a social worker and asked whether I agreed. I did, wholeheartedly.

A fight began at one end of the playroom. Immediately the little nun was between the boys and it seemed to me as though she was trying to arbitrate rather than just to stop the fighting. The boys walked off in opposite directions. (Italian boys — and men too — seem to fight with hands open rather than making fists, which little American boys do so naturally.)

The little nun came to tell me that there was "a great big red car outside." Perhaps it was waiting for me? I looked at my watch in astonishment. Three hours had passed! Yes, the car was for me. The mother superior went out with me and I introduced her to Mitch and Debby. She urged us to come in for coffee. Remembering their poverty and the cost of coffee, I quickly lied that we had another appointment.

One little boy had slipped out the door and looked at the car with wistful eyes. Then the little nun came out to whisper to the mother superior that the children had seen the car from the window and were begging to go for a ride. I went back in with her and a cheer went up from the boys as I reappeared. I made my first Italian speech. "Boys, today is cold and wet, and my husband has business. But someday when the sun is shining, someday when you have almost forgotten about it, we will make a surprise. We will come and take every one of you for a ride in our big car." I left them cheering.

When we drove away, Debby kept looking back at the one small boy who stood beside the mother superior waving us off. "I want that one in our family," said Debby. I did too. That one and every other one I had seen, even the sick little boy on the tricycle. I remembered the little nun asking whether I had come to choose a little boy. Was it really that easy?

I looked back at the sign, "San Francesco's Little Nest for Children." St. Francis of Assisi, saint of birds and beasts and gentleness — how well the sisters in his institution followed his example!

February 22

It was a cold, crisp, sunny day with an almost blindingly blue Italian sky when Mitch and I drove off to one of the hill towns south of Rome, the "Castelli Romani." The drive was lovely – over an excellent winding road that took us through the valleys of agricultural Italy where poppies and wheat and ruins shared the fields, up, up the mountainside to slopes where the crops grew poorer with each mile, while the flowers grew more brilliant and spectacular. The people too seemed different from the Romans. The women's clothes began to look more like costumes – long-skirted, simple black dresses cut on peasant lines, very handsome in their simplicity and honesty. Often the women balanced gleaming copper vases on their heads and their men walked behind them, pipes in mouth and switches in hand with which they tried in desultory fashion to hurry the fuzzy little donkeys half hidden under enormous burdens.

It was a twenty-five-mile drive before we reached the grand and elegant villa of the Contessa Ventrusi. The villa was a castle set on park-like grounds. There were many sub-buildings, mostly humble and unpretentious. I was lucky in finding quickly what I sought. The convent of San Giorgio was housed in what probably had once been the gatekeeper's house. I rang the enormous bell at the gate, a little startled to have shattered the quiet with such clamor. A man answered immediately and led me to the mother superior.

I took a deep breath and made my well-rehearsed speech – I could now do it quite well. "Good morning, Mother. I am the American social worker who has a great interest in observing Italian children. I hope that you have already received the telephone call of Signorina Mannini so that you are expecting me. I do not speak Italian very well. I hope that you have understood me."

She interrupted me before I finished. "You have spoken enough," she said kindly. I felt like a child excused from reciting the last verse of "The Star-Spangled Banner."

I can think of no American parallel to the Villa Ventrusi. Though I lack skill in making such estimates, I would guess that it took in two acres of ground. The land around the castle and the convent was disciplined into an incredibly beautiful park, complete with sturdy Renaissance statuary, fountains spurting water, elaborate rose gardens, shrubs trimmed and trained to form complicated pointed, curved, or squared-off arches. To me the most exciting part was the walk between long rows of camellia trees in full bloom – whites, pinks, yellows, and apricots of all blends and shades. When I exclaimed over them, the mother superior spoke of the great sorrow at the convent. It had snowed last night and the flowers had been nipped by frost. In three days most of them would be gone. "But God was good," the mother told me, "for in a few days the 'somethings' would be in bloom." She pointed them out – thick shiny green, almost waxy foliage with fat buds in them. I studied and I sniffed and she said their name over and over again; our impasse in understanding was harder for her to accept than for me.

Despite the splendor of the grounds, I was unprepared for what the winding, tree-sheltered path was leading us to – a swimming pool that made anything I had ever seen of the private pools of Hollywood stars seem like paltry things.

It was probably centuries old, but flawlessly preserved. I remember that it was done in gorgeous colored tiles to rival the beauty of the camellias in bloom. The intricate mosaic work, in the spirit of, but not exactly like, ancient Roman mosaics, depicted flamboyant fish of all sizes and colors. This, the mother superior explained proudly, was the pool of the contessa who owned the villa. She liked to have the girls of San Giorgio swim there. See, at the far end, the little shelf? That made it safe for the babies who were not tall enough for the deep parts.

As we walked back toward the convent, I asked many questions about the contessa. I'm not sure that I understood all the nun said, but she gestured toward the castle saying that this was where "the good contessa" lived. A widow and childless, she was very religious. She loved children and had given the building to the nuns so that there would be small ones living at the villa. No, the contessa was not there now. She spent much time at her other homes in Rome and Milan. Recently a great tragedy had befallen the contessa, and it appeared that she might be forced to sell the whole villa. She who had always been rich was suddenly poor. Until the villa was sold, the nuns and the children could live on, but no longer could the contessa give them money for food. The nuns worried and prayed. They had heard of another place where they might move but it was far away from the church, and surely I could understand how impossible it would be for the nuns and the children to be far away from church?

Each day and night they prayed that there would be enough food for the children. Now she was "lacking in courage" and when she heard of other children who needed shelter, she turned them away. She said this with deep guilt. She was a very worried nun.

The door of the convent was opened by a smiling, rosy-cheeked sister who led me into a parlor to ask whether I would like coffee, tea, or "a little liquore?" I said that I had just eaten. Her face fell. It was prepared. Remembering their poverty and guessing that tea was the least expensive of what she had offered, I quickly changed my mind. I would, after all, like tea. It was served exquisitely on a little tray with lacy linens and tiny cookies. The mother superior and the smiling nun watched me eat.

A third nun came in with an enormous bouquet of camellias. "We are poor," she said, "but we are rich in flowers." I was to take them home to help me remember the convent of San Giorgio.

After tea, we went to see the rest of the convent. I was beginning to be struck by the sameness of all institution dormitories. This place, having been built as a home, had bedrooms that with the tightest of squeezing would accommodate no more than about seven beds. One draped with white veiling was where a nun slept. The mother superior explained to me: In the night, the little ones called, "Mama!" Though she was not their mother, the nun answered, "Yes, dear," and took care of them. "Little children," said the mother, "especially at night, need to call someone 'Mama.'"

Children of all ages were mixed together in the rooms except in one room with five beds for the oldest girls. No nuns slept in this room. Even here, "seniors" had privileges!

My attention was drawn to the many beds that had large, expensive dolls on them. These were the gifts of the contessa who believed that every little girl must have a doll.

As we entered each room, the nun threw back the shutters to let that clean bright sunlight enter the room. The mountain fresh coldness that had felt so sharp and clean outdoors felt cruel inside. I looked at the bed covers. Oh, surely there were too few.

Haltingly I asked whether it was not cold in the rooms at night. I got the puzzled Italian response. "One is not cold when one is asleep." (This American was, and mourned for the electric blanket she had foolishly left in America.)

We went down the narrow winding staircase. (What a firetrap!) I entered a large dining room swarming with children and activity. The forty girls ranged, I guessed, from three to fifteen. The children were very busy setting the table, tying bibs on the small ones, following commands of one of the nuns. I asked whether there weren't more nuns. No—just these three; but the children were "very capable and could help themselves."

I was motioned into a chair, happy to be forgotten for the moment. The children, except for the very little ones, went unsmilingly about their work. The four tiny ones kept getting in the way. Repeatedly they were pushed to one side and scolded a little.

The impression I gained of the girls of Villa Ventrusi was that they were sad, beaten, submissive, excessively good children. No one passed me without an automatic "Scusi, signora," and one three-year-old who came up to finger my purse was pulled back sharply and told to ask her "permesso" of me.

I asked whether I might watch the children eat. There was a quick consultation and an agreement. I told the mother superior that I knew she was very busy and I wished she would forget that I was there.

But she was too polite for this. She continued to stand beside me and point out various things. She brought a tiny, homely girl to me who wasn't much over five and asked the child to do something. With vacant eyes fastened on a corner of the room, the girl recited a poem in a singsong drone. When I congratulated her, she shuffled listlessly away.

The girls kept sneaking glances at me, only to blush and turn away when I smiled back at them. The rosy-cheeked nun came in carrying a big kettle of soup. The children stood at attention behind the benches and said a long grace. The big girls brought the small soup bowls and the sister half filled them.

Medium-sized girls passed bread—one piece to each. Little girls got the very littlest girls seated on benches with bibs adjusted. All of this without confusion and almost without a sound. My eyes traveled up to the wall where I was shocked to see a large sign, "Silenzia!" Embarrassed, I looked away, hoping I hadn't been caught with my feelings showing.

As the mother superior signaled the children, all except the big ones began to eat. How silent they were, and how earnestly and hungrily they ate! The rosy-cheeked nun came in again with the big soup bowl and almost every little hand in the place extended a bowl for more soup; but there were seconds only for about ten. With inappropriate jolliness she held the kettle up to show that it was empty.

The big girls carried off the soup bowls and brought in the main course. The mother superior stopped a girl to show me what they were having. A piece of thin fried fish about two inches square, half an orange, a piece of bread. She pointed to the fish, then to her own head, saying, "The fish is very good for the brain." This . . . their main meal of the day!

In the silent room, I began to feel especially depressed. I tried to pretend that I hadn't seen the sign that called for "silenzia." "Why don't they talk to each other?" I asked the mother superior.

She looked embarrassed and urged the children to talk. They looked embarrassed, too; she urged and begged them to talk, and this made them tongue-tied. I was sorry I had raised the question. I heard her say to them, "The signora knows that all children have long tongues. Talk, chatter together!" But beyond a few timid whispers they made no sounds.

But I did become aware of one sound. A quiet kind of sobbing that grew louder and louder until it seemed to fill every corner of the room. The mother superior left my side, whispered to the crying child, patted her shoulder, and came back to be beside me. The sobbing quieted for a moment and then grew very loud again. Finally a girl who looked to be about thirteen gathered the crying, limp six- or seven-year-old up in her arms as though she were a baby, and staggering under the too great weight carried her out of the room and toward the stairway. Everybody seemed embarrassed.

With the silence and the quick eating, the paltry lunch was quickly completed. I was certain these children were still hungry. The mother superior explained to the children that I was an American, and where America was. We tried a little conversation back and forth, the children and I, and at some of my errors, I got a glimpse on a few faces of what looked like repressed mirth. I asked who was the latest girl to arrive. All hands pointed to the empty chair where the sobbing child had sat. They responded to me as though I were the teacher and this a lesson. When I asked who was the next newest, a pretty brunette got smilingly and proudly to her feet as though she were being honored.

I explained to them that I was a social worker in America and that I had come to visit their villa. I learned from polite response to my questions that they played tennis and swam in summer and that they were eager for summer to come.

The girls were not in uniform. I felt certain that they were in secondhand clothes—clothes neat and clean but faded and patched. Their shoes, always the quickest give-away of poverty, were almost falling off their feet.

I hated the poverty that made them dress so poorly. I was depressed by my conviction that they didn't have enough to eat. These were things the nuns couldn't help. But most of all, I objected to the sign that called for and obviously got silence.

There was a quality of submission, of broken wills, of hopelessness, that I found intolerable.

The nun who had produced the empty soup kettle suggested that the girls sing me a song. She sang loud, lustily, and tunelessly and the girls followed her apathetically. I could understand most of the words. "We are the girls of Villa Ventrusi. We work and play and pray together here. We have such happy times swimming and playing tennis. And when the good contessa comes with a smile on her lips and candies in her hands, then we thank God that we are the girls of Villa Ventrusi." (So much like camp songs I had sung at their age: "We are the girls from Camp Lakamaga . . .") A less enthusiastically sung group-song I had never heard.

Now we were all leaving the dining room. Little children were again in charge of the littlest children. Next size went to do the dishes. Next size would iron. Next size would mend. I was moved by the pride with which the nuns showed me an ancient Singer sewing machine.

I asked whether any of the girls had to study. Yes, three of the big ones studied an hour each evening. One was learning in school to be a secretary, one a dressmaker; I couldn't get the word for what the other was learning to be. (By upper class Italian standards, an hour's study was nothing. Children of this age probably would be studying four or five hours a day and their parents would be working with them hard in this country where a few failures might mean the end of a child's education.)

I wondered as I walked among the girls at their work what had been done to them to achieve such total submission. How were they punished? Food withheld? Extra tasks assigned? I sensed that some strong discipline must have existed, but what it was, I preferred not to know. I had never before seen such cowed children. Not once an open spontaneous smile. I ached for them.

I wondered too about where they had come from. Another institution, I supposed. And the little sobbing girl? What merited such soul-shaking mourning? Was it what she had left behind or the despair at what she saw ahead?

The mother superior was eager to please me. (The nuns always were. What did I represent to them? Someone who would report back to the agencies? Maybe a rich American who might send them money if I were pleased?) She asked whether I had liked what I saw. I groped for a diplomatic answer.

I was pleased that children could live in a place as beautiful as the villa, pleased at the swimming pool, the tennis courts, and the wonderful flowers. She nodded smilingly and then her face sobered. "It is a very hard thing, signora," she said. "It is not the hard work that matters. It is to want to give bread to the children and not to have enough. It is hard not to know where they will be six months from now."

The reality of bread and hard work was all these three nuns could hope for or ask, either for themselves or their children. This was the only view of life that they could have had out of their experience. How unfair I was to be critical because they were unable to give these children joy!

I left the villa with my huge bouquet of camellias, many good-bys, and a firm request to return in the springtime when the roses would be in bloom to see the villa at its loveliest.

How strange it must be, I thought, to play in an elaborate garden while dressed in rags, to swim in a pool fit for a princess while trying to forget the growing pain of hunger.

February 24

"OGGI E FESTA" is a frustrating sentence to the American visitor who is moving across Italy on a tight schedule. When followed by a frequently accompanying phrase, "anche domani," it is particularly grim news. (Today is a holiday . . . also tomorrow.)

Festas in Italy dot the calendar gaily and are a source of joy to the hard-working Italians. To an earnest American with either a job or sightseeing to do, they can be a source of despair. Banks, museums, travel agencies, grocery stores, bus lines, and sometimes even restaurants close down, regardless of the schedules of busy Americans.

Five years before, festas had been frustrating to our family. A part of our new acculturation was that we had stopped fussing and were learning to yield to them. Festas in Italy may be national holidays like Independence Day but are more likely to be the birthdays of saints. February contained two such consecutive days and so Mitch, Deb, and I decided to use them for travel time to visit a city north of Rome which we had not seen before. I had learned from Father de la Roche that there was an extremely interesting large institution in this city. He would write ahead asking his friend, Father Nicolo Vincelli, to make arrangements for me to visit at nine thirty the first morning we were there.

That Monday morning I taxied to the Institute of San Marco, arriving at the great walled-in place precisely at nine thirty. I gazed at it in astonishment. It had the look of a huge boys' reformatory but with more flavor of prison gates and walls than even the most old-fashioned of American training schools for boys would have.

The taxi dropped me at the gatehouse of the portiere and I began the vigorous ordeal of trying to keep my appointment.

The portiere was a small, greasy, unctuous man whom I disliked at once. I explained to him that Father Vincelli had written a letter and had arranged an appointment for me with Mother Carmella. She was expecting me. He understood me perfectly, I know, but he chose not to believe me.

"Oh, no, signora," he said condescendingly. "The sisters do not like to have visitors in the morning. It would be better if you came back some afternoon."

I explained firmly that Mother Carmella had received Father Vincelli's letter. I knew because I had telephoned her earlier in the morning to confirm it. She was expecting me.

He shook his head. It was much better to come in the afternoon. I found my anger mounting. I pointed to his telephone and demanded that he call her at once. After some deliberation, he shrugged, put through the call and held the phone so that I could hear it ring. "You see," he said triumphantly, "nobody answers." I gestured out the window at the many large buildings. "In all those buildings," I said firmly, "somebody will answer the phone. You must call another number."

We had reached an impasse. He kept insisting that I should come back "some afternoon." Besides, he said as though this would surely cinch the argument, "Oggi è festa." I refused to leave. I knew that "oggi era festa," but I had an "appuntamento!" I could not come back "some afternoon" because I had driven all the way from Rome to keep this appuntamento.

As we argued, another man entered the room and listened. He interrupted courteously and said to the portiere that I was quite right. He knew for a fact that I had an appointment. He had heard the reverend mother arrange it. However, it appeared that she had forgotten because a few minutes ago she had departed in the car. He took in the distressed look on my face.

"Signore," I pleaded, "couldn't you call the convent and ask whether another sister would take me through the institution? I have driven all the way from Rome to keep this appointment."

"But of course," he said warmly, and gestured that I should follow him. I shot a triumphant backward glance at the portiere whose facial expression indicated that I would soon find out that this would get me nowhere. We walked across a gravel road and entered a large red stone building. Inside, we turned left and he opened a door labeled "Parlano" (They speak).

There was a huge table in the center with chairs around it. On the walls were scrolls, pictures of solemn, religious subjects, and a flag of Italy. He asked me to take a chair, and then started to leave the room. I must have had a premonition of abandonment, because I said, "Signore, you will surely return soon?" A glance at my watch told me that I had already lost almost a half hour in my argument with the portiere. He came back and, to my complete astonishment, lifted my hand and kissed it, clicked his heels together, and after a little military bow assured me that I was "very gracious and very genteel."

I wandered around the room trying to amuse myself. I found

the date of establishment of San Marco and it confirmed my impression that these buildings belonged to the Mussolini period when government buildings were erected in scale and quality as though they were to serve the city of New York for centuries.

Time dragged on. No one came. I heard no voices. Boldly, I decided to do some exploring on my own. I left the "parlano" and went out into the entrance hall. Behind glass, I discovered a long honor roll for the alumni of San Marco who had "gloriously lost their lives for the fatherland." Most of the men had been privates, but there was a fair sprinkling of sergeants and lieutenants. I searched in vain for someone of higher rank. Another glance at my watch sent me back to the portiere to recommence my argument.

This time I was luckier, for a sympathetic stranger took in my plight at once, overruled the truculent portiere, and said, "Follow me." This time we walked around what I had decided was the administration building, through open cloisters, past five or six large buildings; after five minutes' walk we were approaching an area where three nuns were supervising a group of fifty little girls playing on swings and slides.

The sisters saw us and came to meet us. They greeted me by name most cordially and referred to me as "that famous American social worker." "So," I thought triumphantly, "I was expected!" After a few pleasantries, one of the sisters asked me to come with her. I did—and after a rapid walk we ended up back at the portiere's! The nun said I should wait "a little minute" and after a bit she came back with a tall, shy man whom she introduced as Signor Verdi. Signor Verdi was a teacher at the school and had been chosen to be my guide because he spoke English. I think he spoke the world's most incomprehensible English. I found it quite impossible to understand him. In vain I urged him to speak to me in Italian "so that I could practice the language." He would respond to such a plea with something like, "Very yes. Tomorrow."

Signor Verdi led me into the administration building and up three flights of marble stairs; respectfully and anxiously he knocked at a door. We entered a room where a short, fat bald man who looked like a miniature of Mussolini sat at a desk barking out orders gruffly and self-importantly at men and women who disappeared one by one to do his bidding.

Few people have ever given me so strongly the sense that I was being questioned about a crime. "So," he said suspiciously, "you are insisting that you have an appointment."

I began to feel that the fate of democracy was at stake and that I would fight this matter through until the last breath should escape me. Yes, Father Vincelli had written to the institution. No, I did not know to whom he had addressed his correspondence. But this very morning I had phoned in and had spoken, I believed, with one of the nuns at the convent.

"Aha!" he said in the manner of one catching me at last in a lie. "And did you speak to a man or a woman on the phone?"

How diabolically clever! Mitch had made the call and afterwards had said amusedly that those cracked, aged voices of telephone answerers were totally sexless. I explained that my husband had made the call so I didn't know. He used his best "a likely story" manner, and continued. I had told the portiere that I had driven all the way from Rome to inspect San Marco. Just what was my interest in San Marco? Poor Signor Verdi looked from one of us to the other miserably.

Suddenly Mussolini slammed his papers on the desk and said, "Oh very well! Take her around." Together Signor Verdi and I fled and began our tour.

I was exhausted emotionally and physically. We toured building after building, up and down flights of stairs, crossed and recrossed the courtyard, choosing buildings not side by side but in a crazy pattern as though we were out for exercise. All the time we walked Signor Verdi talked astonishing English gibberish to me; I kept answering in what was probably equally astonishing Italian.

The dormitories for the boys were as neat and stark as military barracks. Only the plaster statue of a saint with a vestal light flickering beneath it broke the plainness of the rooms. Beds were unmade with mattresses and bedding neatly folded. The children made their beds five minutes before getting into them, and in the morning, neatly unmade them before breakfast. No lolling about by adolescents on these beds!

The chapel was a perfect little gem of Renaissance architecture. No expense had been spared here. A sweet old man took me through, pointing out lovely works of art. I remember especially a wooden statue of the angel Gabriel which certainly was one of the most graceful I had ever seen. It belonged, it seemed to me, in a museum beside the works of Michelangelo and Rodin. Seeing it was probably a rare privilege, for no mere art critic or art lover would ever get past that portiere!

The beautiful spoken Italian of the old caretaker was a delight. In a few minutes with him I learned more than I had in an hour with my "English-speaking" guide. There were six hundred children at San Marco. Five hundred were boys, one hundred girls. The girls were cared for in a separate part of the grounds — only for church services did the boys and girls come together. Attendance at services, except for Sunday Mass, which is obligatory for all Catholics, was voluntary; but the great majority of children chose to attend Mass each morning and Benediction in the evening. Benediction, he told me, is a most beautiful service. The setting sun, he said, transforms the white marble of the chapel into a glorious pink. The service itself is "very artistic." There is the wonderful perfume of the incense which the priest burns, the soft glow of the candles, and most inspiring of all, the hundreds of reverent little children's voices lifted to heaven. The Americana must come back some time at twilight to attend a Benediction. I hated to leave the chapel and the old man who spoke so poetically.

Signor Verdi and I trudged on. We went through several expensively equipped buildings whose purpose was vocational training. I saw the huge printing presses where boys made posters which I had already seen in Rome — multicolored, handsome posters. I remember one that had amused me. There, gazing out seductively, lay Deborah Kerr in a remarkably low-cut gown. The name of the movie was "Tè e Simpatia." Across Miss K's white chest was a sentence printed in red, "Forbidden to minors under sixteen years of age."

Newspapers were printed there—not dailies, but weeklies. There was no evidence that I could see that we were not in a most expensive printing plant for adult professional workers. We saw an equally impressive leather-working shop—unusual because in Italy there is much emphasis on handwork rather than machines. We toured a shoemaking shop.

In and out of buildings we went while Signor Verdi bombarded me with rapid-fire pig-English. I was dependent on my eyes rather than my ears. Except for a lone boy here or there hurrying across the grounds, I saw no children. I explained in Italian that I really had wanted to see the children. I would like to see them eat, and play, and at work in the shops. He looked very unhappy. Right now they were eating their noon meal but for some reason he was not free to take me to see them. (Probably orders from that Mussolini-like character.)

At this point a handsome Ronald-Colmanish-looking man hurried across the courtyard to meet us. He introduced himself as Professor Rusciano, the direttore of San Marco. He was full of apologies because he had not been on hand to take me on the tour himself. He had looked forward to my visit and feared that I had had a disappointing time.

I forgave him, but added that I had wanted to be with the children. Since I had spent four hours at San Marco now, I was tired. Perhaps I could come back late this afternoon and see the children? He was most affable. Would I come at five o'clock and plan to have my evening meal as a guest of San Marco? This would give me time to converse with him, meet some members of the staff, and still spend some time with the children. I accepted happily and said that I would be at the portiere's at five o'clock. Would he inform the portiere because I had found it a little difficult this morning? An angry look—for the portiere, I think, and not for me—crossed his face.

Half numb with fatigue and hunger, I entered the hated portiere's office and asked him to call me a taxi.

At five o'clock I was back again, and said to the portiere somewhat nastily that Professor Rusciano was expecting me. With a not ungraceful bow of defeat he led me to the administration building, up a flight of stairs to the professore's office.

Professor Rusciano was all grace and charm, even to kissing my hand in greeting. We had a pleasant conversation full of generalizations about the problems of institutionalized children. I commented on the excellence of his "plant" and found it easy to ask whether he did not find it hard to put human warmth into the relationships with six hundred children. He looked grave and assured me that it was most difficult.

I said that I would be interested in techniques of discipline. How was the rebellious child handled? For little misdemeanors, he said, a word of correction was enough. The next step was withholding television programs for several nights. Sometimes a few hours of solitary confinement was effective. When all these things failed, the child would be referred to San Marco's social worker.

Of course, I was pleased to know that there was a social worker. Professore said he would introduce me to her soon. I asked how she would work with the rebellious child, wanting to hear his point of view. She would counsel with the child, he said, to learn what was bothering him. Not infrequently, she would work with parents to see what influence their behavior during monthly visiting hours or at Christmas vacation time might be having. If the child's adjustment continued to be poor, the social worker might seek to move him to some smaller, less complicated institution. Some delicate children, the professore told me, could not accept being a part of as large a group as this.

At last at San Marco I had found something beside the lovely chapel that I could like! This was to me a gentle, sensitive, and thoughtful man.

Someone brought in glasses of vermouth, and I switched to the vocational problems of the older boys. Professor Rusciano was proud of what they had been able to teach many of the boys; and those who had vocational leanings in different directions could leave the grounds to go to the schools in the city. When a boy was ready to begin work, he might not be psychologically prepared to live alone. Perhaps he would not even earn enough to feed himself adequately, especially during the period of his apprenticeship. These boys could go out each day to work and return to San Marco's for their evening meal and for a place to sleep. Some boys took almost a year before they felt ready to be on their own at the end of the day. I was able to say that San Marco was here far ahead of American communities I had known, where resources for the youngster in late adolescence were very limited.

As we talked we moved into another room on the same floor that was full of sculptures and paintings. Some were by relatively famous painters and I was unclear just how they had come into the possession of the institution. Others were copies of originals done by the boys of San Marco who were learning to be artists. There was a student's etching of the Mona Lisa which seemed to me the best copy of the mystic smile I had ever seen. All the work seemed to my inexpert eye to be at a professional level.

I felt warmly drawn to Professor Rusciano and was delighted by our easy communication. It seemed to me that I was talking to the soundest social work administrator I had seen since I had left Minneapolis.

There was a knock at the door and Signorina Louisa Fermi entered. She was the social worker for San Marco and had been assigned to spend the evening with me. She was a plain, olive-skinned woman with lovely soft dark eyes. When we were alone she told me bitterly that she was a part-time worker at San Marco — a full-time worker was not needed for six hundred children!

She began by taking me to her office. Her office was one of four desks in a room, with a telephone to be shared by four people, and a kind of inappropriate china closet of which one shelf was for her papers and materials. I asked where she kept her case histories and she surprised me by saying, "In a locked compartment in my home." When I said that this must be inconvenient, she said in a somewhat melodramatic way, "Inconvenient, yes, but much safer!"

I asked her to describe some of her cases and this part of her conversation I found a little hard to follow. She told me of several boys who had problems of excessive fearfulness and melancholia. She had had the great good fortune to have them transferred to a small institution in Rome known as Santa Clara's. Did I know Santa Clara's? I said that I was planning to visit it in a week. She said that the nun in charge, Mother Giulia, was a graduate of the New Roman School, her own very close friend, and that she ran the best institution in Italy. "When a boy with problems goes to Santa Clara's, the problems disappear the first week he is there. Mother Giulia is a gifted woman."

She suggested that we walk outdoors to see the children at play. The boys were coming out from buildings all around the square. They marched in formation and showed off with military maneuvers like little crack squads. A "sergeant" marched beside them with a chanting "Hup, due, tre . . ." and the Italian chopped commands sounded much like English. After each squadron had broken rank, the boys ran to one end of the playground for free play, much of it in a dozen spontaneously formed little groups of soccer. The deepening gray of the evening was defeated by big floodlights that played on the grounds. We must have stood silently for ten minutes watching the new groups come in, go through their paces, and then go join in the free play. "It is pleasing to you to see children like this?" she asked.

"No," I said firmly, "it is too military and big and cold. They should be home with parents, brothers and sisters. It must be especially bad for the little ones."

Her eyes were full of tears. "It is terrible for them," she said, "truly terrible."

A squad passed close in front of us, and stopped to go through its complicated maneuvers. The boys looked no older than ten. Suddenly, almost in excitement, she grabbed my arm. The "sergeant," a boy of about thirteen, was addressing a boy in rank. "See, oh see, how the poor little one holds up his hand as though to ward off a blow? It is a compulsive response. It is not appropriate. No one is going to hit him. I have begged his mother not to hit him when she visits. He is so used to ducking that he now does it to everyone. Except me. With me, he is tranquil. I must get him away from here before it's too late."

When the "sergeant" left him, she called, "Gino!" The boy broke rank and came running to her. "Oh, no," she said, "first you must gain permission to leave rank." Gino ran back, whispered to the squadron leader, and returned. When he began to talk with her she interrupted him. "Gino, greet the signora."

A thin little hand shot out and a thin little voice dutifully said, "Buona sera, signora!"

They talked together softly for a few minutes. Gino did, as she said, look "very tranquil" when he was with her. I heard words like "mother" and "we'll talk together tomorrow." She gave him a little pat on the cheek in dismissal. (I approved the warm gesture serenely used with the boy who feared being struck.) We began to walk among the boys, who interrupted their games to greet her. A dozen different ones came up and she required each one to "greet the signora." I shook a dozen limp, shy hands.

A group of the oldest boys approached with questions about jobs. I was pleased with their looks. Italian boys in late adolescence I always found hardest to like of any Italians I saw on the streets. They seemed to me to affect clothes and manners like those of American "hoods"; if they were wealthy, I often saw something deeply effeminate in them. Both of these traits seemed to me to disappear by their mid-twenties, when they became attractive, warm, masculine men. (Six months' observation of this phenomenon did not yield a satisfactory explanation of it.)

I said to my companion that I had the impression from what I had seen and heard that perhaps San Marco was better for older boys than for little ones. Didn't they do a good job in vocational planning? "The vocational planning is good," she admitted, "but this is a dreadful way for any boy to live. I am the only woman in their lives."

In the far corner of the court I saw a nun scuttle by, her black shawl clutched tightly against the wintry wind. "What about the nuns?" I asked.

"They aren't women," she said coldly.

"Are they kind?" I asked, wishing I had a decent vocabulary.

"Almost never," she answered stonily.

We went into the dining building, where five hundred boys were eating their evening meal. They ate in clean, bare white rooms from sturdy white dishes, about fifty boys in each room. As we walked through the rooms they always started to rise to greet us, but I learned to copy her little gesture waving them down. The older boys were well-scrubbed and smiling-faced. They were eating food as good as could be had in Italy. There was a pleasant sound of talking and joking at the tables. And there were plenty of "seconds."

In one room Signor Verdi, my English-speaking guide, rushed forward all smiles with hand extended. I was prepared to shake hands with him; he planned to kiss my hand. And so I bumped his nose. I had gone forty-two years with an unkissed hand and now it had happened to me three times in eight hours. Despite my confusion I surprised a look of cold hatred on Signorina Fermi's face directed at Signor Verdi. She was going to get into trouble with that "open book" face, I thought.

In another room I was introduced to a big, fat, red-faced man who looked like James Farley—the "director of recreational activities." When he entered, the boys jumped to their feet with something like "three cheers for so-and-so." He boomed a laugh and said to me, "You will find this a wonderful place. The boys are so open with their feelings." Again on Signorina Fermi's face I saw that look of hatred.

Finally we arrived at what I guess might be called the staff dining room. Tables were set for one, two, or four. Professor Rusciano came forward to escort Signorina and me to a table for two and fussed a great deal about where I should sit, did I have a napkin, and so on. I was served about the right amount of food for four people—excellent food. I was embarrassed because I could eat so little.

Well, at least I didn't have to worry about the nourishment at San Marco's. I said to Signorina Fermi that it must be very expensive to feed children as well as this. She said that San Marco's was a very rich institution — one that beside having a large government subsidy, raised much of its own meats, vegetables, and dairy products.

As we left the dining room, we were joined by another member of the faculty — an apologetic man who said that though I had been in the girls' dormitory in the morning, I had not seen one dormitory that was especially "dear." It would make him very happy to escort me to it. It was eight o'clock, and it had been a killing day, but I was curious about the beautiful dormitory and I wanted a glimpse of the girls; so I agreed to go.

As Signorina and I walked across the court, I saw a small boy scurry through the shadows. Two minutes later a man came running after him, shouting that he was "capricious." He was breaking a rule! A boy could not leave his building without his squadron, I was told.

I asked Signorina how the boys were disciplined. Were they ever hit? As I raised the question, two men walked by, and she shushed me in a manner that again made me feel that she was an odd woman who loved children, hated many adults, and acted as though she and I were caught up in some kind of dangerous intrigue. She and I would soon part. I went along with the game. "Do you like Professor Rusciano?" I asked, remembering that I had not seen the hostile look on her face during the time he was with us.

"He is a wonderful man," she said. "He has just been here a year and many things have improved greatly. But what can he do in the midst of so much evil?" As I was wondering whether I could have made a mistranslation, we were joined by the man who was to take me to see the "very dear" little girls' dormitory. Signorina Fermi's face froze again. It was necessary to say good-by to her while she was still constrained in the "presence of evil." I was puzzled. It had occurred to me more than once that she might be a paranoid with delusions of reference, but this was hard to judge. Perhaps I might think her behavior appropriate if I had understood what really went on at San Marco's.

It was a three blocks' walk over the gravel to the girls' dormitory. The wet soles of my shoes felt paper thin between my throbbing feet and the pebbles. I tried to cover up my need to limp.

My guide talked freely and pleasantly. This much I understood. Of the hundred little girls, twenty-six were given special privileges. They had an extra lovely room, more clothes, more candy. These were children who had lost their fathers to the Russians. Maybe the fathers were dead. Maybe they were in a slave labor camp. No one knew. But the government paid an extra sum so that these orphans should be especially well cared for.

When we reached the back door of the dormitory, my guide rang a bell. A maid answered the door. He could not go in with me because he was a man. He told the maid to show me the dormitory for the orphans of men who had been "maltreated by the Russians." He disappeared and the maid led me up the back stairs into a starkly plain room where everything was completely white. That old hospital feeling! Genuinely puzzled, I asked in what way it was different from the rooms I had seen this morning. The maid seemed surprised by the question. "Why, signora—it is all in white! The curtains, the bedspreads, even the blankets. In the other rooms some things are brown, some are gray. Is it not very dear?"

I nodded dumbly. In vain I listened for the voices of the little girls. It was close to nine o'clock. "But where are the children?" I asked.

"They are at chapel saying their night prayers," she said. "Mother Carmella asked me to tell you that if you wish to see them, you should return tomorrow morning at ten o'clock." Again I nodded. I was too tired to observe anything more tonight. Perhaps if I saw just one more thing I would burst into tears.

The maid let me out the back door. Another of those damnable drizzly cold rains had started up. It must be close to three blocks over the gravel to the hateful portiere's room. I cut across the court on the diagonal and had I not hurried, I would have ended up in the center of a last squadron drilling. These were the littlest boys I had seen. They didn't look over seven years old. I heard the squadron leader's calls and heard the careful, rhythmical stamping of feet.

A shadow came toward me. Signor Verdi again. "Good morning, miss," he said. "The boys good exercising. Very happy time. No?"

He took me by the arm and steered me toward the portiere. "Professor Rusciano demand taxi. Now. For you. Here. Thanks." This time he shook hands, taking no chances on getting his nose bumped. "Our doors of San Marco are welcome your heart forever," he said grandly as I got into the taxi.

I slumped back in the seat, dully watching rivulets of water course down the windowpane. I ached with tiredness and with a sudden loneliness for my own son. At this time of night he would be stretched out in our friends' living room, his novel on the floor under the reading lamp and his shoeless feet under the coffee table. He would not be out in a drizzling rain going "Hup, two, three, right, right, left, stomp, stomp."

February 25

A TEN-HOUR SLEEP, a leisurely breakfast, and a brilliant Italian sun had revived me. I approached San Marco's for my ten o'clock appointment to see the little girls with only one trauma left from yesterday — the tenderness of my feet.

The portiere gave me a surly "Buon giorno!" and immediately telephoned the convent. In a few minutes two smiling, apologetic nuns came to meet me saying that they hadn't realized I would be coming at this hour. I explained that the maid who had shown me through the girls' dormitory last night had given me a message from Mother Carmella that I was to come at ten this morning. It was most unfortunate, they told me. Today was the day the girls were to get their hair cut and surely I could see that they could not be observed at such a time? I suggested that I would find it fascinating to watch them get their hair cut, but this unconventional idea distressed the nuns. I sensed that they had been sent on the distasteful errand of politely getting rid of the American and I decided that I should not punish them. They were not responsible for the run-around that I was being given.

The gates of San Marco may have been welcome to my heart forever, as Signor Verdi had said yesterday, but I had spent all the energy I cared to in getting behind them. So I turned away, wondering what it was that the nuns were so determined to keep me from seeing.

I had just one more appointment on this day—at six o'clock to talk with Father Vincelli.

At six I went to the local branch of the New Roman School of Social Work with fresh enthusiasm. The branch in this city (which I am not naming) was much like the Roman branch. Father Vincelli, however, was like Father de la Roche only in his ability to speak excellent English.

Father Vincelli, a young man in his thirties, had Latin coloring—black hair, brown eyes, and chiseled features—but his crew cut and his fondness for American slang made me feel often as though I were talking to a man from home.

He began by saying that he would have been unhappy about sending me to San Marco's had he not been sure that he could discuss it with me afterwards. I enjoyed telling him the story because his expressive face—now convulsed with mirth, now looking agreeably sympathetic—made him a good listener.

I started with questions about Signorina Fermi. Because of my immediate sense that it was safe to be frank with him, I told him that she seemed to me a little paranoid. He looked grave and asked whether I believed that life could present people with such pressures that a paranoid-like response would be the only appropriate one. I said indeed I did.

San Marco, he told me, had been modeled after a Nazi institution that took great pride in skillfully indoctrinating German youth so that they developed a passionate identification with militarism and the fatherland.

"Perhaps, signora," he questioned, "you have observed that the Italian people lack flair for militarism and fascistic behavior? One of your American journalists recently wrote that our soldiers and police dress and act like characters in an Italian comic opera." He chuckled approvingly.

For this reason, he said, San Marco was never a true copy of the German institution, though it had picked up some of the more odious characteristics, such as "all that crazy marching about."

Mussolini had appropriated vast tracts of land and had diverted tax-free income from a large area in the heart of the city into the coffers of San Marco. Appointment to the staff was a political plum and for the most part the appointees were paid ridiculously high salaries for small duties.

"The place is a cesspool of political corruption," he said.

He asked whether I had seen the most elaborate hotel in the city. I responded that we had walked through the lobby and had been impressed by its lavish splendor. He told me that San Marco owned the hotel and rented it to the management at 50,000 lire a month—a good bit less than one would pay to rent a modest apartment in Rome.

"So the hotel management and the board of San Marco join hands in the corruption?" I asked.

He nodded. "You can be certain that vast sums of money end up in the hands of the corrupt through this kind of arrangement. Remember, I have told you about just one of the buildings involved. There are similar stories about dozens of buildings."

I turned back to my observations. I said that several things had impressed me favorably—the vocational program, the good food. It would seem to me that a reform movement to rid the place of corruption might result in the city's having a perfectly excellent institution for vocational and emotional rehabilitation of adolescents. I had completely rejected it as a setting for little boys.

"Gosh!" he exclaimed. "It's fun to talk to an American again. You people have such a cockeyed expectation that everything can be reformed. Now me—I think the only way to handle San Marco's is to burn it to the ground."

I asked him to tell me about Signorina Fermi. "She is a fine, intelligent woman who is breaking her heart trying singlehandedly to do a killing job." She was always being spied on. She would repeatedly find that her locked desk had been broken into and her case records read. If a boy was beginning to relate warmly to her, she would be prevented from seeing him unless San Marco had already written him off. The institution was reluctant to lose children. They needed the full six hundred to constitute "a screen for where all that money is going."

Because the corrupt powers sensed that Signorina Fermi tried to re-establish broken families or to help troubled children get into small, humane institutions, she was spied upon as though she were engaged in criminal activity. Some kind of political pressure had got her her job, but those in charge were determined to keep her confused, unaware of what was really happening, and frustrated in what she tried to accomplish.

I spoke then of Professor Rusciano and my feeling that he was a good man who cared what happened to the children. Father Vincelli drew thoughtfully on his pipe. "Signorina believes, as you do, that he is a good man. It's almost too much to hope. He is not an idiot and so he is not talking about what his plans are. We watch him with hope and prayers for his success because we too are guessing that he is opposed to the corruption."

I told him of my belief that the nuns in the convent for little girls had contrived to keep me out. Should I give up trying?

He laughed. "You may as well. I have read in your social work journals from America about aggressive casework and forcing your foot in the door. Well, you got one in yesterday—but it would take a great deal more effort to get the other in."

The rumors about the nuns' behavior toward the girls, he said, were alarming. Several times citizens' committees had tried to do something about it. It was said that protests had even gone to the pope, but no one really knew. There were just these "ominous rumbles."

"Father," I said, "nothing that I have seen or heard since I came to Italy has distressed me more than your story of San Marco. Is it unique or are there other large institutions run like this in Italy?"

He looked grave. "Our city probably has the distinction of having the most corrupt large institution for children, but there must be quite a few others that rival it." And he named half a dozen.

Father wanted to know about foster home placement in America and the problems I saw in beginning this kind of child care in Italy. This was my first opportunity since I had begun to get my Italian eyes to talk in English about how this might be accomplished. Though our appointment lasted several hours, I was reluctant to have it end. Father Vincelli's point of view was refreshingly realistic. He knew that students had to learn to interview and to figure budgets, to recognize the pain of separation, and to achieve humility before they moved into that "erudite, psychiatric area of casework in which so many of you Americans seem to be dwelling these days."

His secretary interrupted to say that a woman had arrived for her appointment. He got to his feet at once. "A client who is having problems with her daughter," he explained.

This was as close to a client as I had come in Italy and I expressed surprise that the head of a school of social work was doing casework. "This casework stuff," he said simply, "is so hard to understand. I feel as though I can't teach it without having experienced it."

The corruption at San Marco's had made me despair of accomplishing anything for the institutionalized children of Italy, but Father Vincelli himself gave me high hopes that he and his graduates, given time, would be able to accomplish a great deal.

February 27

I WAS GLAD to be back in Rome. Even the little drizzling rain didn't change that. I was glad too that I was going to see the Institute of Santa Clara and the Mother Giulia whom all social workers seemed to respect. This was the woman who had won her diploma from the New Roman School of Social Work before she had entered the convent.

Santa Clara's, not far from the heart of Rome, was behind a charming, ancient, nicely-crumbly wall. (In Rome, one soon learns to distinguish between the structures that look merely run-down and those whose very deterioration is worn like an artful decoration of antiquity.)

Inside the gate, I found an odd little assortment of dwellings — a doctor's office, an unpretentious private home, a building that was shaped like an American barn but was covered with huge, flamboyant religious murals, and a slightly bedraggled mansion which was, as I guessed, Santa Clara's. The garden had its expected flower beds, but off to one side was a good-sized graveled area — a play space for the boys. There was a warm, homey look that I liked.

The door was opened by a nun who couldn't have been more than four feet eight inches tall. She looked astonishingly like my memory of my beloved kindergarten teacher, "Little Sister Rose." This miniature turned out to be Mother Giulia. She had been expecting me. She was sorry that she couldn't speak English but she would try to speak very slowly for me. "You must remind me frequently, signora, because I always move and talk very fast." It seemed to me typical of her thoughtfulness that never once did I have to remind her.

As I came in, Mother Giulia introduced me to a young woman who was leaving. Signorina Lametti was a student from the New Roman School who spent fifteen hours a week at Santa Clara's for field work experience. Her major was in group work. (With Father Vincelli, I had almost seen a client; now I had at last seen a student in a field placement. Ever so slowly, I was beginning to see bits of resemblance to social work in America.)

Mother Giulia asked me what I would like to know about Santa Clara's. I said that though I wanted to see where the children lived, I was even more interested in spending time with them, observing them at work and play.

She led me upstairs into the usual overcrowded bedrooms of

the slightly converted mansion. But these rooms were different. Bedspreads and draperies were in colorful flowered prints, and each child had a locker of his own. Plants on brackets, placed high on the wall to be safely out of the way of scuffling boy-play, softened the institutional look.

"How nice your dormitories are," I said.

Mother Giulia shook her head. "They are not nice at all. There are too many beds in a room, too little privacy. Oh, it's all wrong."

"Perhaps it isn't what you want for the boys," I said, "but it's so much more homelike than I've seen elsewhere."

"It's the best we can do," she said, "but please don't think of it as 'good enough.'"

There was spice and firmness in her speech that went oddly with her tiny stature. Something sloppy in my thinking often starts me out expecting tiny women to be like cute, precocious children.

She showed me the battered splendor of the huge, marble bathrooms and laughed as she described how incongruous it was to see dozens of little boys among the pink marble and gilded fixtures. "You see?" she said. "It's all wrong."

In speaking to her, out of my inarticulacy, I referred to the children as "orphans." She corrected me just as I hundreds of times in America had corrected this misnomer. "Our children are not orphans. Each child has at least one parent. Children and parents have been separated by various kinds of pressure — emotional and economic. Here at Santa Clara's, we work hard to keep family ties alive." She sounded like a direct quotation from me translated into Italian!

I asked whether the parents visited. They did. On Wednesdays and Saturdays and, if they had time, on days in between. Sometimes an employed parent would stop in to take his child out for a walk or a treat. "Parents are valued and always welcome here," she said proudly.

When parents had a suitable home in Rome, the children visited there — after school or for weekends. In the summer, if a child was lucky, he might spend a whole month at home. This interested me greatly because in America our experts have often been afraid to try such liberal visiting schedules.

"And are the children upset after such frequent long visits?" I asked.

"Oh, yes," she said, "they cry and are lonesome. But it is much better to cry with lonesomeness for parents that one sees often than to give up shedding tears for parents that one never sees."

Together we went into a large recreation room where about twenty-five boys, between nine and eleven, sat around a big table. Some were writing letters, some sketching with crayons, but most were reading comic books. The comic books were pinned by brightly colored plastic clothespins to a clothesline that ran on a pulley down the center of the table. There must have been about seventy-five of them. When a boy finished his comic book, he pinned it on the clothesline and pulled the rope along until a desirable book came his way. Two boys willingly showed me what they were reading. "Pecos Bill" (pronounced Paycaus Beeel) and "Topolino" (Mickey Mouse). I told the boys that these comics were made in America. They were immediately interested. "But," a tall boy protested, "the words are in Italian. Americans do not speak Italian." I said that comic book publishers probably hired some clever American who could read and write Italian very well to make the translations.

Mother Giulia offered me a chair and excused herself. I sat down quietly and the boys went back to their reading, healthily forgetting my presence. This was a comfortable group of boys. They called out little jokes, good-naturedly argued over who got "Roee Rojairs" next, and all in all seemed smoothly in tune with each other.

A pale redhead brought me a cheap little globe of the world not much bigger than a grapefruit and asked me to point to the place in America where I lived. He also wanted to see in what direction my ship or plane had traveled in coming to Italy. Putting his finger on the tiny spot that stood for Minnesota, he showed the little globe to other boys in the room. Some were interested;

others were good-naturedly annoyed at being interrupted in what they were doing.

Presently Mother Giulia came back. I noticed with admiration the way she used her hands as she walked among the boys. Now a hand on a shoulder, now a quick soft gesture to gently brush back a stubborn lock from a boy's eyes. Once with a shy, soft-spoken boy who was several inches shorter than she, she cupped his chin in her hand to direct his eyes and speech upward. It struck me suddenly that if a charade player could mock these gestures, her team would know at once that the word she was acting out was "maternal." But the gestures were too real and full of genuine feeling ever to be successfully mocked.

While Mother Giulia sat beside me, a boy came running in breathlessly to ask permission to leave the grounds for a walk and perhaps a treat with his mother. "Certainly," she said easily, and he raced happily out of the room.

It was fascinating to watch the faces of the boys as they talked with her — no adoration here, no fearfulness, no uncertainty. Every look I saw directed toward her suggested security and quiet respect.

One boy had been lightly tossing a Ping-pong ball in the air. Suddenly he tossed it high and as my eyes followed it up I saw that there was an expensive-looking television set anchored almost at ceiling height. I asked Mother Giulia about the "tee-voo" (as it is pronounced in Italy.) She said smilingly that it had altered their whole lives. The boys loved "co-oo-boee" (cowboy) shows. These shows came on at seven o'clock. So the whole schedule had to be changed so that everybody would be finished with dinner and homework. On Wednesdays, there was no good show, and since a benefactor had given them a movie projector they had a real movie every Wednesday night. Sister Renata, who was very clever with machines, ran the projector.

We went downstairs to see the "little boys" — two large rooms of them, grouped roughly according to age. I guessed them to be between five and nine. The recreation rooms in which they played were also the dining rooms. Mother Giulia showed me the little four-place tables, handsome little pieces of furniture whose plastic tops were in gay pastels. Each table wore a flowered tablecloth "for when we eat" and over it a clear plastic covering "for when we play."

An exquisite little boy with hair so long that it fell in soft curls came up and took Mother Giulia's hand, and continued the walk with us. Mother explained to me that Angelo, their youngest, had a stomachache; for this reason he had felt like holding her hand and going almost everywhere with her that day. Angelo was well named. He had the face of an angel. Gregarious and outgoing, he talked with me at a lively clip even though Mother Giulia would laugh and cry out, "Piano! Piano! Angelo! Signora Charnley is just learning to understand Italian."

We moved in among the children, who left their crayons and their art work to run up and greet Mother Giulia. Several of these boys showed that they were younger than the boys upstairs by the spontaneous, unself-conscious hugs with which they greeted her.

I was introduced to each little boy and solemnly shook hands with all. Mother Giulia pointed out some pleasant fact about each child. "This is the boy who could count to 500 before he was five years old. And here is Elio, with the brand-new blue trousers which his mother bought him yesterday. And Gian Carlo, who had his picture on television."

A cork bulletin board with thumbtacks followed the wall on two sides of the room. One small boy mounted a chair and was straining to pin up the picture he had just made. Mother Giulia and I stopped to admire the picture — a garden scene, with very Italian flowers, statues, and fountains. It was like art work I had seen by other Italian children. (Where were the cars, trains, horses, and airplanes that free-drawing periods in America always produced?)

Mother Giulia was praising the picture. "Six weeks ago, when Mario first came here," she explained to him and to me, "he didn't know how to make a picture. He said he didn't even care to learn. And now, Signora Charnley, just look at the fine picture he has made! Wouldn't it be a fine joke if Mario grew up to be the best artist that ever lived at Santa Clara's?" Mario and I looked properly impressed by the idea.

One of the last boys I met was Michele. We had chatted with him for a few moments when Mother Giulia said suddenly, "My goodness, Michele, I almost forgot to tell you. Signora Charnley speaks English. Here I've been trying to tell her all about Santa Clara's when you could have done it much better."

I bent down to take Michele's hand. "Hello, Michele," I said. "Where did you learn to speak English?" He took my hand and said rather hesitantly, "My parents and I lived on the island of Malta. I started to a school where only English was spoken."

"Do you like to speak English, Michele?"

"Oh, yes," he said, "sometimes I'm afraid I will forget how." Mother Giulia, two nuns, and a young assistant came and listened admiringly as we talked.

Mother Giulia explained that Michele's father worked for NATO and his parents were distressed because he was learning to read and write English instead of Italian; for this reason they had sent him to Santa Clara's to be educated. He would go home for vacation this June. I asked whether I might have a conversation with him. Mother Giulia courteously asked his permission and he readily agreed. First he wanted to wash his hands and comb his hair. He disappeared for a few minutes and then returned and whispered something to Mother. She said, "We'll ask the signora." She explained the problem. Michele's shoes were quite dusty and his second pair were even worse. Would I mind having a conversation with a boy with such dusty shoes? I would not.

The four of us walked upstairs together — Mother Giulia, the curly-headed Angelo, Michele, and I. In the reception hall, a number of adults waited to see her. Several seemed to be parents; one was a workman ready to install an incongruously modern reading light in a corner of the reception hall.

Michele and I went off to talk. Mother Giulia, one hand anchored by small Angelo, gestured freely and Italianly with the other. She drew the parents and the workman into a discussion of where the lamp would look best, how long the cord should be, and other such details. The parents seemed as interested as though the home were their own.

Michele had the polite, constrained manner that I have learned to associate (largely from movies) with well-bred British boys. He answered a few questions politely and then abruptly said, "Signora, how do you say 'prima' and 'dopo' in English?"

"Before and after," I said, and he grinned with that "how could I have forgotten?" look.

Interviewing Michele was much like interviewing a child in America. He told me how in Malta his father had not liked his eldest son to learn first to write English. His sister, three years older, had become angry and said, "I don't care if I never learn to write Italian. I like English better." Patiently Michele explained, "It's not so important for a girl." His baby brother was at home in Malta "but that doesn't matter about him because he is too little to write."

"Do you like living here at Santa Clara's, Michele?"

"Oh, yes. I guess every boy likes living here. Everyone is very kind."

"But at first, were you lonely?" Quick tears swam in his blue eyes. I changed the subject, angry at myself for having broken through so fragile a defense. "And in June, you will go home to visit your family?"

"Perhaps my father will come for me."

"How nice that will be!"

"I only said perhaps," he reminded me sternly.

"And will you come back to Santa Clara's next year in September?"

"That is for my father to say. I shall do what he says."

As we were talking, the little blond unhooked himself from Mother Giulia's hand and came to listen to us in complete fascination. He disappeared to come back staggering under the weight of three big books. These were the scrapbooks of Santa Clara's.

Angelo drafted the somewhat reluctant Michele into the job of being his translator. "Dica a la signora . . ."

The three of us looked through the scrapbooks at pictures of the boys and the nuns on various outings—one halfway up a mountain, with Mother Giulia leading the way, her habit tucked inside her rope belt. There they were at the Piazza del Duomo in Florence . . . and there was one improbable picture of boys and nuns together in a sailboat. Every time I found Angelo's picture, he would dance with joy, having invented a new kind of hide-and-go-seek game with me. But not one word of Italian would he speak. He had written my Italian off as impossible.

Mother Giulia, when the parents had shaken her hand and left, beamed her approval at the sight of the two boys and me going through the scrapbook together. She led us into another room where I saw boards and carpenter's tools. "Here we are going to have a caffè," she said. "The boys can serve coffee to their parents and other visitors for fifty lire. We will have chairs, and a cash register, and a big red umbrella even though it is indoors. The boys really wanted a red umbrella." From a closet she took two aprons just the right size for Michele and Angelo. They put them on to show me how they would look dressed as waiters.

"Angelo will serve his mama and Michele will serve his uncle when they visit," she explained. "You must come back in a few weeks, signora, and have coffee with us. It will cost you fifty lire, but it will be very good coffee."

The doorbell rang and Mother Giulia went to answer it. This time it seemed to be a grandfather. She looked behind him and then called to me that there was a very large automobile in the yard. Was it someone waiting for me?

I said my arrivederla to Mother Giulia and to Angelo. "Dica a la signora, 'arrivederci,'" Angelo demanded of Michele, who impatiently said, "Angelo says 'good-by.'"

March 2

THIS SUNDAY AFTERNOON we drove to another of the hill towns near Rome to visit the Orphanage of St. Joseph. This little city with a population of 20,000 was as ugly as the last hill town had been beautiful. My first impression was that I was looking at a town that had not raised a hand against the ravages of time, but closer observation showed that it had seen savage bombing during the war. About every fourth building had a gaping hole, and the ones in between were peppered with strafing patterns.

The sign above the door proclaimed that this was the Orfanotrofio di San Giuseppe. It was the first time I had seen the word "orphanage" used thus. San Giuseppe's, a dirty gray four-story building, was attached on one side to the thirteenth-century village church. I was puzzled about the entrance, so I went in through the church. Toward the front I saw what I supposed was a Sunday school class for about twenty little girls (children of the townspeople, I guessed, because of the quality and variation of their dress) who were memorizing their catechism just as Catholic children do in America. Two young women marched among them guiding the chanting voices: "The church is one; it is holy; it is catholic; it is apostolic."

One of the young women came toward me, and I asked where I could find the padre in charge of the orphanage. She called a solemn-faced child and asked her to take me to the office of Father Speranzo.

The child led me silently through a side-door entrance down a grimy, dingy hall, and knocked on a door. It was opened by a stout young man in a disheveled cassock. (It seemed to me that, except for the pope, I never saw a thin member of the clergy in Italy.) The child, who had not heard me speak, surprised me by telling the priest that I was an Americana who wished to see the orphanage. Father Speranzo was perfectly courteous and pleasant as I explained that I was the Americana about whom Signorina Lombardo had written. He agreed with a little nod to show me through the institution, but it was clear that he was bored by the assignment.

First he led me into a dark, cold room with discolored walls where there were several tables and chairs, a few comic books, and three table games that we Charnleys had nicknamed "table football." We had often seen it played in caffès by as many as eight or ten men at a time. This, I was told, was the recreation room. It served fifty boys!

Next we went into a kind of classroom where eight adolescent boys were quietly studying. They were shabbily dressed, but not in uniform. When we entered they stood up and remained standing though I tried unsuccessfully to imitate Signorina Fermi's trick of waving them down. Father Speranzo explained that these were the boys who had elected not to go on some kind of outing – they had remained at the orphanage on the chance that parents might visit. The boys listened to Father with dull passive faces. It seemed to me that there was little affection between this man and the boys.

As he led me downstairs I raised a question. "Why is this institution called an orphanage when some of the boys have parents?" He shrugged his shoulders uninterestedly. He led me into a basement dining room with water-stained, ugly yellowed walls, gray tablecloths that had once been white, and an odor that could only have been the stench of slowly rotting food. He gestured toward the kitchen and I was pleased not to be invited in. From where I stood I could see garbage on the floor and three big cats prowling in it.

I was happy to leave the horrid first floor. On the second floor, he showed me several classrooms with blackboards and maps where the boys studied, and a dingy, dusty room which he grandly called "the library." It had a few short shelves of books – all cheap paperbacks, which had taken on the gray-brown of the entire institution.

Father Speranzo would fling open a door, briefly explain the purpose of the room, allow me ten seconds to let my eyes wander over it, close the door, and march on to the next room.

We went up an ancient staircase and found ourselves on the dormitory floor. First I saw the bathrooms, three of them. There was just one shower with a nozzle that was dribbling water, dozens of crude, rust-stained wash basins, and about fifteen toilets. I saw no bathtubs at all. The stench of urine stung my nose. When we entered the dormitories, I found that the odor permeated the entire floor.

The bedrooms with their rows of army-like cots were much like others I had seen except for one important difference. These beds were lumpy and badly made. Books, balls, jackets, and clothes were strewn about. Shoes and pajamas littered the dusty floor. In other dormitories I had been repelled by the stark, military neatness, never realizing, I guess, how frantically restless a room becomes that has a little disorder around each of fifteen beds. The answer must be that there is no right way for a dormitory to look.

In one room, a pale and sandy-haired boy, carefully buttoned into a heavy gray sweater, sat up in bed. He was playing with a half-dismantled table radio. The padre did not greet him, but I did. I learned from the boy that he had a bad cold and a fever. He hoped he could get up tomorrow. The padre seemed impatient at my efforts to talk to the boy. When we were out of the room, he said that the boy had "only a little fever." The sensation of the loneliness that I felt hovering around the pale boy with the radio clung to me, and I weighed proposing to this cold, brusque priest that I would like to go back and talk with the sick boy. I never did get up my nerve to suggest it. Partly it was because it was hard to suggest anything to Father Speranzo, but also because my impulse to mother these children seemed to me a little foolish . . . like trying to hold back a flood with a pebble.

I had to work to match my stride to Father Speranzo's. We went up to the fourth floor where there were small bedrooms for four priests and another dormitory for the youngest boys "near to the adults."

After our quick inspection Father pointed to a narrow little circular staircase. I was to mount it, I gathered. (Italian politeness always required that "the signora go first" even in a tour of unknown places. It seemed to me I was forever trying to guess which way my guides expected me to turn and at which door I should pause.)

At the head of the dark stairs I opened a small door that let us out onto the roof terrace of San Giuseppe. The view in all directions was magnificent. Straight ahead was Rome. To the right, the eye traveled up a green mountainside to its peaked top. Most wonderful of all, though, was the gentle mountain meadow to the east. At one corner of the roof terrace, looking down on the town, was a handsome statue of the Madonna, her hand gently resting on the shoulders of a sturdy little boy. Her halo was outlined in electric lights, a crude touch on an otherwise lovely statue. The boys and I could see only the rear of the statue, because the front view was for the townspeople. Perhaps if I could see her at night with her halo lit from the town square, I might forgive the little lights that seemed from close up to mar her beauty.

I drew my eyes from the lovely view and focused on the buildings nearby, some of them with repairs in progress. Here on the terrace a handsome new tile floor was half finished. I asked myself why they tiled the terrace floor before they painted and cleaned the ugly rooms in which the boys lived. I didn't know the word for bomb damage. Father Speranzo watched my eyes travel from one damaged building to another. Perhaps he was thinking angrily that it was American bombers that had wrought such havoc in his impoverished little town. There was no clue in his impassive face.

I wonder whether other Americans experienced, as I usually did, a quick irrational rush of guilt and shame at the sight of bombed buildings. I never questioned at the time of the war that America had to fight fascism. Yet those gaping tears in buildings and a quick image of how it must have been for the townspeople the nights those bombs fell made me shudder. I guess I should have been ashamed not for my own country but rather for the whole human race.

For the first time, Father Speranzo seemed not in a hurry to have me move on. Perhaps it was because this view from the terrace of San Giuseppe was one in which a man could take pride. At a gesture from me, he opened the door and I led the way down the dark winding staircase. Glancing at his face, I deduced that our tour of inspection was ended and that it was up to me to find my way out.

I was not more than ten feet from the front door when I was overtaken by Father Rossi, the head of San Giuseppe. He was a warm, outgoing man who apologized for his absence, invited me back for coffee (which I refused), and wondered whether I had any questions. Perhaps he understood Father Speranzo's shortcomings as a guide.

In a few minutes on the church steps, I learned from him that eighty boys were cared for by day at San Giuseppe's, but thirty of them went home to sleep. None were really orphans, and some day they would get a new sign over the door.

I asked whether they had nuns to help them with the cooking and laundry. Father Rossi said that they hired "the good women of the town" to do this work. "Good, perhaps," I thought, "but not very efficient." Father said that there were two other institutions for children in his town, both for girls. Perhaps he could arrange appointments for me if I would care to see them. I declined, thinking of Debby and Mitch waiting in a caffè in this depressing town.

Three institutions for children in a town of 20,000! I was reluctantly beginning to realize that this was typical of Italy. As I walked back to the square, I wondered how many Italian children must be growing up in places like San Giuseppe's.

This was the dirtiest institution I was ever to see in Italy, though I'm sure there are others as bad. "Is this," I asked myself, "what happens when men in Italy take on women's work? Does it matter deeply to the boys who grow up in it? Can the warmth of Father Rossi compensate for the coldness of Father Speranzo?"

Always, there were questions, questions, questions. When would I begin to feel I knew some of the answers?

March 3

TODAY I FINISHED WRITING, in English, a fourteen-page talk titled "How America Succeeded in Thinning Out the Number of Children in Institutional Placement." Certainly this was the first time in my life that I'd written a speech without an audience or an invitation in mind.

My last month's experiences had left me burning with "messages." Somehow I must get across the essential wrongness of letting children grow up in institutional care. I must break through the fatalistic Italian response that, because this is a treatment plan that dates back almost to ancient Rome, nothing can now be done to change it. It seemed to me that if I quietly told how America had slowly and painfully managed to close down most of its institutions for child care somebody might draw a parallel about what could be done in Italy.

I chose my words thoughtfully, hoping to inspire without producing resentment. My plan was to have my tutor, Signora Giorgiana Ugonio, translate the script into Italian and then give me lessons in how to read it intelligently. Perhaps the staff at SANC or at ICS would attend a meeting to hear me give this "discorso." Maybe Father de la Roche would turn me loose with a group of his students. Already I had many things to say to Italian social workers; my puzzle was how I was to get them said.

I took my manuscript with me when I went to see my tutor. For the last two weeks I had been working with Signora Ugonio six hours a week—three mornings of two hours each. I had been very lucky in finding her. Though she looked little more than twenty years old, and though she was warm and kind, she was also a stern disciplinarian.

She brushed aside my allergy to grammar: "It is true it is boring, but you must know it." She drilled me so hard that in a two-hour period I rarely had a moment even to light a cigarette. When I was practically numb at the end of the second hour, she would allow fifteen minutes of conversation. Even then she would not talk slowly, because I really must accustom my ear, she said, to the more normal tempo of speech. The "homework" she assigned was "at least three Italian movies a week." (I managed only about one a month.)

I am making her sound humorless and harsh when actually she

was nothing of the sort. I could never get over my surprise that I, a mother of nearly grown children, could be driven into such a frenzy of work by someone with a puckish little girl face. She was an excellent tutor, and more conscientious than I wished in seeing that she and I both earned the $1.65 an hour that the Fulbright Commission spent for her tutoring.

For our fifteen-minute conversation periods, I would save up all the questions that puzzled me. Sometimes I would slip into English but firmly she would pull me back into Italian. Precisely when the two hours were up, however, she would offer me coffee and when I had time to stay she would discuss in lovely English many fascinating subjects, one of which was her love of good American novels.

She was sympathetic and helpful about my struggle to understand the cultural meanings back of the strange experiences I was having. She was amused at my confusion about how I'd get started really working and my anxiety about some of Father de la Roche's grandiose ideas. His family and hers were personal friends, and sometimes she would tell me stories about his childhood and young manhood. "His mind is like quicksilver," she would say. "It is exhausting to try to follow it. But you need to have faith in it because it gets to the right places."

Mercilessly as she drove me, she always wonderingly and approvingly commented on how hard I worked. "This Fulbright program for Italy and all you people who work so hard to help us – you are all so generous! So good! Oh, you Americans, how I really love you all!" And then, thoughtfully, "Well, almost all. You have some spoiled rich brats. I tell you it is impossible to teach them Italian. Really impossible. I cannot do it. And I cannot like them."

She had a way of reducing me to the stature of a small, not too bright child. "Now really, Mrs. Charnley, your fixation on the masculine singular verges on the pathological. How am I to cure you?" And she would shake her head in despair.

But then she would lift me up again. As she did today, when she quickly scanned my first three pages of manuscript. "Oh, splendid," she said. "You have a nice, clean honest style—like Hemingway. It will be a pleasure to translate you."

Yes, Signora Giorgiana Ugonio was a hard teacher—the hardest I ever had. I made progress with her that was almost faster than I could endure. Even Maria, our maid, said that it was remarkable. I'm sure that I owe Signora Ugonio for something besides my vocabulary. I loved Italian food and would surely have become fat if she hadn't worked me as hard as she did.

I had learned but never quite believed that mental energy burned calories. But after a workout with Signora Ugonio, a platter of Maria's best pasta didn't even leave a small bulge.

March 6

TODAY I HAD MY FIRST APPOINTMENT at SANC—the Society for Assisting Needful Children. I felt almost as lost as I might have had I been asked, say, to talk to highway engineers about the best way to plan a new freeway. I had given myself little lectures about being flexible and learning to yield to a new culture, but not to the point of agreeing blindly to undertake something I didn't know how to do.

The agency offices were in a middle-aged Roman "palace"—Roman yellow in color, resembling a 1910 American apartment house as much as anything. The building was in a quiet, tree-lined street near the Tiber. SANC's offices were on the second floor.

I pushed open the door and found the long reception hall that was the characteristic architectural mark of Italy's devotion to waste space. Smack in the center was a tiny table where a short, smiling man sat with a telephone. On chairs down one side of the corridor were a few impoverished-looking people—a woman in ragged clothes with two or three small children, a wretched, hungry-looking old man, three adolescent boys with the subtle aura of juvenile delinquency on them, a sad-eyed young woman in widow's weeds.

The little man at the desk gestured toward the chairs and indicated that he would be free in a minute. Since all chairs were taken, I moved up against the wall to wait. To my dismay, the two Italian women quickly rose and with much bowing and scraping urged me to take their chairs. I protested; but my refusal distressed them and merely convinced them that they were not being understood. In the interest of peace I sat down, thinking that nothing can be more painful than to yield to so objectionable an act of caste-consciousness.

I listened to the little man at the telephone, trying to make out his function. Slowly, and with astonishment, it came to me that he was doing telephone intake! I heard him explaining, "But, signora, there is nothing our ente [agency] can do for you."

He put down the telephone, shaking his head in obvious puzzlement at the depths of human frailty; instantly, it rang again. Someone apparently had legitimate business with Signorina Menotti. He asked the caller to wait "un momento" and opened a closed door without knocking. There I saw several women, apparently social workers, at their desks. One of them put down her papers and picked up the phone.

Now the little man approached me; when I told him that I was Signora Charnley, armed with an appuntamento with Signorina Italia Lombardo, he was all smiles. In broken English he settled down to quite a little conversation with me about his brother in Boston, the war years when the nice American soldiers had taught him to speak a little "brutal English," and so on. He was a genial, likable little man, delighted to be showing off his English, and I would have enjoyed him had I not been troubled by the insistent ringing of the telephone and the fact that Signorina Lombardo was waiting for me. Finally the disciplinarian in me could bear it no longer and I said, "Signore, the telephone is ringing."

The telephone man came back to me. "Please follow me to Signorina Lombardo," he said.

Signorina Lombardo greeted me with a handshake. Again I experienced a rush of warmth and liking for her. Here was a wonderful face. I hoped that someday an Italian painter would find the skill to portray the weariness, the compassion, the generosity and worry that made her plain sharp features beautiful.

It was not difficult to understand her. She spoke slowly and carefully, gesturing freely; when words and gestures failed, she would reach for a little scratch pad and sketch a picture for a word I couldn't get. With no one else to whom I talked did I attempt such elaborate communication. Almost from the first we talked like old friends and co-workers; we refused to let the Atlantic of language difference come between us.

I drew from my purse the dog-eared list of institutions I had visited. We were in accord in our feelings about all of them but one – San Francesco's Little Nest. When I told her that I found the three simple, uneducated nuns warm, gifted, and understanding of the needs of their children, she shook her head in wonderment. "But this is a terrible place," she said. "These nuns swallow up a child, so that he is lost to his own parents, social workers and everybody. We have heard that parents are turned away from the door. We have heard that children are told that God is so displeased with the sins of their parents that He wants the children to forget them."

"But," I protested, "when they leave the institution at age six, surely the social workers can get to them?"

She shook her head sadly. "They belong to the nuns of Saint Francis. They are sent to another convent of Saint Francis in Milan or Venice. To be given as an infant to the nuns of Saint Francis is an eighteen-year sentence. There is almost no escape."

My senses, I think it is fair to say, reeled. I remembered the little nun who had sheepishly kissed the naughty boy. I remembered the balls wildly bombarding the picture of the St. Francis. I remembered the patience of the nuns toward the blue-faced boy with the runny nose. I explained to her my feeling. I said, "There is some mistake that probably grows out of my ignorance of your language. I can make serious mistakes with words, but not with feelings. I trust my feelings. And my feelings say that San Francesco's was a good institution."

The olive-green eyes warmed as the laugh wrinkles tightened

around them. "I too trust your feelings, signora," she said. "There must be, as you have said, some mistake. In time you and I shall discover what it is."

Together we admired the gentle gifts of Mother Giulia at Santa Clara's. I said that she represented Italy's highest hope — to educate the nuns and priests who cared for the children to the importance of parental love in the life of the institutionalized child.

She agreed and told me that this was also Father de la Roche's highest hope for Italy. Did I know that there was a branch of the New Roman School that had just one function — to train the nuns to be social workers? I said that I was delighted to hear it. She said, "Someday I shall bring you to the school to teach my classes of nuns about the American philosophy of child care."

"And what about the priests?" I asked.

She smiled. "The priests do not think of themselves as needing to learn anything," she said. (Double negatives are proper in Italian so that the sentence came out delightfully: "Priests don't think they need to learn nothing.")

We moved on to specific questions. I needed to know how much an ente like ICS or SANC paid the institutions that cared for children. To my dismay, I learned that it was 200 or 300 lire a day (32 to 48 cents). Crash went my dream of showing Italy that foster placement could be more economical!

I told her my disappointment. In America, it cost about 1,000 lire a day to keep a child in a foster home, but 4,000 lire to keep him in an institution. She was amazed. What was so expensive about institutional care?

I explained the costs — rent, food, medical care, salaries of many workers . . . She frowned. "In America you pay the nuns a salary?" she asked.

When I explained that we didn't have many nuns and that most of the institutions were not church-connected she looked thoughtful. "There would be advantages," she said slowly, "to living in such a country." Quickly she modified her disloyal remark: "At least, for doing social work."

I went after the big question. By whom were Italy's institutions supported? A little by the government, a little by the church, a little by the rich, and a little by the parents themselves when they had money beyond their own needs.

Could she tell me about a family budget? What if there were a widower with one child who earned 18,000 lire a month?

Such a man would pay the ente 8,000 lire for the care of his child in an institution and would use the remaining 10,000 lire ($16.50) for his own living expenses. I asked whether such a man might not take the child home with him at night to sleep, or perhaps to spend Sundays. How, she asked, could mothers or fathers take children home when they had none?

"But where do they sleep?"

Signorina's description of the way of life of thousands of Rome's poor showed me the hopelessness of trying to apply American solutions to Italian problems. A working man or woman who lived on 10,000 lire a month (and many lived on less) would share a rented room with five or six adults of the same sex. It would be crowded with beds or, sometimes, mattresses. There would be one toilet shared by thirty or forty people. There would be no cooking facilities at all. At all times of day or night there would be people sleeping in some of the beds. They ate by buying a piece of bread and perhaps a little fruit or some cheap wine, which they often consumed outdoors. (Hadn't I seen men walking along the streets eating bread? Of course I had; but it hadn't occurred to me that this was their entire meal.) I could see, couldn't I, that such a parent could not take a child "home"?

I was unwilling to yield easily to the inevitability of separation of parents and children by reason of poverty alone. I described our practice in America of helping the working father of a motherless child to move in with a family and to pay for care of the child by day and often for one meal for both. Parent-child boarding homes, we called them. Could the ente not find some poor woman who would be willing to take in a man and his child for, perhaps, 16,000 lire a month, leaving the man 2,000 for his other needs? She said that the entes did not help clients to make such plans, but sometimes the clients made plans like this by themselves. However, so few poor Italian families who would accept this plan, even for 16,000 lire, had any extra room. All "free" space was usually quickly rented out to other families.

I continued to look for solutions. Was there no government agency in all of Italy from which a widow could get money to feed herself and her children? She shook her head. Then she added that sometimes, if the man had had insurance, there would be a little money. "Only sometimes?" I asked.

"Father de la Roche told you of the company in which Signorina Sletto works? If the agent of the company is well impressed with the mother, he will give her the money. If he is not, he will give it only to institutions. This is why we are so eager to have social workers, not businessmen, do the investigations."

I began to realize that I was butting my head against a rigid legal and cultural framework; but I continued to test it. "The 200 or 300 lire that SANC can give to an institution for the care of a child – couldn't you give that to a mother instead? If a mother had three children and you gave her 900 lire, and she could earn a little, couldn't you try this?" (My sentences were terrible, but she understood me.)

At last she was nodding. "Yes, this is what we are beginning to do here at SANC. Some strong women are contented with this little we can give them and do succeed in holding their families together. We give it only to women who we believe will succeed, because we fear that if there are gross failures that get into the newspapers someone may question our right to give directly to mothers the money that is really set aside for institutional care. But this weak plan is our only hope for keeping poor families together."

I asked Signorina Lombardo how many children in Italy were growing up in institutional care. She dug about in her desk and came up with a government pamphlet. In 1945 there had been 6,563 institutions for children in Italy, with 489,137 beds. She said that no recent figures had been gathered. It was generally believed that these figures were not even accurate for 1945, and that there had been a steady growth in the number of children institutionalized since 1945. I asked whether half a million would be an accurate figure for the number of children in care. She responded that it would be a very conservative figure. She added that she had heard the statement that one of every ten Italian children was growing up in an institution.

No wonder Signorina Lombardo looked so tired and worried. I learned that morning that she was as opposed to institutional life for children as I, and for about same reasons. How strong it was to hate and detest a system like this — but to choose to work within it!

"What is the most common cause of family breakup in Italy?" I asked. "Is it the death of two parents? Is it divorce? Poverty?"

"Poverty is the chief cause," she answered. "Poverty and the very large families. Sometimes a couple can find a way to feed one or even two children. But our poor families have perhaps eight, ten, perhaps fifteen children. Divorce is not a problem because divorce is illegal in Italy — though we have our share of abandonments. Sometimes fathers or mothers run away to avoid having more children."

I was on shaky ground. I wanted to ask this Catholic social worker about birth control. This is a neat problem to handle in English. And how in the world do you say "birth control" in Italian? Think, Jean, think . . . some fancy English word for birth control to which you can give an Italian twist. I gulped and tried. "Signorina, do you know an Italian word that is like 'contra-concettivo'?" She nodded smilingly.

Her quick understanding and her smile seemed good omens. "In America there is a type of contra-concettivo which we call — (Oh damn! How would you say 'rhythm'?) I made what I hoped was a rhythmical gesture. It didn't work. I drew rhythmic lines on the scratch pad. Bless her! She was trying so hard to understand. I backed up to start over. "A husband and wife may come together every week of the month except the one when the woman has eggs." She broke into a broad smile. Now she understood. I continued. "American priests say that this is not a sin. Would not this method be helpful for poor people with big families?"

She shook her head. "Also in Italy it is not a sin. But to use it well, both the man and woman must be well educated to understand it. There must be money for a doctor to teach them. And even then, I have been told, it does not work very well."

I said hesitantly, "Though I am not Catholic, I know that Catholics may not use birth control. Some students of the church say that someday the church may change its mind. It seems to me that this would be the most important single way to help the children of Italy."

I had not offended her. She was nodding in agreement. "Yes, this is so. But it is against the laws of our nation and our church. Perhaps the church may change someday. I doubt it. But even if it does it will take many generations."

I was aware that instead of helping Italia Lombardo, I was taking up her morning in educating me. But when I told her of this feeling, she said that my questions were "interesting and useful." I suggested that I should return on the following Monday to read some records and begin to prepare comments on my reaction to the agency's casework. She was very pleased; she would have case histories ready for me.

She suggested that now I might like to meet some staff members. We went into a room where there were five desks. She pointed to the empty one, saying that I would find the case histories there the following Monday. She introduced me to the four staff members — three attractive women and a man, all in their late twenties. Immediately they pulled chairs into a circle and we began a conversation. Signorina Lombardo got us started, then shook hands and left.

I started by telling them of the institutions that I had been visiting. They agreed with me in general except about the dirt at Orfanotrofio di San Giuseppe. "Perhaps on a Sunday morning things might be a little disorderly?"

How do you say "stench" and "filth"? I had to settle for "sporchissimo" (the most dirty), spoken with great vigor. One pretty woman said that she visited St. Joseph's once a month, that the boy she had placed there was happy, and that she didn't find it too dirty. I pondered to myself the differences in cultural standards. Since I lacked adjectives, I used nouns to describe the cats eating garbage from the kitchen floor, and the "bad smell." The young worker smiled tolerantly saying, I think, that in the evening a woman would sweep the garbage off the floor and they would open a window to air it out.

I tried them on my puzzling favorite, San Francesco's Little Nest. None of them had visited it; but from what they had heard they were amazed that I had gained admission and were baffled by my liking for what I saw.

I also tried to describe the little house with the small girls who were handled like big dolls, but I couldn't remember its name. But yes, they thought they had recognized it. A woman, whom I later came to know as Alta Quello, told an animated story about "the crazy woman" who was the direttoressa. Signorina Quello spoke lovely clear Italian and, though I understood every word I heard, I couldn't believe what she was saying: The direttoressa, Signorina Quello insisted, sewed an elastic band inside a long sleeve of each child. On one end was attached a hundred-lire piece. She would send the children one by one to the open food stands to ask for an orange, a loaf of bread, or whatever she wanted. The child would show the hundred-lire coin between his thumb and finger to the tradesman. When the unsuspecting merchant handed the child the food, the child would release the coin, pretending to have dropped it. As the man searched for the vanished coin, now safely up the child's sleeve, the child would run off, food in hand, and give it to the direttoressa who was hidden nearby.

"But," I protested, "Signorina Mannini of ICS likes this place!"

More discussion led to the solution. They had been speaking of another institution nearby. Not Santa Anita of the big dolls. I pressed, "But there is actually an institution in Rome where children are taught to steal?"

They assured me soberly that there were many terrible ones, not alone in Rome but all through Italy. I would not see them because people who exploited children like this would not let me.

One young woman asked me whether I liked the institutional

plan of living for children. I told her that I did not. I said that I believed that only maladjusted adults could emerge from such a rearing; but, I added, I did not see that Italy had any present alternative. They nodded agreement. I said that perhaps the starting point would be to improve the institutions – make them more like Santa Clara's and less like the huge, military San Marco's. This pleased them. They asked what I would like to change. I was careful to acknowledge that they knew much more about this than I, but that my American point of view suggested some beginning reforms. They pressed me to tell them and, somewhat to my discomfort, two of them took notes.

I said that first of all, I would send every child to the public schools so that he should daily see and know the outside world. Next, I would abolish the system that moved children every three or four years. On both of these ideas, I sensed vigorous agreement. Next, I said, I would mix the sexes – rearing boys and girls together, and having them taught by nuns and priests who lived in the same institution. I'll never know just what I said about "living together"; but suddenly my audience burst into surprised and delighted laughter. They apologized quickly but soon their laughter bubbled up again, and a girl named Sofia needed to wipe her eyes repeatedly.

"Perhaps in America, signora," the man social worker explained kindly, "nuns and priests might live in the same place and work together. But in Italy the idea is most unusual!"

"They would be fighting all the time," Signorina Quello explained amusedly, "about who was boss."

At length I told them I must go, but I would be back to read cases on Monday. Sofia said that Signorina Lombardo had mentioned that, though I spoke Italian very well (that Italian politeness!), I didn't know how to read. I said sadly that it was true – I must come with a dictionary and teach myself. They were all sympathy. As I left, they warmly offered to help any way they could.

March 10

BLUE MONDAY CAME with soggy weather to match my mood. What a depressing feeling it was to start off with paper, pencil, and a dictionary to read a case history!

The smiling receptionist proudly greeted me in English and led me to the desk Signorina Lombardo had assigned. Three of the four workers I had met were there – Signorina Quello, Sofia, and the young man Alfredo.

Optimistically, Signorina Lombardo had left four case histories for me. Happily I noticed that they were less than a fourth the size of American histories. My office mates, all of whom stayed with me all morning, seemed to be engaged in reading cases, taking occasional telephone calls, and doing their recording in longhand. They greeted me warmly, happily accepted cigarettes whenever I passed them, and – though they held their case histories up as though to read them – seemed to be in no mood for work.

After ten minutes of conversation, I picked up a case history and began my struggle. I wrote out my translations word for word. It was interesting to see what an Italian case history was like, even though the discovery involved a long and painful process. Here is the first case history I read in Italy.

The Ammale Case

Child: Ammale, Anna Maria; born 4-24-53 – recording done on 1-26-56 when Anna Maria was less than three years old. [I never did understand why there was just this one child listed when the case referred to problems in planning for four children.]

Complainant: Signora Salvi, [address and telephone number], Rome.

Problem: Signora Salvi knows Signora Ammale well because she often buys her wares. The mother plants chicory [those two words, "plants chicory," cost me about twelve minutes], gathers it herself from the fields, and brings it into the town to sell. Signora Salvi knows that the older children rarely get to school and the two younger ones roam the fields unsupervised and unfed all day long in their mother's absence. Signora Salvi requests that SANC step in and take custody of these "minor and neglected" children.

Signora Salvi was asked the next time she sees Signora Ammale to tell her to come to the agency. An appointment time was given.

The mother, a peasant woman from another province, speaks with a heavy accent and it is hard to understand her and to be understood. She was punctual in keeping her appointment. She had lived for only a short while in a crude little house that she herself had built in the country on the outskirts of Rome. She had built the house with great difficulty. Her children lived with her. [I couldn't tell whether her husband did too.]

She justified her children's not being in school because school was so far away that even if they left early in the morning, they would not arrive until nearly noon, and then would soon have to start the long journey to get home before dark.

I asked why the family had left its original home and she said they had suffered from hunger when her husband returned from war. He was not able to continue his regular employment because he suffered from a crippling kind of arthritis contracted during the war. He had obtained neither treatment nor pension. The woman said that they were both illiterate and had not understood about things like pensions and now it was too late to apply for one.

Beside the two children of school age, there were two littler ones whom she left in care of neighbors. This was necessary because she hoed crops for a living and for this work it was necessary to leave home at dawn while the children were still sleeping. She had been repeatedly warned to take better care of her children but she was ignorant of various kinds of community help, and she didn't know how she could change.

She did not know, for example, that she could leave the two littlest children in a semi-institution where they would be given shoes, smocks, noon meals, a primer reader ["primer reader" cost me seven minutes], and an afternoon repast so that they would not be hungry when their mother came to take them home.

I promised her [a literal translation] that we were interested in her children and that we would work to help them. I said that either I or a colleague would go into the fields to find her children and become acquainted with them but right now unfortunately there was too much work for us to do at the agency. But eventually we would help her. Signora Ammale asked me to put through a telephone call to Signora Salvi (who had referred her).

11-10-56 – Signora Salvi has called many, many times and is very irritated because SANC has not been able to help the children "who are living like hungry little animals." I have explained that they do not have residence in Rome and that I have been writing letters and making phone calls to the commissioner at Fresone (place of legal residence). The commissioner had said [I think] that he might be able to bring the family back to Fresone after he had worked out a plan for them. Signora Salvi is impatient with the explanation and will not be pacified by the social worker's explanation that because the Ammales do not have residence, the social worker cannot put the children in a SANC nursery school.

Treatment Plan: I think these children should be put in a nursery school. At present they are living a very primitive kind of life. The extremely hard part of the case is that they are so very far away and it is so hard for a social worker to get to the place where they live . . .

This was not the end of the case; it was as far as my translation progressed.

When I came on the residence law I wanted to weep for Italy. It was not enough that this poor nation had all its own problems — it also had to struggle against one of America's most benighted systems. I wondered idly whether this law had originally been part of a Roman system of relief that had crossed the Atlantic to America, or whether Italy, just awakening to responsibility for its starving people, had copied the clumsy law of residence from America.

At any rate, it operated in the same ugly fashion in both countries.

I turned to Signorina Quello and asked whether it was ever possible for SANC to persuade the commissioner in Fresone or any other province to send money to Rome that could, for example, be spent in caring for children in a Roman nursery school.

She understood my question but didn't know the answer. She turned to Sofia and the two women discussed it lengthily and unintelligibly. Then the two of them took the problem to Alfredo and his whole manner suggested a role of masculine authority. Now there was a three-way discussion going with rapid-fire Italian words and gestures. The discussion went on and on.

I would have felt guilty at taking three workers away from their jobs except for my disconcerting observation that they weren't doing any work anyway. They had ordered coffee, and discussed Sofia's new scarf for which she had paid 1,000 lire; had visited with a pretty young woman who I guessed was a former employee; had repeatedly passed a roll of candy mints; and had had several long, gay four-way conversations with the receptionist, who made social calls from time to time.

Poor Italy! The law of residence . . . and now gossipy, lazy social workers who didn't know how the law would operate!

After perhaps twenty minutes they seemed to reach agreement, and it appeared that Sofia was to bring me the news. She spoke clearly and carefully and, though I was critical of her for wasting her morning (when she or one of the others could have been out in the fields looking for the Ammale children), I couldn't help melting to her attractive, charming manner.

"Signora Charnley," she said formally, "it is our opinion that sometimes it might be possible to get the commissioner in another province to send a little money for the care of children. It depends on whether it is a backward province or a modern province. But even when they do send some money, it is always too little."

I thanked her. "We have the same silly law in America and we too have problems with it."

Alfredo looked interested. "It is the law, so what can we do?"

"We American social workers are trying to change it," I said.

Signorina Quello joined in. "And can the social workers change the laws in America?" she asked.

I said that we could not all by ourselves, but that we, like any citizens, could work to persuade all the people together to change a law.

Alfredo scratched his head. "Why do you say it is a silly law?" he asked.

"Because," I said, "if an Italian is hungry, or if an American is hungry, he needs to be fed right away, wherever he is. It doesn't matter where he lived last year."

"I think so too," said Sofia, "but most Romans aren't willing to pay for the peasants' children from all over Italy. They would all come here to have their children fed in our nursery schools."

This is not an easy problem to discuss in English. Worn out by the effort I had already put into translations above the hubbub in the office, I was girding for another effort.

But I was saved by the receptionist, who came in to announce the noon break. I asked whether I might stay on a little longer to work. He was sorry, but when they closed they locked up, and would not be open until tomorrow morning.

He moved into English for me now. "Every Monday, every Wednesday, the office is locked in the afternoon. Every Tuesday, every Thursday, it is locked in the morning."

"But why?" I asked. "Are these all holidays?"

"Oh, no," he said, startled. "This is when the social workers go out to visit in homes and institutions. Sometimes they come back late at night."

I bowed to the command of the key in his hand and walked out with Sofia. She told me that she would be visiting an institution in a little town forty miles away to see whether they would take a nervous boy she knew. She would go by bus. I asked when she would get home. "Long after dark," she said.

I commented that her day was very long. She agreed uncomplainingly. She made me more accepting of the time wasting I had seen all morning.

The rain had stopped. The sun was beautiful and the clean cool air tasted delicious. I started toward my bus feeling rather triumphant. After all, didn't I have half a case translated?

March 11

I WORKED ALL DAY trying to learn to read aloud Signora Ugonio's translation of my speech, "How America Succeeded in Thinning Out the Number of Children in Institutional Placement." If I read word by word, understanding each word myself, it was, as Signora said, "terribly slow and awfully boring to hear." If I speeded up, hurrying over the words, the rhythm was all wrong and it became hard to understand. The only way seemed to be to study it so hard that I could look at a whole sentence and recite it instantly.

That was only one problem. There were certain words I had to learn to pronounce, such as "psicologia." The phonetic pronunciation would be something like this: "p-see-caw-law-gee-ah." It was an impossible word for me to say. I felt my mouth wiggling around as though I were trying to dislodge a fly from my nose. In vain, Signora Ugonio and I sought a synonym for psychology. We tried to eliminate the whole sentence. "It is very difficult, you see," she said pleasantly, "because for some unknown reason you are quite incapable of saying this word."

The reading was very hard; the pronunciation of a few words almost impossible. But the worst part was working myself into a lather to learn to give a speech that no one was to hear. Today it seemed to me that the flexibility I was showing in finding a way to do social work in Italy was bordering on insanity.

March 12

I KEPT AN APPOINTMENT this morning with Signorina Maria Mannini at Italian Children's Service. I was to report my progress in visiting institutions, to plan appointments to see more, and to try to find a way, as I was trying at SANC, to insert myself usefully into her organization.

I hadn't seen Signorina Mannini for some time, and I realized happily that I met her with the comfort one has in seeing an old friend. I greeted the six social workers who had desks in her office and began to tell her of my beginnings in Italy. She was easy to talk to, though not as understanding as my excellent Signorina Lombardo. And this turned out not to be one of my fluent days.

She was very interested in my visits to institutions. I described San Marco's and with a flush of pride she said that an order had gone out through ICS to all branch agencies in Italy that no ICS social worker was ever to place a child there. I told her about my unhappy puzzlement over San Francesco's Little Nest. It seemed to me that it was one of the gentlest institutions for children that I had seen in Italy; but Signorina Lombardo, Signorina Fermi, and many others said it was a terrible place. She asked me to describe just what I had seen. When I said "twenty-seven little boys," she halted me.

"Masculine, not feminine?" she asked.

"Yes, masculine." (This was a smart question because one of my special skills was mixing feminine and masculine endings on nouns.)

A few more questions cleared up the puzzle. I had gone to the wrong place. I said that the sign over the door had said "San Francesco's Little Nest," but I agreed that it was old and weather-beaten.

"The place you went to was really Santa Euphemia's," she said. "The poor nuns of Santa Euphemia moved into an old convent abandoned by the nuns of San Francesco. They neglected to remove the old sign. The nuns of Santa Euphemia are sweet, kind, uneducated women. They are truly impoverished. The nuns of San Francesco are prosperous, hard, authoritarian women who are hostile to parents of children and to social workers. At the new convent of San Francesco, which is ten kilometers north of Santa Euphemia's, there are seven hundred children. All girls. We had hoped the nuns might mistake you for an ordinary rich American and let you in."

Signorina Mannini seemed to find it fun to talk with me. I think she was highly amused by my improbable Italian. I would see a smile tug from time to time at the corners of her mouth. Sometime her eyes would stray slyly to the others in the room, hoping that they were sharing her enjoyment of my comedy. This didn't make me at all uncomfortable.

I really liked Signorina Mannini. I told her about the speech I had written. I told her how I had practiced giving it. Would any of her staff members be interested in hearing it? She was very polite and assured me that they would enjoy that very much but did not suggest a time or place.

I told her of our family plan to drive to Florence next weekend and she quickly wrote out the names of "two of the best institutions in all Italy." She said that she would get letters in the mail that night so that they would be expecting me. We arranged a date after our return to visit several institutions in the hill towns near Rome, and I said that Mitch would be willing to drive us.

March 13

TODAY I FINISHED writing a second speech in English. This one was entitled "A Few Suggestions for Changes in Italian Institutions." In it I tried, in the most diplomatic language I could find, to suggest ways of removing the worst of the curses of institutionalized life.

To me as an American social worker, it was routine to say that institutionalization was wrong for the normal child and that social workers in Italy should work toward its defeat. This was a fact which they apparently recognized almost as well as I. By now I had caught the tempo of Italian thinking enough to know that one moves toward social reform with infinite patience. Habits and prejudices move glacially, and it is the job of social work to make the generations of children who must wait as comfortable as possible.

I pleaded for cottage-type institutions with children of various ages and both sexes growing up together, with one nun acting for continuous years as the mother-figure, and with male volunteers, young priests, and even the gardeners visiting like bachelor uncles so that the children could at least see what a man was like. I asked for institutions made up of "little families."

I wanted my manuscript completed so that Signora Ugonio would have the weekend and the days we were in Florence to work on her translation. She was now approaching her delivery date and I was aware that her mounting tension and excitement made it harder and harder for her to concentrate on translation. The child welfare worker in me deeply approved her dreaminess and her little mistakes.

Mitch and I came home from a cocktail party at ten. (Most of the couples had gone on to dine at this fashionable Italian dinner hour.) We had work to do. We divided my manuscript in halves. Mitch typed the last half and I the first so that it would be ready to leave at Signora Ugonio's on our way out of Rome.

The next morning I arrived at a quiet apartment and didn't want to disturb a woman in the ninth month of pregnancy who was asleep. In vain I tried to find a safe place to tuck my manuscript in the door. Then my eye lit on the perfect answer. It seemed to me to offer appropriate symbolism. I tucked it under the handle of her recently emptied garbage can and trusted to luck that she would find it.

March 15 (Florence)

I BEGAN THE MORNING by walking from our hotel to the office of the United States Information Service, where bright-eyed young Signorina Pinucci was in charge of the dozen or so Fulbright grantees stationed in Florence. Signorina Pinucci had been in the Florentine Fulbright office five years before when Mitch had been teaching here, and it was pleasant to think of seeing her again. Florence was at her lovely, springtime best. Walking again through those magnificent Renaissance streets was a thrill.

Signorina Pinucci quickly arranged appointments for today and tomorrow at the two institutions to which Signorina Mannini had written.

I was entertained at her word choice when she spoke to the executives of the institutions that I would be visiting. "Signora

Charnley," she said, "understands Italian very well, though she speaks a little quaintly."

The Institution of the Queen of Heaven was not far away. Because I was so deeply in love with Florence this morning and so reluctant to leave the city to go indoors, I luxuriously decided to hire a carrozza (horse-drawn carriage). First I bargained with the driver. What would he charge to take me there?

"Six hundred lire."

"Five hundred lire?"

"Five hundred and fifty lire."

Since I wasn't sure just how far it was, I accepted his second price. When I arrived at the institution, I discovered that his meter read 400 lire. So I gave him 450. We had a heated discussion – I holding that he was unfair to offer a price to a stranger that was higher than the meter reading, he protesting that I was not taking into account that his poor horse was very tired and a good bit of our journey had been uphill. I was too full of well-being to argue wholeheartedly and so I paid the 550 lire with the suggestion that since I was doing this for his poor tired horse he should see that the horse got a good rest. He laughed happily as he drove off.

At the Institution of the Queen of Heaven I was met by its handsome and gracious director, Professor Grazzini. He told me that many years ago he had been in America for six months of study but had learned very little English. I think this made him especially tolerant of me.

This was an institution for "troubled" children, but I wasn't sure in what way they were abnormal. I asked whether there were schizophrenic children (this was an Italian word I knew). He said – rather critically, I thought – that America was much too free in applying this term to children. He believed that he had just one schizophrenic child. Many of his children were intellectually retarded, thanks to heredity, epilepsy, birth injuries, and incestuous unions. The institution cared for both boys and girls. About fifty per cent of them came from Florence and the nearby villages, the others from all over Italy. Many were Sardinians. In areas of Italy where there were no institutions to treat damaged children, the province and the parents would sometimes join to pay the cost of a child's care. Sometimes agencies paid. There were also rich benefactors who established free beds for needy children.

I asked whether parents visited. Yes, two Sundays each month. Tomorrow was visitors' day and was to be a great festa. The children were having a dress rehearsal this morning of the play they intended to give for their parents tomorrow. It was a very happy thing for the children—this giving of a play. The anticipation lifted the children up for many weeks and they got "a feeling of accomplishment—so precious and important for these children."

It was very difficult to teach "damaged" children to perform, Professor Grazzini said. They had short memory spans and poor senses of rhythm. But he was fortunate in having on his staff a nun who was truly gifted in helping children. It was important not to care too deeply how the show worked out but to remember that the whole point was to give each child a happy experience of accomplishment. "Happiness and security," he explained, "are more important to our children than to others because if they are unhappy or worried they cannot learn."

Had he any social workers on his staff? I was astonished when he replied that he had fifteen. But as we talked I discovered that in his thinking the term "social worker" applied to wardrobe mistress, lay teachers, and nuns. Most of his staff were lay women. He had five nuns to help him, most of them in the kitchen. No one on his staff had attended a school of social work. One of his board members, a Florentine doctor, had been trying to persuade him to hire a social worker. The doctor had said, "They are surprisingly useful." Professore laughed and said, "I'm sure you would agree. But your opinion would be biased."

Our tour of the buildings began with the psychologist's office, which was the first place a new child went. He showed me the tests that the psychologist used and I was fascinated to see the Thematic Apperception Test, the Stanford-Binet Intelligence Test, the Wechsler-Bellevue, the Rorschach—all tests used in America, all printed in Italian. He told me that each child was retested frequently as a measure of progress and a check of the original diagnosis, which might be skewed by "new-arrival trauma."

Next we went into the medical examination room, his own. It looked like any American pediatrician's office. Obviously the children got frequent and careful medical attention.

I asked about the use of drugs. Professor Grazzini said that he did not believe much in tranquilizers for children and he questioned the American use of them. He had experimented a little with them on newly arrived and very anxious children, but he believed that they tended to lessen the effectiveness of the staff in quickly reaching the troubled child. He did use anti-convulsive drugs for children subject to seizures and he found these to be very beneficial.

His services and those of the psychologist were available to Florentine children on an outpatient basis. I asked whether he felt he made more progress with outpatient children who lived in their own homes than with those in the institution. His answer was thoughtful. "The parents of these children are full of problems. The children who live here make more progress in learning to read and to become self-supporting. But it is a tragic thing to take a child away from his own home if there is a way to help while he is in it." This sophistication for the first time in Italy gave me the feeling that I was talking to an expert who would have something to teach American experts.

We continued through charming small classrooms, suitable for six or seven pupils at a time, and across the open courtyard to the shops where older children learned trades — shoemaking and book binding for the boys, embroidery, dressmaking, and straw-weaving for the girls. No children were in sight but I was introduced to a few teachers, both men and women. They were likable people, proud of the job they were doing.

The institution was beautifully planned, with an airy courtyard playground, a room in which to see movies or television, a spotless, well-equipped kitchen, and a sunny, gaily-decorated dining room. I didn't see the dormitories because we stopped to join the audience of children to see the play rehearsal. More than two hours later I was still watching the play in absolute fascination.

It was performed on a stage in the gym. Professore and I sat on folding chairs with the children all around us. The production was amazingly good, and how the children loved it! I was particularly moved by several playlets. One seemed to resemble the story of the little lost boys in Peter Pan. A pale-faced redhead sang a nostalgic song about his yearning to see his mother. A fairy princess complete with wand, glittering costume, and gobs of make-up danced in and sang a long and quite lovely solo in which she assured the little boys that she would help them get back to their mothers. (The theme was heartbreaking in this setting.) Professor Grazzini whispered that just a year ago the little soloist had come to the institution as a totally mute child. "Now she sings solos." I knew why he looked proud.

The playlets went on and on. In the frequent intermissions I had good opportunity to watch the children. In all that group – there must have been a hundred and fifty – I saw only one, a boy about six, who appeared dull and disoriented. The plays didn't interest him, and he wandered aimlessly about with no apparent purpose. Sometimes a teacher, sometimes an older child would take him gently by the hand and lead him back to his seat.

Four charming little girls sat in front of us whispering secrets to each other, giggling frequently, and making gay little jokes with Professore, who was delightful with them.

I noticed that the girls around ten or twelve loved to mother the three- and four-year-olds – holding them on their laps, fussing with their hair, kissing them. It seemed to me that the two age groups were nourishing each other emotionally.

The room was divided vaguely down the middle – boys on one side and girls on the other. But there was a good bit of interchange between the two groups and often a boy would move over to sit with the girls or several girls to sit with the boys. Teachers, nicely dressed women, were scattered through the group; each teacher held a small child on her lap, trading one for another when the first became restless.

Costumes and stage props were elaborate. The big boys did slapstick comedy that seemed to me much like early TV shows in America (or, now that I think of it, much like contemporary TV in Italy). These were lavish productions with dishes freely broken (how this made the audience laugh!) and a fancy and apparently fresh cake dropped on a boy's head. When the girls danced, they carried real flowers.

In the background I could glimpse a nun hustling around handing out properties, whispering forgotten lines to the children, her beads clattering incessantly. I had a farback memory of plays like this in my own grade school, and I recalled that the nun in charge usually got crabby and unstrung at rehearsals. This kind of tension and raspiness obviously didn't happen with this nun. The playlets I was observing were more polished than ours had been.

I was so moved by the performance by these abnormal children who were having such a happy time that the hours passed before I realized it. I whispered to Professore that I must leave. I would let myself out so that he could see the playlet through to the end. He rose immediately and led me back to his office, saying that he had seen it several times. He liked to observe the interactions of the children in the audience and to strengthen his relationship to them.

Before I left, Professore gave me a booklet about his institution which he urged me to read carefully, "so that you will understand the story behind what you have just observed."

Riding back to the hotel in the taxi, I studied a chart of diagnoses of the children in the Queen of Heaven. It showed a large number of children with post-encephalitic behavior; next most frequent seemed to be "frenzied behavior with a biopathic basis" (I could only guess what that might be). There were about twenty cases of mongolism, though I had suspected it of only two children I saw; several kinds of epilepsy were listed; there were false psychosis, abnormality of character, and a small number of children described as having "abnormality in social development"; five children were simply "nervous" and one schizophrenic.

I was so interested in the Italian diagnostic terminology—some familiar to me, some totally strange, some I could guess at—that I had done a most improbable thing. I had ridden through the streets of my second favorite among Italian cities with my nose in a book.

Perhaps I had become even more fascinated by Italian children than by Italy itself.

March 16 (Florence)

As I RANG THE BELL at the gate of the Institution for the Holy Innocents, I looked around at the breathtaking view. Ahead were mountains snow-capped and gently outlined against an intense blue sky. Behind was an almost airplane-like vista of the enchanting city, the Arno flowing through the center and beyond it the pattern of spires, domes, and towers. I wondered how I had become so disloyal as to prefer Rome.

The door was opened by a most typical woman door-opener in Italy—old, withered, dressed in widow's weeds, a nice flush of pink in her wrinkled cheeks. Was it all that red wine that gave even the very old in Italy such rich skin?

She led me to Direttoressa Nomentana, a handsome soft-spoken woman of perhaps forty, who greeted me in broken English. We talked for a while in English and then in Italian before she said, "Your Italian is a little better than my English. Perhaps we should speak Italian. If I puzzle you, we can move back to English."

This institution, she told me, had been established primarily for babies—newborns up to four-year-olds whose parents or grandparents had had tuberculosis. I made sure that these children's parents didn't have it currently. No, these babies had not been exposed to t.b., it was merely a factor in their heredity. A word like "preventorium" was used. I said that t.b. was slowly dying out in America, in part because of the use of drugs. She said that this was true in Italy too. In fact, the Institution of the Holy Innocents was more and more taking on a new character. She expected in time that the place would lose its "preventorium" aspect.

The building itself was lovely. It had been, she told me, the thirteenth-century castle of a Florentine count. The most recent contessa had been American-born. She had brought the American concept of charity—especially to the children of the poor—from America to Florence. At her death, her bereaved husband had given his castle to be used for the poor and sick children of Italy. Thus it was an exceptionally rich institution. The castle was known throughout Italy, and many years ago the government had declared it a national monument, which meant that no structural change that would mar the original pattern of the buildings could be made. Signorina Nomentana seemed to have mixed emotions about this—pride in the history and beauty of the place and annoyance at not being able to alter it.

I failed to see the problem, for every room I saw seemed sunny, charming, and functionally sound for the lovely babies who were being cared for in it. The place was summer-warm on a chilly day. It was sparklingly clean and the plaster on the walls looked new. There were wonderful Della Robbia ceramics of cherubs on the walls, and other lovely little statues everywhere. I liked particularly a whimsical long-legged, big-beaked bird that had pried open a giant oyster shell and was looking quizzically at an exquisite newborn baby sleeping inside it. I asked whether Signorina knew the English name of the bird. "Americans always ask and though I once learned I cannot tell you. But no—it is not a stork."

This place had all the cleanliness, convenience, and sanitariness of the grim place I had visited in Rome, but none of its spiritual frigidity. The babies were in little rooms that looked like nurseries—five babies to one attendant. The attendant moved quickly and warmly when a baby cried, picking it up, rocking it gently, and talking to it. Signorina and I moved in among the babies, stopping to talk with them as we went. She would point out that this baby had lovely eyes, that one a strong back . . . and "this little Elio was both beautiful and intelligent." The babies were most responsive – wiggling and squirming with pleasure as we spoke to them.

I remarked that some institutions kept me behind glass windows. Did she not fear my germs?

She smiled. "Signora, we live in a germy world. The nicest things and the nicest people are simply covered with germs. Even babies must start getting accustomed to them if they are to be happy. Perhaps you are bringing our little Celia some new American germs." I had offered a finger to Celia, who had wrapped her little fist tightly around it. I had an impulse to pull quickly back. Signorina laughed. "Oh no," she protested, "Americans are very nice people. Celia should get acquainted with your germs."

We walked through the room for newborns, who were all lying on their backs. "Do they sometimes sleep on their stomachs?" I asked. They did. Two hours in the morning and two hours in the afternoon until they were old enough to let the nursemaids know which they preferred. Leading out from the dormitories were French doors which opened on a terrace. The beds were on wheels so that when the weather was fine the babies could sleep and play in the fresh air. "The fresh air on this high Florentine hill is especially pure and health giving," Signorina told me as she led me onto the terrace to sample it.

The view from the terrace was so outrageously beautiful as to be almost in bad taste, like a Maxfield Parrish sunset. Though I knew the babies couldn't understand such beauty, I liked to think that their nursemaids did and that this made them extra serene in handling their charges.

We moved back into the dormitories. Carts with food were being pushed into the rooms. It was odd to see tray upon tray of nippled bottles. Signorina drew my attention to the solid food for the older babies: ground meat that looked like fine-cut hash, a thick vegetable soup about the consistency of pudding . . . and, to my amusement, Parmesan cheese sprinkled on top to train the new palates to Italian cooking. (When I told Debby about it that night she laughed and said, "I'll bet they sprinkle a little on the mother's breast for the littlest babies.")

Next we went through the rooms for the creepers and the crawlers. These were bubbling, outgoing babies who jabbered and squirmed ecstatically when we stopped for conversation with them. They were in playpens, strollers, and the Italian equivalent of teeter-tots. One little girl was crying impatiently and the nursemaid was soothing her. She explained that Sylvia had seen the food and was impatient. "Such a little pig," she said fondly. "Always she eats and eats and eats, and she never believes she will surely get another meal."

We went to see the "big" babies. The schoolroom was equipped with nice nursery-school-like toys. There was no school today because it was Sunday. Here, I was informed, they learned to count to five and sometimes ten; they learned their colors; they learned to identify animals in picture books.

In the next room we found "the big ones" seated around horseshoe tables listening to a woman tell them a story. They had no toys but were giving her very close attention.

As we entered the room Signorina greeted the children and asked me to shake hands with each one. Most of them loved this game, and each one beamed as he said his "buon giorno" to me. But six or eight ducked into the center of the horseshoe and hid their hands behind their backs. Signorina gave me a quick, nervous glance. Would I be one of those stupid adults who pressed shy children? I didn't, and she was reassured. "Rosa doesn't want to salute the signora," she said pleasantly to Rosa.

Now everyone felt relaxed. They left the table to inspect me thoroughly, finding the pockets in my coat, stroking my soft wool scarf, counting my buttons. Young Giovanni, after counting five buttons which he found readily, acted as though he was going to undress me in his quest for more to show me that he could count beyond five. A little girl grabbed my purse demanding, "What's this? What's this?"

"Questa è una borsa," I replied.

"Una borsa! Una borsa!" several of them chanted.

Signorina Nomentana lifted my purse up so that all could see it. "The signora has a big, black, beautiful purse," she explained.

"La signora ha una grande, bella, nera borsa," many of the chil dren said solemnly.

Then the signorina explained to the children that I was a visitoı who had come to meet them and to see where they worked and played. What else should they show me? "The toilets," exclaimed a brown-eyed blond triumphantly.

"And who," asked the signorina, "would like to show the signora where the toilets are?"

It turned out they all would, and as they clustered around me, leading and pushing me, I felt like a Gulliver swept along by Lilliputians. A talkative little girl was the first to think of showing me how they flushed, and we all admired the operation of the little toilet. A shy-looking boy pointed at the lavatories and said, "For washing our hands." Signorina hugged him spontaneously murmuring, "Bravo, Carlo!" (Carlo, she told me later, was retarded.)

I wanted to spend the rest of the day with these children — so gay, so outgoing, and, a voice inside me kept insisting, so well adjusted. I squirmed at my heretical response to the dogma of the psychiatrists, psychologists, and social workers — the "saints" of my adult professional life — who had convinced me that institutionalization of healthy little children almost invariably produced psychological cripples! They had written and I had believed that infants reared as these children were being reared wasted away, refused to eat, even died from the lack of will to live that came from lack of a constant mother-figure.

I looked at the happy children's faces around me and found myself dreading to think of the time that they must leave. I asked Signorina about it.

"When they leave they cry; we have heard that they cry for a long time and want to come back to us."

"And where do they go?" I asked.

"Many of them go home, especially those who come from parents with histories of tuberculosis. Some, who do not have suitable parents or homes, move on to other institutions."

I described the symptoms of murasmus, the wasting-away disease, to Signorina. They had never had a disease like that, to her knowledge, in the last thirty years. I asked about deaths. There had been none in the past four years. The year before that two babies had died. But they had been very ill when they arrived.

We had been moving toward a formal Italian parlor. When we were seated on dark red velvet chairs, a maid came in with coffee. We talked about many things, Signorina and I. I asked about when toilet training began. "Around eighteen months," she said. "It varies from one child to another. They teach each other. They are good teachers," she added. Then she surprised me by asking, "Is this right?"

"It's close to what we do in America," I said, "but our children rarely live in groups so that they cannot teach each other quite so well. I am beginning to think that children teach this lesson better than adults can."

Our coffee finished, we walked out into the yard so that she could show me the new building.

The building, so new that it was only half finished, blended nicely with its thirteenth-century companion. It was to be a surgical hospital for babies – babies who needed elaborate surgery like "repairs to the heart, the intestines, and the stomach. But children with infectious and contagious diseases cannot come here."

I saw the miniature X-ray table, the small operating table, the little oxygen tents. I saw the bedroom especially prepared for the doctor who would "stay all night for seriously ill babies." This, Signorina explained, was to be a new function of the Institution of the Holy Innocents.

As we walked toward the gate, I told Signorina that I had felt the babies I had seen were "well adjusted." She said, "They approach strangers with security. They eat and sleep well. Their color is good. They laugh easily. Yes, I think that they are happy babies."

Signorina offered in English to call a taxi, but I had decided to walk a few blocks to a bus stop. I kept going farther than the first stop, full of the beauty of the day and the setting, full of my own thoughts . . . Most of those warm, happy four-year-olds had lived in this institution since they were newborns. Surely these were neither incipient schizophrenes nor sociopaths. Would the uprooting process which some of them were soon to begin initiate the personality-scarring from which my profession was trying to protect babies? Somehow I was deeply sure that I had not been spending the morning among damaged children.

I had a sensation that reminded me of late adolescence, when so many childhood beliefs on which I would have staked my life began to totter before new knowledge.

What was the answer? What was the difference between these babies and the American babies who had been so damaged by institutional care? Culture? Heredity? A different manner in those who cared for the children? This kind of questioning was disquieting now as it had been in adolescence.

I was walking by an ancient garden wall over which some early spring roses were spilling. "A rose is a rose is a rose" . . . "Una rosa è una rosa è una rosa" . . . The rhythm was all wrong in Italian. Well, try this: "A fact is a fact is a fact is only sometimes true."

March 20

THIS MORNING'S NINE O'CLOCK APPOINTMENT had been arranged with Signorina Mannini by telephone, which meant that I was unclear about many things. Mitch was free to go with us as chauffeur, and we were to head "somewhere south of Rome."

Our destination turned out to be thirty kilometers into the Alban hill country—the Institution of the Immaculate Heart of Mary, a division of Italian Children's Service staffed by nuns. The buildings were situated on a beautiful big farm-like estate complete with vineyards, cattle, chickens, and huge vegetable gardens. Men were working the fields. Signorina Mannini told us that the institution produced enough milk, eggs, and meat for all its own children and a surplus for some of the other ICS institutions.

We were met in the parlor by the mother superior—a handsome, cultured woman who charmed Mitch completely. She soon discovered that his Italian was better than mine, and she addressed most of her remarks to Signorina and to him. She refused Signorina's invitation to describe her institution to me, apparently thinking I wouldn't understand. So Signorina described it: "The Immaculate Heart of Mary serves 247 girls, whose admission is always arranged by ICS social workers." (This was a modern innovation of which the nuns and the social worker were proud.) "The children go to school on the premises. Parents visit twice a month while school is in session, and ICS and the institution work hard at seeing that each child visits at home for Easter, for Christmas, and for a whole month in the summer."

"Signorina Mannini has taught us," the mother superior explained to Mitch, "the importance of keeping alive in the parents' hearts and minds a love for the children who must live away from them."

There were obvious affection and respect between these two women. When Signorina explained to the mother superior that I was an American social worker "dedicated to the well-being of children," the mother superior nodded approvingly. "Just as you are in Italy," she said.

It was a well-run institution. In the handsome, efficient kitchens nuns and lay women worked side by side. The dormitories were attractively furnished. Each youngster had a little chest at the foot of her bed for her personal treasures and her clothing. I saw dolls, teddy bears, collections of letters tied in ribbon, pictures of movie stars, pieces of embroidery which increased in size and complexity with the age of the owners.

The dining room, sunny and gay, had pasteled tables for four in graduated sizes. There was a little bouquet on each table. When Mitch said to the mother superior that he would like to live here, she burst out in pleased laughter.

I had my first view of a wardrobe room. Here six lay women and three nuns kept four sewing machines—Singers—humming. At one table a nun was cutting out stacks of navy blue serge to be made into spring capes for Easter. One woman sewed lace edging on white Peter Pan collars. The ball of lace she said she would use up that day was the size of a pumpkin.

The mother superior opened wardrobe cupboards to show rack after rack of identical costumes. The quality and the workmanship seemed excellent, but I was bothered by the sameness. When she opened another closet to show me summer dresses, I was greeted by a rainbow of many-colored, many-patterned cotton prints. I admired them freely and said I was glad to see that the children would be having dresses that were different from those of their mates. "Children need," I preached, "to find their individuality in their names, in their possessions, and in their clothes." The nun and the social worker liked my approval and seemed unaware of my tacit disapproval of the winter uniforms.

We attended the classrooms one by one, beginning with the preschool group. These little girls were open-faced, secure children who approached us in a friendly fashion. One little charmer quickly got Mitch involved in playing ball with her. The teachers were attractive, soft-spoken young women, most of whom lived in the nearby village. We were shown a kind of free-play room where seven little girls were busily keeping house. Their well-made miniature equipment included doll beds, bathtubs, tiny brooms, mops, scrub boards, clothesline, and dishes. A low sink full to overflowing with clean fluffy suds was shared by two little girls who took turns scrubbing doll clothes on a ribbed board. A most permissive atmosphere prevailed. One solemn-faced child had carried a bucket of soapsuds out to the terrace and was pouring the water on an old rug and scrubbing it vigorously with a brush. Signorina Mannini asked the teacher whether it wasn't too cold to be playing with water outdoors. The teacher asked the child whether she was getting "a little cold" and when the child said "no" she was left to continue her job.

While we were there, a bell rang and the seven little cleaning women put away their tools, dried their hands, and went back to the schoolroom. Seven new candidates came running in to continue the housework.

The next group, of kindergarten age, was engaged at various kinds of handwork at little tables. One child was drawing with crayons; another made countless tiny f's on the small squared-off paper that Italian children use in learning to write. One child, following a simple design on an embroidery hoop, was sewing tiny beads. The most "brava" and highly praised of all was knitting. The stubby little fingers gripped the azure yarn as tongue, shoulders, and elbows strained to twist the yarn around the needles properly. The children were contentedly engrossed in hard work—too hard, I thought. When we were out of earshot, after carefully expressing my approval of most of the institution, I said, "Your five-year-olds do very skillful work. American doctors believe that it is better for little children to do less fine work. When our children sew, they sew big stitches. When they make letters, they make big letters. Fine work, the doctors think, strains nervous systems and vision of small children. Mostly they need activity that uses big muscles." This was my first attempt to offer direct criticism and though I had walked on eggs in choosing my words, I had displeased Signorina Mannini. She liked pleasure and acceptance, but not criticism. "The little girl who knits," she explained, "will soon be so skillful that she will not have to look at what she's doing." She dramatized the gestures of an expert knitter.

As we went from classroom to classroom, Signorina Mannini greeted the children warmly and expertly. I watched her capturing the attention of each group, making an interesting story about the visitors from America, finding a dozen ways to reach the children individually. Now a hand on this one's shoulder, then a comment that a girl had changed her hair style. As I saw in room after room the happy responses she drew, I thought, "This is a universal—this skill of the expert group worker."

The children showed off for us. They sang songs, recited long verses, displayed their art work. In each of two rooms I found a boy. I felt sorry for them. Later I learned that they were sons of the farmers who lived at the institution. "It is good, this mingling of boys and girls, is it not?" she asked.

And I, who was preaching coeducation in the institutions of Italy, silently begged those two boys' forgiveness as I nodded in false agreement.

I was aware from the first of the elaborate, multicolored hair ribbons that the girls all wore—great butterfly ribbons of a kind that haven't been in fashion in America for a generation. Signorina Mannini told me that they served an important function beyond decoration. The nuns used them for discipline. A troublesome child would be deprived of her hair ribbon for a day or two. Then Signorina, actress that she was, showed me how the child would cry and promise to reform and the nun would yield and let her have the hair ribbon again.

"And when withholding the hair ribbon doesn't work?" I asked. Signorina explained. "The nuns have little talks with the girls in much the same way as you and I would, signora. These nuns are sweet and gentle by nature. There is no harshness in this institution."

She lowered her voice. "Five years ago there was a harsh mother superior of another order of nuns in charge here. I tried to persuade her to be different, but without success. Finally, and with a very heavy heart, I had to ask for her removal. It was a desperate measure. I was fearful of doing it. But when I see the happy faces of the little girls now and think of how they were before, I'm glad I found the courage."

I sympathized with her. "Your job calls for courage and diplomacy. I should think you'd be very proud of what you have accomplished."

"Doing social work in America must be very pleasant," she said wistfully.

"It is good to be doing anywhere," I agreed, "but never easy. We always want better things for children than we are able to give."

When we drove out of the grounds of the Institution of the Immaculate Heart of Mary, Mitch turned left, toward Rome, but Signorina corrected him. He must turn right to keep our next appointment. Mitch gave me a quizzical look, shrugged, and turned right. How many appointments had I agreed to, I wondered.

We had been in the foothills. Now our little bus was pointed straight toward the heart of the hills and for ten kilometers we climbed steadily until it seemed our narrow road had nowhere else to go. It hadn't. Our destination, we found, was called "Institution on the Top of the Mountain."

The setting and the way the buildings old and new were built into the mountain top would have charmed a modern architect. From my point of view, there was little else to recommend this institution.

It was run by a group of north European nuns who spoke Italian with heavy accents. (Nothing made me feel so proficient in my new language as to be able to identify a foreign accent.) I met the mother superior and her assistant, both gracious and eager to please, but both senile, frail, half-crippled. They climbed some of the myriad flights of stairs with us, puffing and straining at the effort. On every second or third level we stopped for tea or conversation. I was shocked at the effort these stairs required of them. Some of the saints, I have read, offered their suffering up to heaven for the release of the souls in purgatory. To have built a convent on a continuous flight of stairs seemed to me really reaching for a hair shirt.

Signorina and I, both distressed at the effort the poor old women were making, asked whether we couldn't go on alone. After much discussion a bell was rung, and a pretty nun in her late teens skimmed up the stairs with the ease of a skater to complete the tour with us.

This was a most unhappy place for children. The temperature couldn't have been above fifty-five. We kept our coats buttoned up, and I expected to see my breath.

Much of the building was brand-new— so new that bits of scaffolding and plaster were still about. The rooms were fresh, clean, and simple. The chief extravagance had been in the lavish use of windows which made one feel as though he were outdoors on a mountain top.

Most of the children were still at school in the village. How many miles of stairs did they climb to go to school, I wondered? The boys we saw—about twelve in all—were playing games in the sparsely furnished recreation room. All of them wore short pants (the universal costume of boys in Italy until their late teens), white shirts, and light pullover sweaters. All those bare legs were, as I had anticipated, purple.

"I hope," Mitch said to the nun, "that before your building is completed, some method of heating it will be installed."

She smiled and pointed to the ceiling where there was a small electric heater. (We used one twice this size in our small dining room in Rome.) "But is it enough?" I asked.

She assured me that winter in Italy was brief, that the noonday sun warmed the building marvelously, and that the air on the top of the mountain was "so very healthy" that nobody worried if it was "a bit fresh at times."

The boys greeted Signorina Mannini enthusiastically. Once again I saw that gifted woman move into a group of children and somehow capture the interest of the entire group while she was making each boy feel singled out. I caught a whispered aside to a boy about "when your mother visits."

Even though the boys were enjoying Signorina Mannini, I saw some unhappy faces. After a little conversation, our guide suggested that the boys sing for the visitors. This they did, shouting out their words tunelessly. I was beginning to feel like an expert at sensing how institutionalized children were feeling. If this were my job, I thought, I would really need to do just two things. One was look at the faces of the children when they were not talking. Many of these faces bore flaccid despair and sadness. The other criterion would be to hear a group sing. Its excellence had no diagnostic value; the important clue was whether there were heart and enthusiasm in the singing.

Mitch and I both thought that despite the courteous remarks that passed between the signorina and the young nun, this was a miserable group of boys.

We were shown a terrace so large that "the boys could ride

their bikes on it." "What boy wants to ride his bike on a damn terrace," Mitch whispered to me in English, "no matter how wonderful the view?" He was having his own firsthand experience with the institutional blues that I so often felt. The other institution hadn't done this to either of us. "There are good institutions and bad," I thought. "In them one finds happy children and sad." Fairly obvious thoughts, but they came to me as a surprise. I had always assumed that institutions for normal children were always bad and that in them I would always find only unhappy children.

It was one thirty. We hadn't eaten since breakfast. We were cold. And the institution on the mountain had depressed us. "Let's get back to Rome," Mitch whispered.

I had thought of taking Signorina Mannini out to her noon meal but feared quite appropriately that she had other stops in mind and that if we were to pause now to re-fuel she'd keep us going all day. I was right. She did have another stop in mind after lunch, a "very dear place" that was "just like a simple little family."

Because we had left home expecting to be gone for only a few hours, I begged off. I feared at the moment, and I know in retrospect, that I offended Signorina; she was never close to me again.

On the drive back to Rome she asked whether I didn't think it generous of the nuns to give the newest and best quarters to the children and use the old run-down ones for themselves. My noncommittal comment satisfied her. Secretly I thought that there was altogether too much mortification of the flesh by these aged executives. How crabby they must be!

I had learned to present negatives sparingly to this woman who, in her love of her work and her pride in it, wanted mostly admiration. After several pleasantries I said cautiously, "I am thinking that the Institution on the Top of the Mountain was very cold inside. I shiver at the little boys' bare legs."

She smiled affectionately, as though I had said something rather quaint. "I have been told that you Americans worry about bare legs on our boys—that your boys wear trousers like little men." She laughed—not scornfully but as though she found the comment amusing. Then she added kindly, "Do not concern yourself. They are used to it and would be unhappy in long trousers."

Thinking about these nuns, I was remembering that I had heard of Irish nuns, French nuns, German nuns, even nuns from the United States who had convents in Italy. I asked Signorina why they should come from all over the world to so Catholic a country. Surely other countries had greater need for missionaries?

Her explanation was simple. "They feel content to live so close to our Holy Father the Pope," she explained.

We would drive for perhaps five kilometers in silence while I tiredly selected the vocabulary for my next question. I asked her what a parent would need to do to be able to take his child from an institution. Her answer was that the parent need only say to the social worker that he was now able to support his child and care for him.

Only about ten or twelve were reclaimed each year from the Institution of the Immaculate Heart of Mary, however. This was not because parents were indifferent but because poverty was so hard to overcome in Italy.

Did many of the boys and girls from the institution become nuns and priests? She surprised me by saying that it was exceedingly rare.

As we were approaching Rome she called to Mitch, "Professore, pull off the road! Stop the car, please."

It was after two. We were starved. But Mitch unquestioningly obeyed. She pointed to some of the early Roman ruins that break the landscape so picturesquely along the road to Rome. She was pointing to an almost complete arch of an ancient aqueduct half obscured with vines and shrubs. "In there," she said, "right in there, three years ago, we found a baby boy and a little girl about a year old . . . all alone . . . dirty . . . crying." Her expressive face portrayed her distress at the memory. "An ICS social worker took them to an institution. Now they are beautiful and bright. But nobody knows whose children they are."

What more appropriate place to be abandoned than among those two-thousand-year-old arches!

The part of my brain that handles Italian suddenly gave out. I begged Mitch, "For goodness' sake, make some small talk." So he added to the not inconsiderable burden of coping with Roman traffic the task of being pleasant to Signorina Mannini.

I liked this warm, skillful Italian social worker very much. But I found myself "molto contenta" at parting with her. She demanded of me skill in Italian, plus diplomacy. By the time she stepped down from our Microbus, I was fresh out of both.

March 21

THE DAY BEGAN with another two hours of hard work on the first talk I had written, "How America Succeeded in Thinning Out the Number of Children in Institutional Placement." Signora Ugonio said that she thought I should now be able to present it to an audience. "Unh-hunh," I thought. "What audience?" She had completed the translation of my second talk, "A Few Suggestions for Changes in Italian Institutions." She was pleased with both of them and made quite a touching speech of her own about what it meant to her that Americans would come to Italy and work so hard to share what they knew.

After the tutoring sessions I felt justified in loafing a bit. I went out to lunch with Mitch and Debby one day to a superb outdoor restaurant. We ate cannelloni and drank red wine in a garden on a hilltop that looked as far as the eye could see down the ancient Appian Way. There the cobblestones laid down before Christ still formed the basis of the road and there bits of ancient walls, battered but still lovely statues and columns, and shells of old Roman mansions blended into the fields now besplattered with vibrant wild poppies.

My first introduction to a foreign language had been in Latin at age thirteen. The frontispiece of my textbook had been a picture of this highway. The memory of that picture, coupled with finding myself actually here struggling with the modern language of these Romans, gave me my own peculiar sense of personal antiquity. Surely it must have been at least a hundred years ago that I mimicked Sister Mona when she said, "Italia est patria mea." How would I say it in Italian? "Italia è la mia patria."

I rested for an ordeal that lay ahead—an appointment with Father de la Roche.

It was a good thing I had rested. Our appointment began at the normal Italian business hour, five thirty. At seven forty-five I said wearily, "But Father, I'm taking up too much of your time."

An airy wave of his hand and a typically bombastic "Nonsense, Mrs. Charnley" released a fresh torrent of astonishing plans for my immediate future. Our meeting ended at five minutes to ten.

I had prepared carefully for this encounter. I presented him a neat outline of what I had done—the eleven institutions I had visited, the two talks I had written. It was followed by some "proposed activities" including titles of "talks I could write."

He was pleased by the neatness of my outline. He talked long and brilliantly about the institutions I had seen, and seemed deeply interested in my comments on those in Rome. But he was rather indifferent to my observations of institutions outside Rome. I think it was the "not my problem" kind of response. When I pressed in expressing my enthusiasm for the institution in Florence where boys and girls lived together, he said, in tones of faint annoyance, "Now don't get off on that coeducational kick. We don't have time for a crusade. It's against the cultural mores. It would only be permitted for abnormal children who aren't valued highly."

I asked then what kind of crusade for reforms in the institutions would be appropriate. He said, "The first step is to get all institutionalized children to attend the public schools in their communities. This gives them at least some knowledge that a world exists outside the convent walls. The second step is to give social workers easy access to them and to help design a system so that the children won't be mislaid."

"Mislaid?" I asked.

He illustrated his point with a case history fresh in his mind. The child Luciana had lost her mother when she was five years old. She had four older brothers and a crippled elderly father. Luciana was placed in an institution because of the acute poverty in the family. The boys were left at home to help the father run the farm. "If the social worker had had one ounce of sense," Father complained, "she would have seen all those males as potential wage earners. She should have labeled the child's record 'Return to home in five years.'" Instead, nobody remembered to return her until she was eighteen. So at eighteen Luciana was being returned to the really prosperous farm to which she could have gone at fourteen.

I agreed that the social worker certainly should have kept in touch with the brothers.

"What for?" Father asked puzzledly.

"To keep alive their interest in Luciana and to know when they were ready to take her home."

"Ah ha!" He chuckled. "But that doesn't matter. When we say they must take her, they must whether they want to or not."

"But," I asked, "shouldn't a social worker be seeing them at least once a year?" (Once a year! How could I betray my own standards so shamelessly?)

"What for?" he asked again.

I gulped. "When families are physically separated a psychological separation takes place too. It is the job of the social worker to cherish and nourish the natural cohesiveness of a family and keep everybody in that family aware of the bonds that link them together so that they will feel the comfort and rightness of the plan when they are reunited."

He stared at me analytically. What was he thinking? "She's feeble-minded? She's so American she'll never understand us? Yankee go home?" After a long pause, he began again. "Oh, the nuns can do that when they visit."

"Then, what," I asked, "would you see as the job for Luciana's social worker?"

He said, "There's where we want your help, Mrs. Charnley."

I brightened. Perhaps after all he saw separation trauma as the legitimate concern of the social worker.

"You must help us to make a system so that children like Luciana won't get lost."

I was stubbornly clinging to the psychological implications. Surely "get lost" was a refreshingly clear psychological phrase. But no. The social workers did, I learned, keep case histories on the Lucianas of Italy, but they filed the cases away and forgot to pull them for years on end.

"Tell me," I asked again, "how can I help?"

"You must teach us one of the fine, efficient American systems of bookkeeping so that these cases will be read in five years, not in ten." As he described his real admiration for how efficiently Americans kept track of both things and children, I was crazily picturing a series of huge calendars that I would paste around the walls of an agency. On the square for June 10, 1964, I would make a notation, "Read Verdi case. Send Giovanni home." And on August 23 of 1967, another notation, "Send Pietro Verdi to his father." The Fulbright Commission should have sent a bookkeeper who wouldn't be troubled by the confusion I felt. Pietro and Giovanni would need help with their feelings during these five years, not just bookkeeping. Though perhaps if they could have only one thing, bookkeeping or casework, the bookkeeping was the starting place.

As I thought these scrambled (and inefficient, un-American) thoughts, Father had shifted gears and was off on another project. With an effort I abandoned the bookkeeping to get aboard. It was a study I was to make. I should read case histories in agencies in ten Italian cities. I should study the schools of social work from which the writers of the case histories had graduated and, having a clear picture of each curriculum, I should define the area in which the social workers had remained constant to the basic principles they had learned, and those where they had been corrupted by the realities of the job. It was a marvelous idea. It seemed to me it would make an excellent five-year project for a real scholar with gobs of money . . . It wasn't easy to get into the conversation. By nature I am strictly a noninterrupter. But interrupt I must.

"But Father," I broke in, "I have only four months. I don't have time to do a study like this."

Again I got that penetrating look. I felt mean to shatter with reality the soaring dreams of this scholar. He caught his breath. Just that. That was all it took to set him off on another equally elaborate and improbable project.

I must have listened to seven or eight. All were brilliant and thoroughly impossible. I began to focus on how long it took me to read a case history. This he brushed aside. (It must have been hard for him to understand. He was a fine linguist. I had heard that he worked comfortably in five different languages.)

I managed to find a kind of bulldog tenacity in making one point. "Father," I said, annoyed to hear a plaintive note creep into my voice, "my talents are limited. Time is limited. Why don't you use me in a way that I think I can make a contribution?"

I began to point to the place on my work outline where I had described the two speeches I had prepared and the others that I could write. He didn't like them. "Perhaps," he said reluctantly, "I could let you give them to the nuns." I remembered having heard that the nuns were taught only the easy and obvious in social work and that, though they might go to school as many years as the social workers, they emerged with neither title nor diploma.

"These subjects," he sputtered. "How to select foster parents, how to begin a foster care program, when to use foster homes, when to use institutional care . . ." He looked disappointed.

"You don't think they'd be useful?" I asked.

"They're so easy," he complained.

Quietly I tried to explain that able American social workers who had done this work for years didn't find them easy. We had made many mistakes in finding our way in America. I would like Italy to profit by our experience and start its program of foster care right, avoiding our mistakes.

Poor Father! He hated anything that seemed easy. "We could read about these in books," he said.

"What books?" I asked, being aware of the paucity of our literature.

"Yours, Dorothy Hutchinson's, Henrietta Gordon's," he answered, showing me rather casually how thoroughly he knew the literature of American social work. If he knew it, I wondered, why did he deny the necessity of doing basic things well?

Every time I paused long enough to digest a thought, he was off on another idea. His projects were characterized by real brilliance, and utter and magnificent indifference to such realities as cost of travel, time available, and my inability to cope with a foreign language. He was having a fine time. His blue eyes danced and shone as he dreamed up one Ph.D. thesis after another. As nearly as I could make out, I was not to choose among these impossible alternatives – I was to do all of them. Perhaps, I thought, he will talk himself out. I gave him an hour and though his cassock grew steadily whiter down the front from the cascade of cigarette ashes, he showed no sign of slowing down. I was remembering a movie I had seen in my childhood in which I had been fascinated by the mad monk Rasputin. This man seemed marvelously and brilliantly mad in the same way except that his focus was not on political power but on solving the ills of Italy with research.

I promised myself that the next time he paused to light a cigarette I would make one more desperate effort. "Father," I blurted out, "these are wonderful plans. You must use them sometime with a research scholar who speaks brilliant Italian and who has years to give. But I cannot do these things. Please listen and I'll tell you what I can do." (And to myself, "Don't pause for commas, Jean. Keep going.")

"I can teach your students ways to ease the pain of institutional living for children. I can show them how to start a program that can grow into something very important for the children of Italy. I can help Signorina Mannini and Signorina Lombardo with problems of office management, recording, interviews with clients, and casework thinking."

My progress was zero. "But these things are so simple, Mrs. Charnley."

"No," I insisted firmly, "they are not simple. They are very hard. I can do it best in four months by consultation and by lectures. You must look at the fact that the first step is to do these basic things well." He wouldn't hear me. He was off again.

I ignored what he was saying and only listened for the chance to break through. "Your students must know these fundamental steps. The future of social work in Italy depends on them. I am a good lecturer. In America they pay me a hundred dollars a day for teaching these so-called simple things." (My manners were terrible. Imagine being driven to brag about fees. But it worked!)

"Signora," he said, "I know your reputation in America. In May, you will give a seminar to the heads of the major agencies in Rome and you shall teach us all you know about foster home care."

I was speechless in surprise at my victory. "Fine," I said. "I'll start writing speeches now."

"Oh," he said airily, "don't write any speeches. You just sit and chat from a little handful of notes and I'll help you with the language."

("And give my speeches for me," I thought.)

On and on we went. It was approaching nine o'clock and it felt like midnight. The projects multiplied like amoebas. I had mentioned my distress at the lack of discipline in the office at SANC. This interested him.

"You must educate Signorina Mannini and Signorina Lombardo. Tell them they don't know how to supervise and then show them how." I thought despairingly of the fragile ego of Signorina Mannini and her allergy to negative criticism.

"I'd like to give a lecture on techniques of supervision," I said softly.

"Lectures, bah!" he exploded. "You are so infernally humble!"

He dreamed on and on. I should check a government study by

one agency against case histories and criticize it . . . I should make a study of a series of already published magazine articles and consult with the author and tell him that what he wrote was all poppycock . . . I should . . . I should . . . I should . . .

I abdicated. "Don't fight it any more, Jean," I said to myself, "just flow along with it." I settled back to enjoy him – he really was a marvel to watch in action. By a kind of free association his mind slithered from project to project – all brilliant, all quite impossible.

"We could use you in America, Father," I thought. "You could be president of social research for our whole nation. You could set a nation full of outstanding and ambitious scholars to work for years and years on just what you have planned for me tonight."

Signorina Quinzi stopped by carrying an article that had been presented at the last Italian National Conference on Social Workers on "Casework with Children." Would I like to see it? I would indeed.

"But can you read it?" she asked gently. I wanted to hug her. This breath of realism was as welcome as a drink of cold water after three hours in a scorching sun. I explained that my husband would help me with it. She said that it was her only copy and she would need it back.

I reached out foolishly to her. "May I have an appointment to return it next week?" I asked.

"An appointment to return it?" she asked amusedly. But she apparently accepted my request as American eccentricity and drew out her calendar to make the appointment. I wanted to get to a realist, a realist who knew how to work with this insatiable man. She and his staff must have found a way. Maybe she would let me in on the secret.

Father watched us benignly, apparently pleased to hear me speaking Italian. He switched back to English. "Signorina Quinzi, Signorina Charnley and I have made some decisions. These are the projects that she will do . . ."

Quickly Signorina took out a notebook and pencil and wrote down his ideas. Seeing her pencil going added fuel to my anxiety.

I had comforted myself that the next morning Father would have forgotten all his grandiose plans for me. Now I was too tired to take in all that he was saying. My memory is that he decided Signorina and I would do a seminar that would consider the deterioration of the social worker after leaving school, what's wrong with supervision in Italy, how to establish in twenty cities in Italy a pilot project on foster care, and on and on.

Signorina Quinzi's face was pleasantly impassive as she took her notes. I began to feel her slipping away as my foothold on reality, especially when she suggested that our base be seventeen cities instead of twenty. Three other staff members starting on their way home paused to greet me and discuss last bits of the day's business with Father. I got a sense of mutual liking between him and them. It added to my puzzlement. I tried to imagine how I would feel if in a school in America I were the member of a faculty run by such an eccentric, mercurial executive. "There must be something deep in the culture that I'm missing," I thought.

The others went home. Poor Signorina and I stayed on and she took page upon page of notes. When Father said, "This is a seminar that you two can give jointly," she actually looked pleased.

Finally the evening ended. Father shook hands with me warmly. "You are pleased," he asked pleasantly, "at some of the little ideas I have about how we can utilize your skills in Rome?" I nodded in numb dishonesty, and found myself homesick for my sensible agency in America where we never try to do more than two impossible tasks at a time.

March 22, 23, 24, and 25

THESE DAYS I operated in a low emotional gear halfheartedly reading case histories, working with my tutor, and yielding often to my id's clamorous demands to drink plenty of coffee in the sunshine. It seemed to me that I gave only about half my attention to everything I tried to do anyway. Most of the time my mind was preoccupied with my harrowing meeting with Father de la Roche. What should I do? I could go to Signorina Scalzo at the commission, describe my problems, and suggest that the commission send me around Italy to lecture before social workers much as English and American literature teachers took off with lectures on e. e. cummings or Edgar Allan Poe. Or I could go back to ICS and SANC, read and criticize case histories, and make myself useful to them. Perhaps if I never saw or called Father de la Roche again he would forget me. I could resign. The two possibilities that never occurred to me were trying to do any of the projects that Father had dreamed up and going back to try once more to get my objections across. I was in a bad spot. But somehow the beauty of my setting was so pervasive and soothing that I reacted more like someone who has a little toothache that twitches only momentarily than like a patient facing overwhelming surgery.

This was a period of pleasant sociability for Mitch and me. Several Fulbright families invited us to dinner parties that combined Fulbrighters with Italian scholars who spoke English. We Fulbrighters plied the Italians with questions about their culture which we found baffling.

One enriching evening I especially remember. With us there were two Americans — a political scientist and a rural sociologist — and an Italian cultural anthropologist and his wife, a distinguished modern historian. We Americans worked the attractive, obliging Italians hard; we set up, defended, and sometimes saw shattered our own hypotheses about what their culture meant.

One of that night's ideas that came home with me was that Italy is not truly a democracy. Here — in my words — is the Italian woman's expression of it:

"Our class system is still vigorously in force. Because Italy offers outward manifestations of democracy, Americans are puzzled by what seems to be general apathy in the face of the distress of some of its citizens. Unfortunately, the misery of a group of Calabrian peasants does not excite the industrial populations of the north. The value and dignity of the individual, as a humane and philosophical concept, puzzles many Italians, especially if the 'individual' involved is of the unprivileged class.

"The poor people of Italy — the hungry, the barefoot, the cold — are being wooed by the Communists. But the 'poor classes' move slowly. For one thing, they appropriately distrust the promises of political parties, and therefore have little interest in voting. 'Political pledges are forgotten by the politicians as soon as the polls close,' they think. 'Why should we be so foolish as to listen to them?'

"The church, often innocently, reinforces this apathy. The church teaches that we live in a vale of tears, that pain and suffering are steppingstones to eternal bliss. And the *status quo* means strength for the church. Many of our wealthy citizens who scorn to pay taxes feel strong pressure to build churches, support church institutions, uphold the clergy.

"Not all the clergy, of course, are so innocent. As among laymen, there are left-wing as well as right-wing clerics. There is a vigorous, sharp-sighted group that is frankly impatient for the death of Pius XII. But this group, though it is at liberty to pursue its own political beliefs as long as it stays on the right side of canonical law, finds itself a weak minority at odds with a rich and powerful majority."

I raised a question about the influence of the church on schools of social work. I mentioned a Vatican-dominated school which everyone to whom I had talked, including several priests, considered a poor one. I was told that this was a sound estimate, but that the other schools which were more acceptable to the enlightened members of the clergy were probably Trojan horses. The church wanted to control this budding profession which might conceivably become a powerful force in Italy.

The historian told an anecdote to illustrate the point. Some years before, several Italian social workers from another city in Italy had gone to America to study. They managed to teach Italian to a distinguished American social worker and had persuaded her to come back with them to help set up a new school of social work following American structural patterns and philosophy. After thirteen months, she went home but persuaded an Italo-American to come back and carry on the work. In four years, they had established what was one of the best schools of social work in Italy.

Then "odd things began to happen." A trusted employee made off with some funds. The husband of a teacher was told he might lose his job if his wife continued to work. The executive was fired without warning. His replacement was a bullheaded authoritarian who knew nothing about social work. Most of the staff replacements were Communist party members. It took less than a calendar year to destroy a superb school.

The fine women who had built it were puzzled. They were guessing it was the Communists who had destroyed it. It was true that the Communists had moved in, but, the historian said—and she reinforced her statement by quoting a prominent Italian journalist—this school was the victim of petty jealousy. The clergy and a leading right-wing political party had been unwilling to see a school that had no church connection soar so far beyond the others. The right-wing party had taken the strategic steps that made it possible for the Communists to move in and destroy it.

I had heard another version of this story before from Signorina Scalzo. As is so often true in stories of intrigue, all the "facts" didn't jibe. I do not offer this evening's conversations as facts, for I have heard too many Americans try to explain McCarthyism or what happened at Little Rock to Italians not to know that the likelihood of meeting truth head-on at a dinner party is slight. But these opinions of educated Italians, right or wrong, I was glad to use as a backdrop for my understanding.

During our sidewalk caffè sitting we heard other opinions about various aspects of Italian life. One Saturday morning as Mitch and I sat at coffee on the Via Veneto, Father Nicolo Vincelli walked by and was happy to join us. He asked what I was doing professionally and I found him as easy and comforting to talk with as I had the preceding month when he revealed to me the corruption at San Marco. I wanted to pour the whole problem of my three dozen research projects out to him. But since he was a friend of Father de la Roche, I didn't. Instead I tried to raise questions whose answers would help me sharpen my own views.

"Father," I said, "of all the social workers to whom I have talked in Italy, you seem the one whose thinking is closest to mine. May I ask you some questions?"

"Shoot," he said in one of his startling lapses into American slang.

I told him of my concern that social workers didn't know how to meet a client, how to evaluate the pain of the first interview, how really to hear a simple request a client was making. It seemed to me that the request often got lost as the social worker zoomed off into half-baked Freud.

He laughed. "Keep on, Mrs. Charnley. It's music to my ears."

I said that I found myself among social workers who wanted to dance before they knew how to walk. I thought that walking was good and honest and honorable. But when I tried to teach them to walk, they were offended.

He smiled sympathetically. "So," he said, turning to Mitch, "your wife has really come to Italy in the last four weeks."

Father assured me that I was right. This "intellectualization" was an important problem. "Phony intellectualism, really," he said. He added that he believed my ideas right and that I shouldn't let anyone deflect me from teaching the fundamentals of good casework.

"It will make you unpopular," he said, "but when you get up to lecture, you do it anyway. We are a polite people. We will listen and may learn something from you. Also, if you act as though what you're saying is fancy, we may even think it is."

He explained that he was doing just what I was urging, and that among other schools he had a reputation of being "a stupe," but that agencies were enthusiastic about the graduates he sent them. "My students are practical caseworkers." He chuckled. "They know how to look at a baby's bottom to see whether he's getting good care." He finished his coffee and insisted on buying a cup for us.

Choosing my words with care, I sketched out to him Father de la Roche's idea of beginning the foster care program in Italy with a vast study, followed by a public relations campaign, and then a grand opening of homes in seventeen cities in Italy. I said that my impulse was to do it quietly, just a few agencies here in Rome, just a half dozen homes. What did he think?

He became cautious. I had put him on the spot. He shrugged expressively and then said, "It is what we have been saying, isn't it? You, I suppose, must do it your way. He must do it his. But yours can happen sooner. Much sooner."

To change the subject, I told Father that I expected to be lecturing at a school of social work set up to educate nuns. Did he know the place? He did and was most enthusiastic. "You ought to like that," he said. "It's getting right to the people who care for children and who meet the parents." I said that after meeting Mother Giulia I thought that educating nuns might be a most important hope for Italy's child welfare program.

He nodded enthusiastically. "I'm glad you have met Mother Giulia. Someday they'll canonize that woman. Then we'll have a patron saint for social workers. About time, too. Some of us are a pretty godless lot." He laughed.

Mitch asked the next question. "Jean thinks that someone ought to start a school of social work for the priests who work with the boys. What about that, Father?"

Father Vincelli was entertained. "That would be tough, plenty tough. The nuns are nice humble women, eager to learn. Especially those in some of the smaller, loosely organized orders. But we priests are proud and vain. We say we are enlightened by the Holy Ghost." He paused to light a cigarette. "There's just one problem with that. The Holy Ghost doesn't know a damn thing about child welfare!"

With that he left us. We sat awhile longer in the sun and I remembered that when I was a child playing with a bow and arrow I had once put an arrow through the fleshy part of my hand between the thumb and index finger. After disinfecting it, our family doctor had told me to sit outdoors and expose the wound to direct sunlight. "It's a great healer," he had said.

I found Italian sunshine healing, too — healing to the psychological wound that throbs in anyone who wrestles overlong with "What'll I do now?"

That night at a cocktail party I met an extraordinarily charming and beautiful woman — an American Negro in Italy on a student Fulbright grant, taking courses at the League School of Social Work. She and I lost no time in swapping observations. She had worked as an untrained social worker in San Francisco before she came to Italy. It was, it seemed to me, a crazy way to educate an American social worker, but she at least was enjoying it.

She told me that she had been hearing about the "fascinating and brilliant Father de la Roche." She was eager to meet him. Could I arrange an introduction?

I heard myself saying, "You'd better ask Signorina Scalzo at the commission to arrange an introduction. I don't intend to see him again for quite a long time."

I startled myself. What a balmy solution to a dilemma! Anybody who meets problems slaunchwise like that needs help from a good social worker. I wondered where I could find one.

March 27 through March 31

FOR THESE FIVE DAYS I scrupulously kept the same working hours as the regular staff members at SANC. I spent most of my time reading records to the tune of the swishing pages of my dictionary. I began to sense a growing vocabulary; I must now be whizzing along at the speed of a third grader. One day as an experiment I brought Signora Ugonio along with me to see how well it would work to have her do sight translations on cases while I took notes in English.

The results were comical. She had the healthy disgust and boredom of the intelligent but untrained mind meeting up with a social case history for the first time. For a few sentences, she translated literally and then she began making editorial comments. "Oh no," she'd protest, "this is really too dull. Not another discussion about one silly psychological test . . . ridiculous!" Then she would translate another sentence or two and explode again. "There is simply no excuse for all this fussing about does he or doesn't he love his father. Of course he doesn't. His father beats him!" Americans reading their first unedited case histories are just like Signora Ugonio.

By this time I had come to think of SANC as *my* agency. I knew more and more workers by name. I saw their clients come and go. And when they turned to each other for help in solving a casework problem, I was invited into the discussion. I identified then some of the problems with which I could help. I saw that in finding answers to major casework decisions they turned to each other instead of to their supervisor. I saw also that Alta Quello, the azure-eyed caseworker I had first thought to be such a time waster, was really a hard-working woman.

During these days I had frequent chats with Signorina Lombardo. Sometimes I offered comments and suggestions about cases I had read. Sometimes I plied her with questions. The problem of communication continued to dwindle. Was it her olive eyes that were so eloquent? Was it her gift for telling gestures? Or her extra-clear pronunciation, her easy use of synonyms? All these were important. But most important, I thought, was deep rapport and respect between us. I felt as though we would have understood each other had she spoken Dutch and I Greek.

On the last day on this week, I gave her the two manuscripts that Signora Ugonio had translated and typed for me. She took them eagerly and with a characteristic "communicating gesture" swept her desk clear to show me that she would read them immediately. In about an hour she called to me, her eyes shining. She would have them mimeographed and distributed to her staff. In two weeks, she would call a staff meeting and we would begin discussions based on them. We would start with the American social work history one because "that will be less threatening to them."

Signorina asked permission to show them to Dottore Alberghi, the national executive director of SANC. She assured me that he was a man who was "molto bravo . . . molto simpatico" and that he had been delighted to know what the visiting Americana was suggesting for the strengthening of his agency. He would like to have a conversation with me after the Easter holidays.

"So there, Father de la Roche!" I thought, "my speeches are to have a use after all!"

The Easter Holidays

OUR MAID MARIA showed me that her religious calendar was dotted with festas before and after Easter. A quick family consultation decided us to take advantage of the festas and plan a trip. Maria stormed in indignation at our lack of loyalty to Rome. "From all over the world pilgrims come to Rome for Easter—to buy the little crickets that sing so cheerily in their little cages . . . to eat hot snails in the square at Santa Maria's Church on Easter Monday . . . to see the penitents kiss every step of the Holy Stairs . . . to see the Spanish stairs with thousands of azaleas in bloom . . . to be blessed at Mass at San Pietro by the pope himself . . ." She sputtered and became most eloquent. When she saw that we were firm about our decision to go back to some of the other parts of Italy we loved, she amazed us by bursting into tears and sobbing that she would be lonesome.

These volatile floods in Maria troubled me. When I talked of them with Signora Ugonio she assured me that they merely meant that Maria was fond of us. Signora Ugonio said that what Maria was showing us was what Americans who stayed long in Italy came to refer to as "Italian temperament."

"It gets modified a little," she added, "for those of us who go to college. But only a little. Our emotions are close to the surface. We laugh, love, hate, sing, and cry more easily than you northerners do. You puzzle us, I'm sure, as much as we puzzle you." She was thoughtful for a minute. "But I must say that you are nice and spontaneous for an American."

As we started south on our leisurely journey, I really enjoyed the little traffic dramas which illustrated so well what Signora Ugonio had been telling me. Two cars would bump at an intersection. The drivers would jump out, apparently livid with rage, each proclaiming the stupidity of the other in shouts and unmistakable gestures. In all directions traffic would halt. Drivers from other cars would spring out to join the argument. A beaming Roman policeman resplendent in his comic opera costume would enter the scene and play a jester's role on the sidelines, enjoying, mimicking, and offering critical comment on the controversy. Horns would honk from all directions — not so much in impatience as in evidence that the lively spectators were themselves getting into the act. The discussion would grow heated and for a moment you would expect blows. Then a comedian would call out something funny. Smiles would break out around the crowd. The two opponents would happily shake hands, perhaps embrace, and get back into their cars. Only then would the policeman assume his graceful and artistic role in unscrambling the traffic tangle.

We had decided that this was to be a thoroughly vacationy vacation — slow moving, following our impulses, no deadlines. I left my Italian dictionary at home and took a Hemingway novel and a whodunit. I had planned to see just one institution on the entire trip — a correctional institution for "fallen girls" — and this only if it should rain when we were near it.

I must discipline myself in describing the joys of that trip. I find that it is impossible for me to write of the charms of Italy without sliding immediately into the purplest of prose.

But perhaps with care, I could describe just one episode. We had been following the coast along a new highway between Terracina and Formia when we came upon an enchanting strip of beach complete with bits of Roman ruins, jagged, inviting climbing rocks, and that wonderful mixture of red poppies and white daisies that had been turning every field we passed into a garden.

"Oh, please . . ." Debby asked.

Mitch pulled off the road. Debby and I carried the picnic things down to the seashore and Mitch, calling he would be with us in a minute, went the other way. He was soon pulling wild ivy vines away from a crumbling gray wall in order to read its B.C. Latin inscription.

Debby was wearing an Italian peasant costume she had bought at a street stand in a little town, a lovely full skirt alive with delicate designs that were somehow simultaneously bold and soft. In three minutes she had kicked off her shoes and was skimming fast and hard through the water's edge.

I sat down on a smooth rock, sometimes watching Debby, sometimes Mitch, who was moving now to another outcropping of ancient walls. I was amused at the fine personality analysis situation. Mitch, of course, would go first to the ruins. Debby, of course, would run to find her union with the wind and the water. And I, of course, would choose a midpoint between where I would rest the picnic lunch and be content to look admiringly from one to the other. If only Blair were here, he would be halfway up that biggest jagged rock that rose from the sea and I would be watching him, heart in my mouth, restraining my impulse to be old womanish.

Debby had found a Debby-sized rock, climbed a few feet, and jumped down making a splash. "Debby! Your new skirt!" I called.

Hands on hips she protested. "Ma madre! La donna me ha detto che l'aqua non farebbe male a questi belli colori." (But mother! The woman said that the water would not harm these lovely colors.)

Mitch came and sat beside me full of excitement at what he had discovered. He had found a recently excavated summer villa of Tiberius. After lunch we must all explore it.

"Yes," I agreed, "but right now just settle down and look at your lovely daughter. Doesn't she look like a Botticelli painting?"

She really did. The sun on her red hair, her pale skin, the swirling peasant skirt, and the exotic scenery behind could not help but suggest one of the fragile ladies on the walls of the Uffizi.

"When we get back to Florence," Mitch said, "we must look hard in the art shops. We can find her portrait."

Debby began to dance back from the ocean. At first she burlesqued a modern dance, but her mood changed and she seemed an entrancing sea sprite to her parents.

"Last night," Mitch said, "she told me that she wants to live most of her life in Italy."

"Oh, no," I moaned. I had a sudden humorless image of myself complete with rocking chair and black shawl and the whole Atlantic ocean between me and my child. "We never should have taken her to this enchanted place once—much less twice."

Mitch laughed. "And where did you want her to live when she's grown? In Chicago? Or next door? How long do you plan to make your apron strings?"

Debby came up, breathless. She plopped down, protesting, "I'm starved!" From our picnic basket came sandwiches of Gorgonzola cheese and of that wonderful cold meat called mortadella, the inevitable small bottle of Chianti, and for dessert, blood oranges as red as the reddest wine. Day after day this was our picnic feast and sometimes we wondered how many years it would be before one of us would want to change the menu.

From behind the rocks came an elderly Italian couple, each carrying an armload of fagots. Their chestnut faces were not so brown that the rosiness of their cheeks did not shine through. The old man tipped his hat to us and made a courtly bow.

The old woman smiled and called, "Buon appetito!"

All three of us were pleased. "When I get back to school," Debby said, "I'll go politely through the school cafeteria wishing everybody a good appetite."

"Miss the cafeteria?" Mitch asked curiously.

"Never that," she said. "But wouldn't it be *dee*-vine if I could have all this and Janie and Molly and Cindy and Emily?"

"And Blair," Mitch and I said in unison.

April 7

THE DAYS SLIPPED BY in the golden way of wonderful vacations. Each lovely hour passed in thirty minutes, but every wonderful minute had at least two hundred seconds in it.

The call to return to work was as clear as though it had come from an archangel. We awakened one morning to a cold gray rain in a town that had the kind of museum that merits hours of time. "Since it's raining," Mitch said, "let's spend the day at the museum. If we get bored there's a Gina Lollobrigida movie."

Something in my conscience prickled. I had promised myself that if it rained, in this town, I would . . . "And while you do," I said, "I'll visit the Institution of Santa Marguerita."

And that is how it happened that I went alone up the stairs of the huge reception center, presented myself to the nun who answered the door, and made the speech beginning, "I am a social worker who does not speak Italian very well. I have come from America to Italy to study . . ."

The cordial nun took me to a parlor where I was greeted by the sweet-faced, elderly mother superior. She told me that she had several sisters in her convent who were missionaries from America. Sister Alice Irene would be pleased to escort me through their institution.

Sister Alice Irene was young, a handsome big woman with thick eyelashes blackly fringing slaty eyes. She looked at least five feet eight and I thought she must have felt a giant in this country of short people.

My memories of the Institution of Santa Marguerita and of Sister Alice Irene are full of conflict. This was an institution for girls who had been drawn to the attention of the court for sexual misdemeanor. Mostly their motivations had been innocent. They had been misused by fathers or brothers in poverty-stricken homes where six people might sleep in the same bed. Or they had been sent out on the streets as fourteen-year-old prostitutes by famished adults.

Their ages ranged from nine to twenty-one. They were brought to the institution from several provinces of Italy at the time their "crimes" became known; regardless of their deportment, they did not leave until they were nearly twenty-one.

Sister Alice Irene was proud of her institution and most ambitious for it and, I thought, for herself. As we talked, the idea occurred to me over and over that I might be talking to the next mother superior. This was a rare opportunity to teach and preach in my own language to someone who someday might be free to improve conditions. I warned myself not to antagonize her.

The building was handsomely and expensively equipped. There was a fine basketball court, a tennis court, a sweater loom shop, and a dressmaking shop. Sister told me proudly of the influence of the American nuns, all of whom had had experience in similar institutions in America and who came to Italy to teach and modernize Italian institutions for delinquent girls.

As we walked through the institution, I met many girls. They struck me as immature in contrast to American girls of their age, and it seemed to me that many of them – both those in their early teens and the older ones – were fixed at that normally brief phase in adolescence when teen-agers go into gales of silly giggling at "secrets" in the presence of adults, try unsuccessfully to check their artificial mirth, and then, in false embarrassment, burst again into gales of laughter. Several groups of girls greeted us thus. Some of them had been in the institution for six or seven years, others for shorter periods, Sister Alice Irene told me. She apologized for their silly behavior and scolded them openly. I puzzled her by my questions. "Yes, they often do that with visitors . . . yes, often without visitors . . . yes, sometimes when they are angry and being criticized." My probing apparently seemed dull to her, and she was eager to get on with showing me the excellent equipment and telling me facts about Santa Marguerita. I weighed giving her my interpretation of the behavior – that this inappropriate childish way of showing anger was bad for the girls and that they should be helped to speak out honestly – but I was sure that this philosophy would be in conflict with this convent's belief in patience, obedience, and penitence.

Sister Alice Irene told about the "modern" thinking she and the other nuns had brought from their experience in some of America's most progressive institutions. The ideas had to do with equipment, housing the girls in small groups, and giving them allowances for clothing. With some self-discipline she added, "They get plenty of hard physical activity in competitive sports to help them curb the newly awakened and sometimes urgent sexual drives."

As we talked we moved from room to room in the huge institution. Whenever we came on a group of girls, we stopped to talk to them. I am no group worker, and I envied Signorina Mannini's easy skill. But compared to Sister Alice Irene, I was a whiz. She seemed to intrude her presence and her questions with a mallet. After we had left one group, I said to her, "The looks on the faces of this group were different from those of others we have seen. They looked sullen and depressed. What is different about them?" I froze in horror as she turned on her heel and walked back to ask them. She was answered with a heavy silence, and the hostility at which I had first guessed became apparent and intense. She gaily coaxed them to tell her, her manner implying that it couldn't be anything very serious. I watched the little monologue from a distance, full of shame that I had stupidly brought this humiliation to the girls. I had been trying to teach this nun some of the things that I thought were wrong about the institution, but my questioning technique had certainly been a failure.

We stopped to look at the exquisite little chapel, and I noted half a dozen young girls scattered throughout the dimly lit room. They knelt with heads bowed and faces half hidden by small black lace scarves. "Was this piety or a way to achieve privacy?" I wondered. As we left the chapel a girl followed us out. Sister stopped her.

"Bianca!" she called. The girl turned toward us. She had a lovely, fragile face. It seemed to me that her eyes were red-rimmed, though it could have been caused by the bright sunlight on coming out of the dark chapel.

"You *are* called Bianca, are you not?" Sister asked. "It's a very pretty name, though not the name of a saint. Perhaps you can be the first Saint Bianca." She spoke not unkindly. The girl twisted a little smile.

She explained my presence and the girl gave me an interested stare. I felt more at ease with her alone than I had with the groups. I said I was sorry about my "brutal Italian" because I would have enjoyed becoming acquainted with her. I explained that in America I had chosen to spend more of my time with girls of her age than with any other groups. She listened attentively; the corners of her lips twitched almost imperceptibly when I mangled the pronunciation of the word "adolescents." I sought her help, but Sister Alice Irene broke in impatiently with a sharp correction. The moment of understanding between Bianca and me was shattered.

She said good-by to us courteously and turned to leave, but Sister called her back. "Bianca," the nun explained with a restraining hand on the girl's arm, "has only been with us for three days. Tell the Americana how you like it here."

Tears swam into Bianca's eyes and she faced us mutely and miserably. Sister Alice Irene laughed softly in that "your-tears-are-not-important" manner that adults so often mistakenly use to cheer up depressed children. Sister urged her to "speak frankly." I reached out to touch the girl's arm just above the nun's hand. "But of course Bianca cannot tell us as hard a thing as that when this is all new to her. She cannot tell us because you and I are strangers to her, Sister. It was very nice to meet you, Bianca," I said trying hard to get a tone of dismissal into my voice. And then, to make the period on my sentence firmer, I added, "Addio"—the word of farewell. I quickly switched into English with Sister Alice Irene. Bianca left.

"She wouldn't tell us how she felt," the nun said. "Some of the girls come right out and say that they hate it here and that they miss freedom."

"Careful, Jean," I warned myself. "If you antagonize this nun, you won't be able to plant any ideas at all."

Aloud I said, "I imagine you are pleased when this happens. If the girls can express their disappointment at lack of freedom, they'll be better able to get along here."

"Yes," she said dubiously, "some of them are quite bold in the way they express their anger."

"That's nice," I said. She gave me a startled look.

Then she lowered her voice and said, "It's terribly sad, Mrs.

Charnley, but quite a few of our girls are pregnant within a year after leaving – illegitimately pregnant."

I found myself choosing my English with the care I usually used in selecting Italian words. "It is very sad," I agreed. "In America, we are all aware that there are a few children who seem compelled to make bad mistakes despite our wish to help them. But most of the experts there would feel that so many years in institutional care away from contacts with the other sex, away from contacts with their families, might really cause this quick careless way of getting to know boys."

Now she defended herself. "In my order in America I have seen the futility of a court order for six months of institutional care. Imagine six months in which to rehabilitate a girl who has had this kind of experience! Here we have a better chance."

I said that of course it was so much harder in Italy – the harsher poverty, the lack of psychiatrists, the lack of social workers to work intensively with the parents, the lack of foster homes to serve as halfway houses between the institution and a girl's own home. Happily I saw her defensiveness softening.

As we walked together I found many bits of equipment and facilities that I could wholeheartedly admire. We came into a charming dining room with tables for eight. I learned that the girls lived in eights in the dormitory and that there was a process by which the groups kept rearranging themselves, voting this girl out and that girl in, until eventually they got themselves arranged in patterns that would remain comfortable for perhaps as long as a year.

I asked Sister whether she had learned the American term "sociometry" or seen the charts the sociometrists used to depict this same process. She said she had not, but she was extremely interested. None of the sisters had been fortunate enough to have had college work past the fourth-year level, but they were interested in broadening their understanding by reading. Would I send the name of a book or two that described this process? She and two other American sisters would take turns doing sight translations for the Italian nuns who enjoyed being read aloud to in their study groups. I quickly and enthusiastically agreed. I would send a list of books on sociometry and also on new patterns of thinking in institutional care.

As I looked around the dining room, I asked, "At which tables do the nuns eat, or do they just mix in with the girls?"

"Oh," she said in surprise, "we couldn't expect the nuns to put up with eating with the girls."

"Why not?" I asked innocently.

"The anti-clericalism is really vicious in Italy," she explained. "This is especially true in the impoverished homes from which these girls come. If a nun were to eat in this room, the girls would make cruel remarks. They would say, 'Look at her eating all that good expensive food! She is rich and corrupt. Why should the poor give money to the church so that a fat old nun can eat so well?'"

I was shocked into silence. I didn't dare confirm it but I assume that this meant that the nuns ate better food than the girls. But even if I put the kindest possible light on it and chose to think that girls would jeer at nuns who were eating what they were eating, I still got a sense that the breach here was so great that no real atmosphere of trust could develop.

As Sister Alice Irene talked on, I studied the meanings of her words. I guessed that she was proud of being an American and had a dream of becoming the mother superior at Santa Marguerita's. I thought that what she hoped to bring to the job was "modern" American methods. I also observed that she was exceptionally defensive about negative criticism.

She asked me for my reactions to Santa Marguerita's. I praised what I could. Then I said, "Through the years, as you and the other Americans are able to bring your influence to bear, you will, I know, try to start the girls going out into the world little by little for brief excursions. They should drive to Rome in a bus someday to see San Pietro. The best adjusted girls might try going to the village school. You might even someday get so modern that once a month you would have boys from some nearby institution come to your institution for an hour's carefully supervised dance period.

"It will be hard work, but it will be rewarding. Your girls will adjust better with little tastes of life outside the institution. You will need to get the help and cooperation of agencies like SANC and ICS."

She laughed. "Mrs. Charnley, you and I know these things would be good. But Italy doesn't. The Italian mentality [what did she mean—temperament or basic ability?] will never adjust to that."

I tried to look pleasant. "You must forgive me, Sister. I come with the brashness of the visiting expert who knows all the answers. Believe me, I don't know them at all. But I think that Italy is changing. Television, radio, and movies are changing it fast, and so are many other forces. If you have faith, little by little, I believe that you and the other American sisters will accomplish these things."

April 9, 10, and 11

I SPENT THESE DAYS in the SANC office, reading and commenting on records and acting as a spontaneous consultant to the workers who, discussing their cases in little groups, often invited me in.

One day when I asked for Signorina Lombardo, I was told that she was at the New Roman School of Social Work talking with Father de la Roche. Perhaps it was Irish intuition that led me to think that she was discussing with Father the use to which my lectures would be put. It turned out that this was exactly right. She came back to ask whether I would be willing to lecture to a class of nuns at the School of Social Work for Religious Persons. I quickly agreed, thinking wryly that Father was holding to his view that my lectures would be "too easy" for his students but all right for the nuns who operated at a less scholarly level. Since I believed that the education of the nuns was important indeed, we arrived at a happy compromise in our unspoken disagreement.

I had been doing a good bit of thinking about the "seminar"

based on SANC records that I was to give in May or June. "How," I kept asking myself, "do you give a lecture on casework to teachers and executives who bask in abysmal unawareness of the simple fundamentals of casework practice?" I decided finally that I would choose an Italian case history and use it to show "how we do it in America."

I read half a dozen cases before I stumbled on the Giobbe case. It was twenty pages long, and I spent hours boiling it down to the essentials I would need to make my point. I wrote my summary out in English, inserting false names for clients and institutions, and gave it to Signora Ugonio to translate. This was my manuscript:

The Giobbe Case

NAME OF CLIENT: Fernando Giobbe
AGE AT INTAKE: Eleven years, two months
DATE OF INTAKE: October 6, 1956
WORKER ASSIGNED TO CASE: Elena Monachesi
REASON FOR CASE: The mother is sick and unable to care for the boy.
REFERRAL: Signorina Facchetti phones that the mother has approached Father Pelligrini, who is opening a new small institution for boys at Albano. Last year Fernando was in the first class at Viterbo, where he didn't do well because of lack of discipline by the teacher. Father Pelligrini is inclined to grant the mother a reduction in fee and to take the boy in. It is requested by Signorina Facchetti that the agency study the case for referral to Father Pelligrini's institution.
ECONOMIC SITUATION: The father is a waiter in a caffè. The mother, ill with gallstones, will soon have to undergo her third operation. There is a twenty-two-year-old sister in the home who does not work because she has "a very serious stomach disturbance." A nineteen-year-old sister, married and pregnant, lives in the home with her husband, who has intermittent employment as a plasterer.
ENVIRONMENT: The home is roomy enough for the number of people in it. It is neat and clean.
HOME VISIT: On October 25, I visited Signora Giobbe. The married sister and her husband were present. Signora Giobbe was cold and reserved. She told me of the operation she had had four months ago and said that she would have to have another in about four days. She asked whether I would be able to make a plan for her boy.

I asked about Fernando's schooling. From six to ten, he had gone to school on Via Nomentana and had done well. Last year he had gone to school in Viterbo but because of "too much liberty" he did not attend to his studies and he had failed. What Fernando needed was somebody to dominate him. Many times at night he slips out of the house and goes to the movies with older friends. He returns home after midnight. Once he was brought home by the police because he was found loitering in the streets at dawn. Last week he was brought home with such severe wounds on his head and legs that he had to be taken to the hospital, where a doctor sewed up the wounds. The boy's behavior worries her greatly. Fernando is not afraid of anyone and will benefit greatly by being put in an institution where he will have to mind.

She would really like to keep him at home but the older sisters are afraid to take responsibility for him. The mother cannot rest when she thinks that any minute he may be doing a bad thing. The father, very preoccupied with his work, has very little time for the boy. All Fernando thinks of is playing and sometimes he will get up in the middle of the night to play with his ball. The mother thinks that institutionalization of the boy is absolutely necessary because at home he isn't watched over and won't obey anyone.

Signorina Facchetti thinks that Fernando should go to the institution at Albano, but Signora Giobbe would prefer a closer one in Rome. She "begs me to concern myself about her son." She returned to a discussion of her illness and her fear that the doctor has not told her the truth about it. The married sister says sadly that she cannot handle Fernando when the mother is in the hospital.

I said that in order to know what was best for Fernando I would need to know and understand him. The mother says Fernando knows that they are thinking of putting him in an institution and he acts indifferent.

I went into the next room where Fernando was playing with his ball. He greeted me "with a very vulgar gesture" for which his sister slapped him. I explained to him that the purpose of my visit was to help him choose the kind of school that would please him most. He said that he would like to go to an industrial school so that he could become a mechanic. He continued to play ball as he talked. I invited him to come to the agency, where it would be "more calm and peaceful" for talking. He turned to his brother-in-law, asking whether he would help him find his way there. The mother scolded him for his behavior, then embraced him, kissing him repeatedly.

OBSERVATION: The boy clearly shows irregularities in behavior. I think we need to take into consideration the good of the boy and the need of the mother to enter the hospital in "a tranquil state." I need to discuss with Fernando his choice of an institution and then to visit one with him.

DISCUSSION WITH FERNANDO AT THE OFFICE: Fernando came accompanied by his sister and brother-in-law. I began by telling him that he would be going to an institution. The school his mother is interested in has a shortage of space so we'll have to look for another one. Fernando told me about his liking for older boys, comic books, and movies with stories of war or animals. He says that staying at home annoys him, so he goes out to seek companionship. He would prefer to go to a day school but he is afraid that if he is at home his mother will not have "sufficient tranquility" for her operation. He says he has heard that in some institutions they are organized for trips and competitive games.

I asked him if he knew of a place called "Joseph, the Carpenter." [This is an agency a little like an American settlement house that has organized play activity for groups of boys for about three hours each afternoon.] I said Fernando could go to day school in Rome, then go to Joseph, the Carpenter for the games he liked after school, and still live at home. Fernando said he might do this next year "if my mother recovers" but that he really must move into an institution now "in order to give my mother the tranquility she needs."

OBSERVATIONS ABOUT FERNANDO: He began the interview shyly and then warmed up. He is a compassionate, sensitive boy who wants to help his mother.

INTERVIEW WITH THE SISTER: She is very unhappy about her brother and cried. He used to be a good boy. Now he is "just terrible." She is worried about her mother's health and her older sister's illness. (She described all the symptoms.) She feels bad to have her only brother growing up this way — undisciplined and rude — but somehow, she cannot control him.

PLAN OF WORK: Get Fernando to an institution; follow him there; keep alive the work with the family.

12-5-56: The sister told me about having found a suitable institution in Rome which was ready to take Fernando in. But she was troubled because Fernando didn't want to go. I said that I was sure Fernando would go. I reminded her of the need of the family to pay every month and she said they would be glad to. I invited her to accompany Fernando and me to the institution.

PLAN OF WORK: Take Fernando to an institution. Listen to his wishes and desires. Keep alive his wish to move in. Have monthly visits with the family.

12-12-56: Visited the Institution of Jesus the Divine. During the trip Fernando spoke little but said that he would be content to go providing he would surely have his Christmas holidays at home. At the institution the director asked the boy questions which he answered reluctantly but precisely. The boy said little on the way home except to comment, "My impression was right!" He spoke of our promise that next year he could go to day school. He reviewed the problems of his mother's health. He shook hands and thanked me for the trip.

OBSERVATIONS: The boy seems content to enter the institution. I think his willingness derives clearly from his worry about his mother. I have the feeling that he didn't like the institution very much. In following his placement, I will check these impressions. If it turns out that I think this institution isn't good for Fernando, I will look for another.

1-3-57: The director of the Institution of Jesus the Divine called to say that he had not heard from the Giobbes and therefore he had just given his last vacancy to a former student who wished to return.

1-7-57: After much telephoning, I found a vacancy at San Tomaso's but the family said that this was too far away.

1-10-57 to 1-12-57: I telephoned dozens of Roman institutions but found no vacancies.

1-19-57: I returned to the family the money they had deposited for the care of Fernando at the Institution of Jesus the Divine.

1-20-57: Case closed. The boy will remain at home in the care of his older sisters while the mother goes into the hospital. [Her hospitalization had been delayed three months.] He has been enrolled in a day school which I recommended.

FINAL STATEMENT: The problem of the boy is not resolved. Perhaps it is alleviated because at least he goes to a school that teaches industrial arts. The environment of the school is not very good; however, it may be able partially to satisfy his need for leadership. I have allowed ample latitude in this family to make final plans for this boy. The family doesn't have further need of a social worker.

This was the Giobbe case with which I was to live so intimately in the role of teacher for my remaining months in Rome.

A better case for teaching I have never found in America. It had almost all the typical family problems in it. The clients spoke clearly of their troubles but the social worker wasn't able to evaluate what they were saying. The social worker was almost uniformly wrong in everything she did, said, and planned. I had a strong hunch that she was wrong because she hadn't been taught – or, rather, because she had carefully been taught the wrong things. I began to think that untrained social workers might be acceptable in Italy because of families like the Giobbes, who themselves seemed to have some sparks of ideas of what to do about Fernando.

My mind went round and round. How do you take hold of such a problem? Sometimes it helped to put the basic problem in another context. Suppose I had come to Italy to teach cooking, and had decided to criticize a recipe. How would I do it? What would be the recipe for Chicken à la Giobbe? What if I started with something like this –

Chicken à la Giobbe

Select a chicken that has been killed at least two weeks before. (The farmer will try to persuade you that freshly killed chickens are better, but do not be influenced. They are not as pungent.)

Place whole chicken, unplucked, under a hot flame until the feathers are burned off and the meat is black. Plunge the blackened bird into a weak solution of coffee and boil for five hours. Sugar liberally.

Remove chicken from kettle. Cut off wings, legs, and white meat on the breastbone and throw away.

Serve in soup bowls with roast beef gravy used as a topping.

Now, how would you teach people to cook chicken when they were accustomed to Chicken à la Giobbe? You wouldn't start by telling them how revolting it sounded to you. Wouldn't you say that, though it is quite different, you think they might be interested in the American way of cooking? Perhaps you'd make some reference to the American theory that chicken killed two weeks before cooking may cause nausea? You could draw them out on this. Could any of them remember an incident of nausea after eating antique chicken? Then, you might describe "the newest American technique" of killing and cleaning a chicken – the method that the real gourmets were using. "The most distinguished chefs in America," you would say, "are now agreed that all feathers should be removed from chickens before they are cooked."

It was a roundabout path, but I felt that I had begun to get hold of something.

The next step was to select the important points of casework technique from the case. I selected seventeen. (I'm sure I could easily have found seventy-seven.) I wrote out my comments in English and had Signora Ugonio translate them. Then, using our little Olivetti typewriter, I typed out my English comments in blue and the Italian translations in red directly beneath them.

Debby suggested that I nail up my seventeen points on a church door in the manner of Martin Luther.

Instead I took them to Signorina Lombardo. The use of the *mot précis* can be very important in discussing casework, and I felt sure that in making a trial run with her I would discover whether I was saying exactly what I wanted to be saying.

April 14

SHORTLY BEFORE I HAD LEFT Minneapolis, Gisela Konopka — one of America's leading writers, teachers, and lecturers on institutional care for children — had asked that I call on Sister Mary Patricia, an American nun who was completing work for an advanced degree in social work in Rome. Mrs. Konopka had carried on a correspondence with Sister for several years. She described her as a delightful woman with a lively sense of humor. Mrs. Konopka had been right.

I met Sister Mary Patricia in an institution for delinquent girls in Rome.

She was reassuringly like the nuns I had known in my childhood — kind, spontaneous, humorful, and direct. She took me through her institution, the House of Santa Teresa, and as we made our tour I described my sensation that in structure, planning, and setup it was much like the Institution of Santa Marguerita which Sister Alice Irene had shown me the week before. But a difference, I told her, was in her attitude toward the girls and their problems, so that I didn't experience the hopelessness that I had felt at Santa Marguerita's. Sister Mary Patricia knew what I meant and was pleased, I'm sure, at my observation.

In both institutions the girls were received at the time their sexual maturation was beginning and left as young adults. Sister Alice Irene had seen this as a great advantage, even though the results were bad; but Sister Mary Patricia recognized the long incarceration as a problem that grew out of the cultural attitudes of a nation which considered institutionalization good. When the girls at Santa Teresa's mourned their lost freedom, a nun like Sister Mary Patricia accepted it as normal. In fact, she joined them in their mourning, and she worked and dreamed of the time when she would be able to bring about reforms. Among those she had already achieved was a system under which the girls not only earned money and used some of it for clothing and spending money, but also put away a part so that when they left the home they would go with a suitcase, a wardrobe, and a nest egg. Another advance made it possible for the girls to choose dress patterns from current fashion books and to select their own materials for their clothes. The result was that the girls (who wore clothes as modish and attractive as those of middle-income girls of the same age outside the institution) did manage to achieve some degree of individuality in appearance.

The House of Santa Teresa had wonderful equipment for vocational training. There was an expensively outfitted beauty shop. Handsome knitting machines chattered in one large room, where girls made sweaters and knitted dresses which were later either used for themselves or sold in the city. Sister Mary Patricia told me that one of the first "reforms" that the excellent mother superior had instituted was to put an end to embroidery work. "These girls have too much inner tension and anxiety to do such fine, painstaking work," she explained.

Except for the solemn shadow of long-time incarceration, the differences between the House of Santa Teresa and the Institution of Santa Marguerita were enormous. Below the surface at Santa Teresa's, one discovered sympathy, informed common sense, and a professional attitude toward the unfortunate girls who had to live so unnaturally long away from home.

But the most interesting part of the experience really was talking with Sister Mary Patricia herself.

She was full of enthusiasm for her assignment. She brought with her rich experience in a modern correctional institution in the eastern United States. The contribution that she hoped to make in Italy was to bring advanced American thinking to her institution and to the other branches of the House of Santa Teresa throughout Italy.

In line with this thinking, when she had found one of Mrs. Konopka's excellent books at the American library at Rome, she had begun a correspondence to arrange for the translation and publication of the book. I asked whether I might buy a copy to mail to Sister Alice Irene. She wrote the address of the Institution of Santa Marguerita in a little black notebook and assured me that when the book was available she would see that Sister received a copy. Even though the two nuns belonged to different orders, there was a way that she could arrange to pay for it.

Sister Mary Patricia was almost girlish in telling me of her anxiety about the coming oral exam that would lead to her diploma in social work. She brought out her thesis chart of "the ideal institution for delinquent girls" and we studied it together. The relationship between social worker and the institutional staff was clearly charted. In the ideal institution the social worker would be very active at the time of a girl's admission, would become less active as the girl adjusted to the home, and would heighten activity again as the time for release neared. Certain nuns were designated to inculcate the thinking of the social worker into the treatment plans for the girls.

"But this is marvelous!" I said. "How much do social workers come into the House of Santa Teresa now?"

"Only to bring a girl here and tell us of her background," Sister said. "Don't forget that my chart is labeled 'ideal.' It looks toward a future when reforms are to be accomplished."

I asked whether she would have a hard time persuading the examiners on her oral examination board of the wisdom of her plan.

"Hard!" she exclaimed. "It would be miraculous if I should succeed." And then she added, "But important goals are never easy to achieve, are they?"

Several years ago in America I worked in an agency that had at times served delinquent girls in the Minnesota branch of the House of Santa Teresa. I told Sister that in Minnesota her order was no further advanced than in Italy. When the juvenile court sent a girl to the House of St. Teresa in Minnesota, the casework relationship was inevitably cut off for the duration of the girl's stay. Only after the girl had been dismissed could the social worker begin to plan for her again. I said that for this reason not only social workers but also psychiatrists in our community were opposed to these placements. In Italy, it was easy for us to see how deep a part of the cultural pattern the restriction was; but it was hard for me to explain why it should exist in Minnesota.

Sister Mary Patricia looked grave. "I'm glad you have told me this," she said. "There is something that I as a member of this order can do about it."

We laughed and shuddered together at the coming ordeal of her oral exam. It would be given on a stage where she and seven examiners would sit. In the audience would be the rest of the faculty, the total student body of the school, and any social worker in Rome who was interested in the material that she was presenting. I remembered how frightened I had been years before at the thought of my oral exam. I had only to face three faculty members, and this in privacy. She would have to take on the burden of an entire audience plus the complication of answering her questioners in a foreign tongue. Her Italian was excellent, but even so there would be a frightening quality to doing such challenging work in a second language.

I told Sister Mary Patricia about my current language jitters.

Tomorrow I was to give my first lecture at the School of Social Work for Religious Persons. I explained that my tutor was in the hospital having her baby and that, as far as I knew, no one in the audience would understand any English.

She commiserated with me humorfully about the anxiety anyone feels on giving his first lecture in a foreign language – and then added that she would be very happy to attend and stand by in case I needed help! If she had said, "I'd be glad to give you ten thousand dollars in case you'd have any use for it," the effect would have been similar. I realized then how firmly I had been repressing my anxiety about this meeting. Now, having been rescued from the brink of my precipice, I felt the waves of relief. She saw this with sympathy and humor, and we laughed together like old friends.

April 15 and 16

I ARRIVED at the school at five minutes to five. The portiere gave me directions to the classroom. I was glad that I had allowed the five extra minutes, for five long flights of stairs meant a lot of huffing and puffing. I wondered idly whether all that exercise during a period of anxiety might not be therapeutic. Primitively, we want to run when we're afraid, and our glands secrete the kind of juices suitable for an energy spurt. But our glands haven't yet learned that today we are not fearing tigers and so, as I understand it, those unnecessary juices contribute some of the physical symptoms with which doctors struggle. As I used my runaway juices on those stairs, I wondered what effect it had when we put them to work to move toward the thing we want to run away from.

Dressed in a handsome dark green dress with a tangerine scarf at her throat, Italia Lombardo stood at the head of the stairs smiling down at me. Seeing her was reassuring, for she had become a symbol of successful communication. She sympathized with me over the climb and took me into a parlor to catch my breath and have a cigarette. To my surprise, she brought members of the school faculty in to meet me and we began a leisurely conversation. I looked at the clock in puzzlement. It was five fifteen, but Signorina Lombardo assured me we were early. I wasn't a very relaxed conversationalist. I had my lecture in a black plastic envelope case and I discovered that the hand with which I clutched it was perspiring freely.

When we were alone for a moment, I confessed to her. "Ho paura" (I'm afraid).

She said that I had nothing to fear. My Italian was better than that of any Fulbright grantee she had ever worked with. "You must think much how important what you are going to say is," she suggested, "and think little about how it will sound. Your Italian isn't perfect, but it is understandable. We think it has a charm that is more entertaining than perfect Italian."

At five twenty I was introduced to Signorina Gabriella Ogne, the teacher of the class. We went to the five o'clock class about twenty-five minutes late. I looked over the "students." They were a score of nuns in their twenties, some perhaps younger. (Who can guess the age of a nun?) Mostly they wore different habits, which meant that what I had to say might travel into sixteen or more orders.

Just as we sat down, Sister Mary Patricia came running in and breathlessly introduced herself to the teacher, explaining that she had promised to help me if I needed her.

As the teacher introduced me and explained Sister Mary Patricia's role, I kept looking at this improbable group. Only someone educated by nuns as I had been could understand the schizophrenic feeling I was experiencing. At age five there was one thing I had learned very well. That was that the nuns were the teachers and I was the pupil. And here was I, Jean Charnley, standing up to teach the teachers!

"Spaventoso!" (A great mistake) my tutor would have said.

When Sister Mary Patricia indicated that it was time, I began in a voice that matched my quavering kneecaps. (Lucky I was sitting down!) I knew the manuscript well enough to dare look up at commas and periods. I was greeted by such a sea of warm, sympathetic faces, all nodding with each word I spoke to show that they were understanding, that my anxiety began to disappear. This was good, for I had started out grimly thinking, "Faster, faster — get the damn thing over with!" and I felt that I was sounding exactly like that.

As the warmth of the group reached me I relaxed and talked more slowly; I think the group relaxed too. Undoubtedly they had picked up my anxiety. "Much better," whispered Sister Mary Patricia.

I stumbled where Signora Ugonio could have predicted . . . blind . . . psychiatrist . . . placement . . . foster mother. Sister Mary Patricia, who followed me on a carbon copy, gently helped me over these tongue twisters and once, when I sputtered hardest, read three or four words for me.

Miracle of miracles, my audience was understanding so well that it was beginning to think about what I was saying instead of putting its energies into waves of support to the miserable linguist. A hand went up. And another. There were questions, discussions, arguments. I had achieved a participating audience, something I had been repeatedly told an Italian teacher rarely managed.

Some nuns who spoke carefully and slowly I could understand fairly well. Maybe one or two words I would need to guess at. I'd quickly give my answer in English to Sister Mary Patricia and listen as she translated it. She would add her own comments, too.

One nun asked whether it was all right to interrupt with questions. We might not get through the manuscript, she said, and they did want to hear all of it. But on the other hand, my American ideas were so unusual that they needed to question me. Signorina Ogne and I quickly set up a plan that we would meet at the same hour tomorrow evening, so that we could take as long as we wanted to with the questioning.

In the manuscript, I had referred to the fact that Marilyn Monroe, "that famous blonde American movie actress," had grown up in a series of foster homes, often changing from one to the other, and that this had been very painful. Marilyn Monroe is a great favorite in this nation of movie-goers and I had already enjoyed seeing her in *Fermata per Auto-bus* (*Bus Stop*). It never occurred to me that she would be unknown to these young nuns. Not one of them, including Sister Mary Patricia, had ever heard of her. My saying that she had been the wife of the famous baseball player Giuseppe DiMaggio helped only Sister Mary Patricia. Sister said soothingly to me and the group that it was probably that constant changing of foster homes that made Marilyn Monroe "a bad woman." "But," I protested, "I have no reason to believe that she is 'a bad woman.'" I faced a roomful of puzzled faces. "But she is an American movie actress!" one nun said.

In English I said to Sister Mary Patricia, "Please tell them that though I have not made a study of her life, I do not believe her to be a bad woman." How I regretted having introduced the complication of this unknown character!

Every few sentences I read brought on more questions. They were good questions. Wouldn't it be better to spend five adolescent years in one institution than in a series of foster homes? What kind of people become foster parents? Can social workers really succeed in weeding out those who become foster parents only for the money?

There was a great deal of approval as I explained my belief in the importance to a child of having only one mother-figure. And when I pleaded to get a few men into the institutions for girls and a few women into the institutions for boys some of them proudly told of gardeners, chauffeurs, and janitors who associated with the children in their institutions. They laughed joyously when I told them that they would need to persuade priests and seminarians that playing ball with little children of both sexes was a way of doing God's work. Sister Mary Patricia told me in English, "They are entertained at your implication that nuns can persuade priests to a woman's point of view."

"Tell them . . . oh, tell them . . ." I kept saying to Sister Mary Patricia. We had just ten minutes left. She smiled at me gently and encouragingly as she greeted my last "tell them" with, "No, I won't. You tell them."

And tell them I did, and as I did, I found it only a little harder to say several sentences in a row to a group than to an individual.

I returned to my manuscript. In their sweet, supportive response to my struggle with their language, it seemed to me they were nodding pleasantly at some pretty heretical ideas. For example, in explaining how we must approach unmarried mothers, and parents who fail their children through drunkenness, abandonment, and inability to love, I stressed environmental determinism in contrast to free will and sin. I explained that such parents need to be seen for what they are — the result of homes barren of love. We learn goodness and the ability to give and to love from our own parents. Most needy children in our communities bring us the marks of the failure of parents who were failed by their parents, and grandparents in turn failed by their parents — a chain of one loveless generation following another.

"And so," I said, "social workers approach the failing parents not in any accusing way that points out their failures, but with the same tenderness and willingness to understand and help that we offer to their unloved little children . . ."

The class was over. The nuns applauded. Sister Mary Patricia told them that this was the first time Signora Charnley had spoken to a group in Italian and they applauded again.

I came out of the classroom in a daze. "I did it! It worked! I did it!"

The next day I approached the group without a tremor and we had a good session as I finished my manuscript. One nun told the group to their great delight that she had explained to the mother superior that Signora Charnley was going to cause "a great surge of leisure among the nuns of Italy." Signora Charnley thought that it should be either the mothers of the children or other women called foster mothers who should get up in the night when the children cried, who should care for them when they were sick, who should do their laundry.

I enjoyed her joke with them, but added that there would always be certain kinds of children — some handicapped children, some delinquent children, retarded children, mentally ill children

—who would need skilled women like themselves to care for them in institutions.

"You see," Sister Mary Patricia laughed, "Signora Charnley doesn't expect us to become lazy. She wants to give the good and easy children to the foster mothers and leave us the hard ones!"

I concluded by saying Sister Mary Patricia was right. This really was what I wanted. And because I wanted them to be able to care for damaged children in the institutions of Italy, I was delighted to see so many taking college work to enhance their knowledge. The job I had in mind for them would require all the skill and knowledge they could possibly achieve. It was not a job for just any good, kindhearted woman. It was a job for a woman who had these qualities and, in addition, professional education.

As in a lecture in America, a few nuns came up to talk with me afterwards. (Sister Mary Patricia had excused herself to attend another class.) One asked whether I knew that nuns who took courses in social work couldn't achieve professional status. I told her that I had heard this before, that it seemed unjust, and that I was going to "protest vigorously to everybody in authority whom I met." They giggled as though they had heard a child say a cute but somewhat naughty thing.

The second nun's question came out as a blur. Try as I would, I couldn't understand her. But here came Signorina Lombardo. She listened to the question, rephrased it, and gave it to me with her wonderful clarity so that I could answer.

At a third question, she held up her hands. "It is hard for us to imagine, sisters, the degree of tiredness that the signora experiences in speaking our language. Now we must let her go home and rest. But you have liked what she had to say and so we shall invite her again and again."

April 21

BACK IN MY "OFFICE" at SANC to finish reading a case, a fascinating case that I had begun over a week ago, before I got swept into preparing for my lecturing ordeal.

The case was the moving story of an eleven-year-old girl who was sharing a room with her nineteen-year-old prostitute sister. Apparently the social worker, who knew of the prostitution but could not prove it legally, had only one hope of getting the eleven-year-old into an institution. The older girl would let the child go only if she would say she wanted to. The social worker must develop a relationship that would let the child express this wish and a willingness to accept the grueling "lack of self-government" that institutional living necessitated. It was the first case I had discovered whose success rested entirely on the quality of the relationship that the worker could attain with the child. I was eager to finish the story not only because I was fascinated with it but also because I wanted to use it in a lecture. I was enough faster at translating now to be doubly impatient at my slowness. I felt as though I was trying to read an exciting novel with molasses in my eyelashes.

My roommates were maddening. They were so noisy this day that I had to hold my fingers to my ears to concentrate on the translation. From time to time they glanced at me with interest. I suspect that they found my unswerving concentration on my work quaint foreign behavior.

I tried hard not to show my irritation and disapproval because tomorrow I would lead my first staff meeting at SANC and I was reluctant to antagonize these members of my audience.

I turned a page and came abruptly to the last page of the case. It ended, "I went to the room of the two girls and learned that they had moved away. I think the neighbors knew who I was and why I was so concerned about their whereabouts but they would tell me nothing. I made a number of efforts to find the girls but all were unsuccessful. Since the clients have disappeared, the case may be closed."

I was sick with disappointment. And I was annoyed by the distractions in my office. I decided to declare a holiday so that I'd come to tomorrow's speech in a happier frame of mind.

When I turned up at home, Debby, who had been as interested

as I in the beginning of the case history, put into words what I had felt often: "Case histories don't exactly have smash endings, do they?"

April 22

I HAD BEEN sufficiently elated by my lectures to the nuns not to fear my first staff meeting at SANC. The staff would have read my article on "How America Succeeded in Thinning Out the Number of Children in Institutional Placement"; at the meeting they would raise questions about it.

As it turned out, I should have been quite concerned. Signorina Lombardo called the meeting to order. There were some fifteen staff members present, my chattering roommates among them. She began by giving a careful synopsis of my manuscript. I could follow it well, but I wondered why she did this for a group who had already read it. An uncomfortable thought occurred to me. "When had they read it?" I remembered the sociability in the office and it seemed likely that many of them had never seen it.

When she completed her summary, she got to her feet and left. I wanted to reach out and hold her there. She was my translator. She was leaving me alone with all these Italians!

I decided unhappily as we went along that this was as poor an audience as the nuns had been good. They looked bored and asked their questions in desultory fashion. When I could persuade them to talk one at a time, it was usually possible to understand, but when several talked at once I was lost.

Time and again I raised my hands to say, "One at a time, please." Then the azure-eyed Signorina Alta Quello moved her chair next to mine and began to discipline the group and simplify the questions for me.

Finally the questions began to come clearly. "Would an agency in America have the right to take custody of the child?" "What was the relationship of social work to the court?" "When a parent neglected his child was he liable to court action?" "What kind of acts might be described as neglect?"

The questions were appropriate and I did my best with them. It was hard because I hadn't got a firm grasp on the word "court." But what made it especially hard was my sudden realization that I was talking to a hostile audience.

"Oh, what word have I misused?" I thought. "Maybe I am telling them they are harsh when I mean to call them kind. Or is it that they sense my displeasure at their time wasting in the office?"

It seemed that this was closer to the answer, for the questions suddenly focused on how things were done in my agency. "How many hours do the social workers work?" "Do they have to write their recordings out in longhand?" "How many clients do they see each day?"

When I answered that an efficient social worker managed from four to five interviews of about fifty minutes each a day, I was greeted first by silence and then by barely masked anger as they demanded, "And how much is she paid?"

When I said that by Italian standards American social workers were extremely well paid, they laughed as though that explained everything. That was the answer! And I had an answer too. They were paid about 38,000 lire a month (about $65). Since we paid Maria 25,000 lire as a maid, I could sympathize with their anger. It was appalling, but not un-Italian. I suspect that they were paid about what Italian college professors were paid.

Their questions continued, and with Signorina Quello's help I understood them fairly well and managed some answers; but I felt that they were not really interested. When I described the dictaphone machines that social workers use in America they said that that would be wonderful. I agreed that it must sound wonderful to anyone who had recorded with a pen, but the truth was that American social workers, much like them in hating to record, were always getting far behind in their case histories. This helped. They found American social workers more palatable when they weren't doing too well. I thought wryly that I could please them greatly with a speech about mistakes American social workers make.

The meeting broke up fifteen minutes early. I was glad to have done with it, but was really puzzled about the way I had failed.

This kind of angry, cold, bored audience was a new experience for me.

But once we gave up formalities the group genially drew me into light conversation. "What did I think about the Roberto Rossellini-Ingrid Bergman divorce now pending?" "Did I believe as many Italians did that Americans wouldn't accept Roberto from the first because he was Italian?" On this non-social work subject, they were both interested and persuadable.

Why this and not social work? "Maybe," I speculated to myself, "these social workers don't like social work!"

Later when I talked over my unhappy experience with Signorina Lombardo, she convinced me that I was nearly right in this guess. She had left the meeting because she thought they would talk more freely to me when she wasn't there. The supervisor whom she had replaced a year before, an untrained social worker, had made the agency into a regular playground. When Signorina Lombardo had tried to impose discipline and supervision, some of the workers were angry. Because they were trained social workers, they also felt guilty. Sometimes out of guilt, they would work very hard and give outstanding service to the occasional client who caught their sympathy. But mostly they refused to exert themselves because they were paid more poorly than workers in other agencies in Italy.

Signorina convinced me that they didn't dislike me personally. They enjoyed hearing me talk. But they heartily disapproved of the industry with which I worked. It made them feel guilty.

Signorina described her problem long and earnestly. She said, "You could help me with many things, signora, but it is here above all that I need your help. This is such a hard, hard problem that I get tempted to quit and run away."

When I went back to my "office" to get my things I was greeted by as pleasant smiles as though my talk had charmed them. They wanted to talk more about Roberto and Ingrid and how divorce operates in America. I excused myself—my husband was waiting below to give me a ride home. Good-naturedly they accepted my excuse.

Signorina Lombardo had been right. It was my message, not me, they were rejecting. I couldn't decide whether it would have been better to know this before my lecture.

"How was it?" Mitch asked.

"Horrible! Ghastly! Terrible!" I responded truthfully.

April 23

ONE WAY in which my days as a social worker in Italy differed from those in America was that I usually planned only one major activity a day in addition to sessions with my tutor. At home a day at the office might be made up of two conferences with other agencies away from the office, a supervisory conference, a staff meeting, two client interviews, an hour or so of recording or letter writing, perhaps half an hour of making rough notes on a future talk. Here I tended to spend a day reading records, another day visiting one or two institutions, another writing a talk, and still another learning to read it in Italian.

But this day, April 23, was pleasantly full of a number of things. It began with the phone call at breakfast from Italia Lombardo. She said that the nuns had been "very lively with discussions" ever since I had spoken to them. The School of Social Work for Religious Persons would like me to give another talk, this time to "the second-year nuns," on April 29 at five thirty.

My first stop was at SANC to finish taking notes on several cases I thought might be useful in the seminars that Father de la Roche had so grandly dreamed up.

My office mates greeted me warmly. Three of them were trying to solve a casework problem of Sofia's. Maybe I could help? The problem concerned two little girls. One was a newborn, the other three years old. The father was in prison for stealing. He was almost always in prison. As soon as he was released, he would impregnate his wife, steal, get caught, and go back to prison.

I said that prison was a far more comfortable place for some people than life on the outside. Often it was no accident that they kept arranging to go back.

At first they laughed, thinking that I was making a joke. I laughed with them, agreeing that it seemed comical, but added soberly that in reality it was sad and that it was important for social workers to understand such twisted thinking. Interested, they moved into a serious discussion. They weren't rehashing something they had known before, but feeling their way to a new view of a client.

Sofia continued with her case presentation. The mother of the children lived in a "little box" with a dirt floor—no windows, no stove, no table. The three-year-old had been in a hospital for a long time, so long that now she could not remember her mother. The mother was a stupid woman who could neither read nor write. In fact, she could barely talk. It was time for the three-year-old to leave the hospital. Sofia must either put the older child and the newborn in an institution or leave them in the "little box" with the inadequate mother. Sofia was remembering what I had said about the importance to little children and babies of having mothering from one woman. On the other hand, she was afraid that the children would be cold, would maybe even starve or die in the little box. The mother loved the children and wanted to care for them in the way a mother animal wants to care for her young. Sofia had read my two talks. Now she felt guilty about taking the two children off to an institution for life. At the same time, she was afraid that they would become sick in the mother's poor home. What was she to do?

Three pairs of social-worker eyes looked to mine for an answer. "This," I thought to myself, "should be called facing your cultural reality."

I said, "I do not want to make you feel guilty about doing what you must do. In Italy and America too, we must often do second best. You cannot send the children to a little box that has no bed, no clothes, no food. Perhaps you should choose the best possible institution and, while the children are there, help the mother to find work so that she can build a better nest for her young. Perhaps you might ask the father why he keeps coming out just long enough to start one more baby and then get himself back in jail. How many times does he plan to do this?"

The social workers looked interested. "But will asking him this do any good?" the blonde with the dark eyes asked.

"Sometimes," I said, "asking a man the right question will start him asking himself other questions. It is a very little thing to do for a very big problem. It is not enough, but it may be the right beginning."

As we were talking Italia Lombardo joined us. Sofia described the problem and told Signorina what I had said. Sofia said that she had been thinking of Villa Ventrusi for the older child.

"Oh, not that one!" I exclaimed, to my own surprise. I explained my feeling that the littlest children got completely lost in the beautiful grounds, the swimming pool, the hunger and hardship faced by the three overworked nuns.

Out of our conference it was decided that Sofia would arrange to bring the mother some food, two cribs, some blankets, and some clothes. She would leave the mother with both of the children. Then she would return in three days to see how they were doing. She would look in frequently, and encourage the mother to ask advice of some competent neighbor. If she failed, the agency would at least have tested her ability to mother. I was pleased, but I had a new puzzle. "They *do* have relief money to help mothers keep families together!"

When I asked about it, they all explained at once that the first money would come from special philanthropic funds – that they couldn't often do this, but that once in a great while there was a way. I think, but I am not certain, that one of them said that later they might be able to use some kind of government fund for children of imprisoned fathers.

My next conference was alone with Signorina Lombardo in her office. She wanted to talk over that day's problem in intake. A wealthy widow wearing large diamonds had come to ask for two children to be taken into her home. Since the widow was almost fifty, there would be no legal problem. But her specific request was not easy to meet.

She wanted two children under four years old, a boy and a girl who were brother and sister. The boy must be the older. They must be children of legitimate birth. She would legally adopt the boy, give him her husband's name, and raise him as her own with "full rights of inheritance." As for the girl, that was to be quite different. The girl would receive care and education, but would not be allowed to use the family name, nor would she inherit from the estate. She was merely a property to keep the boy from loneliness and from suffering the emotional disadvantages of being an only child.

The widow was described to me as harsh, cold. She spoke of the little girl as though she were selecting a puppy. She did not want the girl to use the family name because she might someday become illegitimately pregnant; furthermore, she did not want any complications in the boy's inheritance.

I asked Signorina a number of questions. Was this a woman who could be helped to soften and change? Her answer was an unswerving "No." Would these children probably be reared primarily by warm, kindly servants? The answer was "Perhaps, but the influence of the widow would certainly be great."

I asked whether the choice for these two theoretical children was between a distorted experience with a harsh destructive woman, coupled with excellent physical care and complete financial security, and a life in a series of institutions where they would be separated as brother and sister, where they would lose all touch with each other and their family, and where they would emerge at about eighteen impoverished and unprepared for life. This, Signorina agreed, was exactly the problem.

Together we tested again her firm belief that the widow would not soften after she came really to know the little girl. Accepting her belief, I asked her to tell me, since I could not know this answer from servantless America, how much security two such children could gain from their contacts with warm servants. Would it be enough to sustain them against the onslaughts of a calculating mother-figure? Italia thought it might help but pointed out the probability that a harsh woman would choose harsh servants.

We talked and thought for a long time. Finally, Signorina said, "Institutional living is like malnutrition and hunger. It eats away at children slowly. Some of them as young adults do recover from it. But what the widow wants for these children is a quick poison. The damage is immediate and deeply destructive. I think the children will have a better chance to recover from the damage of life in institutions than from the kind of damage the widow offers. The institutions are for only eighteen years. The widow is forever."

The Italian word for widow is "vedova." To this day, when I hear it, my picture is of a harsh, domineering, witch-like woman, glittering with diamonds.

Back to my desk, my notes, and the sociability of my office mates.

The brown-eyed blonde had just answered the telephone and, though her voice was decorous enough, her clownish gestures commanded the other two social workers to listen in. Sofia and a plain girl whom I had seen only once before came to the phone and took turns. Though they were perfectly silent, they obviously found what they were hearing extremely funny. From across the room I could hear the squeaky rasp of a high, irate, fast-talking feminine voice. After the blonde had put down the receiver, the three women had an animated, giggling conversation. Their gestures were those of puppets in a Punch and Judy show.

After a few minutes the plain girl gathered up her things and left, wiping tears from her face. The phone rang again and once more the high scratchy voice threaded through the office. The blonde responded courteously, then clamped her handkerchief over her mouth. She hung up, and again she and Sofia went into giggling laughter, this time leaning on each other for support. As their laughter quieted, they smiled into each other's eyes, and then spontaneously and warmly kissed each other on the lips.

Forgotten, I watched them in complete fascination. I tried to imagine any two social workers I had ever known who could either laugh together like this or unself-consciously embrace. I failed.

"They really are profoundly different from us," I thought. I was reminded then of the lecture I was to give on how supervisors should help social workers in the appropriate use of time. I wondered whether any American theories of supervision could ever apply to Sofia and the brown-eyed blonde.

The receptionist with his imperious key ended their comedy and my speculation.

This same evening at seven o'clock I kept my silly appointment with Signorina Quinzi at the New Roman School of Social Work, ostensibly to return the magazine article she had lent me. We had had to break the appointment a number of times — once because I was caught later than I planned visiting an institution in the hill towns, twice because of her illness.

Apparently Signorina Quinzi had appropriately analyzed my eccentric wish for an appointment to return a magazine as being what it really was — a wish to work with her toward the May seminar. She and Signora Sacco (Father de la Roche's left arm) were waiting for me — with plans.

We began speaking English, but it quickly developed that this was shutting out Signora Sacco, and I resolutely switched to Italian. (I still hated to use Italian with anyone who could speak English.)

Signorina Quinzi wore a beautiful Italian tweed suit cut on those magic lines that make Italy seem to me to have France bested as a world fashion center. She looked tired. Her hair was a little mussed, her lips were pale. Perhaps this combination of perfection and imperfection in her grooming made me easier with her than in other meetings.

But my chief pleasure in the meeting was discovering how much I liked and admired Signora Anna Sacco. It was almost as easy to communicate with her as with Italia Lombardo. She had, I discovered as our evening went on, an especially orderly mind that moved some of Father's amorphous plans into a sort of workable structure. He was wise to call her his left arm.

Signorina asked me to tell both of them what I had been doing at SANC. When I finished, she amazed me: "How splendid! You have completed the study that Father de la Roche wanted on why social workers deteriorate, and now you are ready to present this in the seminar."

I gulped, gasped, and tried in vain to understand what she was saying. With a sinking feeling, I realized that she must have an intellectual marriage with Father de la Roche.

"What seminar?" I asked weakly.

"The June seminar," she responded casually, as though she were saying, "Today is Friday."

"But what about the May seminar with the agency executives to plan the strategy for introducing the idea of foster home care at the national conference?" I asked, stumbling over two hard words and trying to keep the frantic confusion out of my voice.

"Oh, that!" She paused. "Let's combine them!"

It took me a full half hour to understand that the plan to introduce the concept of foster home care at the National Conference of Social Workers had been postponed "a few years."

Signorina Quinzi's mind had the unpredictable mercurial quality of Father de la Roche's and I was often lost trying to follow her Italian. Fortunately her phone rang, and while she talked Signora Sacco re-explained the problem. Father had decided that foster care could not be started without first making a study. He wanted me to talk about techniques in doing foster care work for the benefit of the audience who might use this information in various ways. But I need not concern myself with the propagandistic problem of "selling the idea" to the nation.

As Signorina Quinzi put down the phone Father de la Roche bustled in, looking more than ever the mad monk of my imagination. His eyebrows were swirled into little devil-like peaks, his watery blue eyes searched the floor, the ceiling, the desks. "You must excuse me, Mrs. Charnley," he said in English. "I need to turn the organizational problems of your seminar over to these two capable ladies. We have run into a snafu and now we must wait until June to hear you. The May seminar must be canceled." His eyes ran over Signorina Quinzi's desk; he rumpled the papers a bit and came up with a small pamphlet. "There's the damn thing.

And my class is waiting!" He hurried off triumphantly, waving the pamphlet.

I suddenly realized at this moment that not only Signora Sacco and Signorina Quinzi but also Signora Charnley were smiling at him affectionately!

I turned back to the two women. Signorina Quinzi looked less alarming to me now. I made about as little progress in trying to protect myself when she was asking the impossible of me as I did with Father, but at least she didn't frighten me. And just a moment ago, I had discovered that Father didn't frighten me any more either.

I managed to get in a question to Signora Sacco. "Signora," I asked, "how have you visualized this seminar?" Bless her, she gave me a direct, clear answer. Signorina Quinzi kept nodding in agreement. "Perhaps you might choose three or four main areas — foster care, casework with parents and children, supervision, or any other you like. If you would lecture on each of these, using as much or as little time as you choose, the New Roman School would proudly provide the time, the place, and the audience."

I said that I had some ideas for two — one on foster care, and perhaps a second on "Supervision Focusing on the Use of Time." The two women were nodding happily.

With much help from Signora Sacco, I explained my deep wish to comment on casework, too, and to relate it to Italian cases I had read. But I was puzzled about how to achieve this. It would be necessary for the entire group to read the cases. In the grand Italian manner, Signorina Quinzi airily volunteered to have five or six cases mimeographed for the group to read — about three hundred typewritten pages.

Doggedly struggling to move from the grandiose to the possible, I worked it down to two cases I would summarize in English and send to Signorina Quinzi. I would disguise the cases. She would translate them into Italian, have them mimeographed, and distribute them to the members of the institute.

"I'll have to ask Signorina Lombardo's permission to use her agency's cases in this way," I said.

"Why?" Signorina Quinzi asked. Before I could answer the astonishing question she added, "I'll phone her tomorrow and tell her you are going to do it."

Firmly I put in, "I'd prefer to ask her permission myself." She gave a small shrug of grudging acceptance.

Then Signora Sacco began to act like an efficient American. She got out her calendar to choose a date, talked about hours, how much time I needed, and so on. We settled on three meetings of two hours each, with the three subjects to be chosen by me. The women drew up the list of people to be invited—all agency heads, leading teachers of casework in the four Roman schools, and a number whose names had no meaning to me. It added up to about twenty-five.

I remarked that Signorina Sletto, the woman who supervised in secret in northern Italy, was not included. I had thought of her from time to time somewhat guiltily. I pictured her hiding out among a set of ruins on bright moonlit nights, secretly whispering her supervisory suggestions to frightened and shivering social workers. Father had said months ago that she wanted to "cry on my breast." I had agreed to let her—and now, my time in Italy three-fourths gone, I hadn't even met her.

"Peccato!" (Too bad!) said Signora Sacco, using that musical Italian word that seems equally appropriate for a broken fingernail or a broken back. "We certainly must invite her!"

The little man brought coffee and I sipped mine with some ease. All the improbable things I was supposed to do as the grand finale of my work in Italy seemed to have been condensed into six hours. Almost anything could be endured for that long.

I have heard clear thinking described as "clear as a glass of water." I wanted even higher praise for Signora Sacco. A comical phrase I had read in an oddly translated bit of travel literature came to my mind. "Her thinking," I decided, "is clear as gin." Maybe she could perform one more miracle.

I pointed at the guest list. "I shall be lecturing to a most distinguished audience," I began. The two women nodded agreeably, not seeing where I was leading.

"In America one prepares a careful manuscript and reads it to such a distinguished audience," I said.

Both women frowned. "But the lecture read from a manuscript is usually dull. Besides, Father specifically didn't want it to be read."

I tried again. "It takes great poise and skill to lecture on three such impressive subjects without a manuscript," I pleaded.

Signorina Quinzi smiled. "We know about your record in America," she cautioned.

"But in America," I protested, "I lecture in English. I'm afraid to lecture in Italian."

They both began to act like inexperienced young social workers giving reassurance to a client. And like most clients, I was not reassured. I dodged and twisted. But they held firm. I descended finally to my trump card: "But my tutor is in the hospital having a baby!"

"Father de la Roche and I will help you if you don't know a word or two," Signorina Quinzi offered complacently.

I ended my three-hour appointment to return a magazine by giving it to Signorina Quinzi. She accepted it with a knowing grin. I also gave her a copy of my book, *The Art of Child Placement*, as a gift for the school. Signorina Quinzi seemed pleased. "I shall read it this very weekend," she promised.

My spirits rose. I had an idea. "After you have read it, perhaps you would tell me of the parts that you think would be suitable for a lecture in the seminar."

She shook her head pleasantly. "I wouldn't care to be that presumptuous."

I shook hands with Signorina Quinzi and restrained an impulse to kiss Signora Sacco Italianly on each cheek. "You have been very helpful," I said in the understatement of the month.

As I told Mitch my sad fate — that I was in for six hours of ad-lib lecturing before a distinguished audience on controversial and difficult subjects — he showed his customary serenity. He knew I could do it. He said that he kept being amazed at the increasingly easy flow of my Italian.

"But Mitchell," I protested, "I'm not sure I could do this in English!"

"Oh," he said, "in that case there's only one thing to do. We'll have to make a visit to Amalfi and Capri and soak you in Italian beauty until this sensation passes."

And that was just what we did.

April 27 (Naples)

OUR THREE-DAY HOLIDAY in the brilliant scenery along the Amalfi coast, with two nights in enchanting Positano and a side trip to the warm majesty of Paestum's Greek temples, proved to be the perfect tranquilizer. At nine on this morning I presented myself at the Naples branch of the New Roman School of Social Work. Mitch and Debby were headed for Vesuvius and Pompeii, and I felt reasonably sure that my day would be less demanding than theirs. How little I knew!

I wasn't, as a matter of fact, particularly optimistic about the day. I knew that Signorina Quinzi had written ahead, and what I expected was that the Naples school would give me the addresses of three or four institutions and turn me loose. Already I had discovered that Neapolitan Italian and I had little rapport, and I pictured myself half lost all day, perhaps even arriving at the wrong institutions where jaundiced eyes would look at me as though I were a Communist all set to start infiltrating.

I couldn't have been more wrong. The most cordial director of the school introduced me to Signorina Primavera Filadoro. What a fairy-tale name! Primavera is "springtime," and filadoro means "thread of gold." She was well-named—young, lithe, quick-moving, and though her hair was brown instead of Rapunzel-color, it had a golden sheen about it in the Naples sun.

Signorina Filadoro was the one on the faculty who spoke a little English. She had volunteered to be my guide on our tour. The school's car and chauffeur were waiting.

Signorina and I had a rough first hour. She insisted on speaking what I decided must be Neapolitan English. Proudly she showed me the tiny 200-lire English-Italian dictionary she had just bought and she got so busy looking up every third word that it took her twenty minutes to tell me she was pleased to know me. When she had been a child, she said, she had had an English-speaking nurse. Now her English was a little (long pause) "rigid."

It soon became apparent that English would get us nowhere. So I switched resolutely to Italian, and for the first half of the morning we each mangled the other's language. Only after she became gradually aware that I could converse with her chauffeur did she finally give up her dictionary.

It developed that my schedule for the day included four institutions. Three of them I'm going to describe only briefly – not that they didn't add to my store of knowledge. But they did have a good many similarities to other establishments I had seen (and have already described); and I want to save my breath for the two major experiences of the day.

The first of the three was a vast institution still abuilding – a brand-new place for a thousand boys that reminded me unhappily of San Marco's. It was sanitary, expertly and expensively equipped, rigid, and cold; it seemed to me that a youngster there would emerge knowing nothing about life except how to run a printing press. The second was a small preventorium for boys who had been exposed to tuberculosis. Here the nuns were warm and eager – they knew that their charges were individuals, and had rights to something better than institutionalization. These nuns wanted to know about foster homes, and could see what they might mean to children. And it was here that I had a brand-new experience: The mother superior asked me delicately, before we left, whether I'd like to use the bathroom. A wise and thoughtful lady!

Lunch was on the agenda after institution number two, and I suggested to Signorina that she would make me happy if she would allow me to play host to her and our driver. "That's impossible," she said in clear English. (I was amused. About the first thing I had learned to say in Italian was "That is possible" or "That is impossible.")

She told me that we were headed for a water front restaurant "very characteristic of Naples." On the drive she described an institution that we would visit that afternoon called Casa dello Scugnizzo. I tried silently to translate. "House of the . . . something masculine and singular."

"What is a scugnizzo?" I asked.

And how that poor woman tried in English and in Italian to answer my question, and how hard I tried with my questions to guess the answer. A scugnizzo, I learned, was a boy—very brave, very intelligent, very beautiful. He was extremely poor. He was not delinquent. He was "only delinquent enough to survive." Sometimes he had parents. Sometimes he didn't. He didn't usually live in an institution. He was a boy of the streets. I think the thing that confused me most was her insistence that there were no scugnizzi in any other city in Italy. I pointed to the little dictionary in her hand, but she assured me that I wouldn't find the word there.

Now we had arrived at the water front and the signorina dismissed the chauffeur for two hours and a half. When I asked, "Why so long?" she responded, "You must rest or you will become too tired."

We entered the garden of the restaurant and took a table right above the water of a little harbor edged by unpretentious restaurants and filled with fishing craft not much bigger than American rowboats. Suddenly I became aware of a dozen boys playing in the boats. All wore skimpy diaper-like swim trunks knotted casually at the sides. It was chilly enough that spring day so that I was wishing I had a coat over my sweater, but these little boys, somewhere between eight and twelve, clad only in loincloths, were jumping easily and happily in and out of the boats, swimming under them, indulging in boisterous horseplay with each other. The signorina watched me as I studied these fascinating children. They were like water animals. Never before had I seen humans and water so intimately and perfectly related to each other. The signorina sighed contentedly. "These," she said triumphantly, "are scugnizzi!"

I asked whether they weren't cold. She said that they were like this — naked and always in the water — in January too. They were, she told me, real products of the Naples water front. There were in the entire world no other boys just like these.

One of the boys spotted us and dived under his boat, emerged, and began to climb up a wire netting like chicken wire. He held out his hand to beg from us. "Stai buono" (Remain good), said the signorina, using the phrase with which Italians so often greeted children.

The boy gave us an impish grin and dove back into the water. My attention was drawn to another scugnizzo who was beginning to row a boat out of the harbor toward the sea.

"Whose boats are these?" I asked.

"They belong to the fishermen who have gone home to eat," she said.

"But that boy out there. Isn't he taking that boat away? Perhaps stealing it?"

Signorina shook her head sadly at her not very apt pupil. "But I have told you. The scugnizzi aren't delinquent! He will bring the boat back presently."

The waiter had brought us a menu and was waiting for our orders. At this point the signorina unhappily returned to English. "I want you to be my . . . my . . ." she swished the pages of her dictionary frantically, "host!" she said triumphantly.

I looked at the dictionary. Sure enough, the Italian word for "guest" also means "host."

In Italian I explained to her and the waiter, who seemed interested and in no hurry, the linguistic impasse. I repeated that I would like to be her host. "Impossibile!" she said again, and to show her opinion of the dictionary, she gaily threw it into the sea.

I asked her to choose for me a small luncheon of typically Neapolitan foods. She and the waiter had a long discussion. When they had finished she said in Italian, "The waiter thinks you should drink beer."

"Is that because he thinks Americans prefer beer to wine?"

The waiter was embarrassed. "I thought you were English, signora."

I explained that I was an American who loved the wines of Italy, and asked whether he had available the famous Vesuvian wine with the beautiful name, "Lacrima Christi" (Tears of Christ.)

"Brava!" said the waiter and Signorina in chorus.

We had a most elegant lunch of crisply fried sea foods — shrimp, clams, baby octopus, other wonderful things I couldn't name. In order to make conversation as I sipped the delicate wine I tried to tell the signorina that "Lacrima Christi" as a wine label might be considered sacrilegious by some Catholics in America. I taught her to say her own name in English, "Miss Springtime Thread of Gold." She thought this very funny.

She was one of those lovely Italian women so full of mirth that the tiniest stimulus makes them bubble. We enjoyed ourselves immensely, making little jokes for each other, eating the wonderful food, drawing the waiter in on our conversation, and never forgetting the laughing, shiny-brown water boys with the great dark eyes.

When we had finished, Signorina said, "Now it is time for your rest." I half expected her to lead me to a bed — not, at the moment, an unattractive idea. Instead, she stopped at the water's edge to hire a boat. What a wonderful show of Italian-bargaining-with-Italian! She called the barefoot boatman a robber and he said she was a hard, hard woman. On and on they went until she stalked off in indignation and I followed in poor imitation of her eloquent walk. Halfway up the stairs she looked back. "Oh, well," she said pleasantly, "he really is not coming down any further. A ridiculous price — but we will pay it."

"This time you have won, sir," she said pleasantly, handing the boatman some money. Smilingly he accepted the paper currency and helped us into the boat. She was to row, she said, and I was to lie back and rest. To my surprise this tiny woman turned the boat straight out to sea and rowed expertly and well. She explained that she loved the sea. It nourished and refreshed her to be on it.

She talked of many things as she rowed. It was an intimate and friendly talk. Sometimes I became drowsy from the sun and water, and weary with the incessant translating, so that I didn't always know everything she was saying. I did know that the life she was describing was a good and full one, scarred the previous year by the death of her father, a distinguished scholar, whom she had loved very much.

"He would have spoken to you today in perfect English," she said, "and he would have been horrified to hear my terrible use of it!"

Much too soon the boat returned to shore and we spent the next two hours on the day's third visit — to a home for the blind. Signorina Filadoro beamed with pride in it, and she was justified. It was pathetic and moving and wonderful, and what it was accomplishing for its old men was worth shouting about. But why did they take an American children's social worker to it — especially one whose feet, as I thought sourly, were just about on their last legs?

The truth is that by this time I wasn't at all sure I really needed another institution. But the indefatigable Signorina Filadoro would have been too disappointed. She had saved the Casa dello Scugnizzo, like a dessert, for the last.

We stopped in front of a tobacco shop while she made a phone call. The chauffeur had left me, too, so that I was alone when I had my first conversation with a scugnizzo. He walked, almost swaggered, up to the car, a curly-haired, black-eyed boy wearing the swim cloth of the scugnizzo and over it but wide open a sheepskin jacket — very old, shabby, and dirty. "Signora," he demanded, "give me a cigarette."

I responded hesitantly that I thought he was too small to be smoking a cigarette. He studied me like an uninhibited psychologist. I was obviously an interesting case. He scratched his head thoughtfully. "Signora, you give me a cigarette for my brother? He is very tall." He raised his grubby hand high over his head. I shook my head. He seemed not to mind — in fact, not to have expected anything from me. "Signora, you are not Italian."

I agreed that I was American.

"Americans have very good cigarettes," he said conversationally.

"Americans believe that children should not smoke," I contributed.

At this moment the chauffeur reappeared and yelled the Italian equivalent of "scram," and my fascinating scugnizzo sauntered insolently off.

Signorina rejoined us and we began to find our way deeper and deeper into the slums of Naples. Both the signorina and the chauffeur were lost. The streets grew dirtier, as did the children who played in them and the laundry that flapped from upstairs windows. The chauffeur must have asked a dozen people for directions, and I was aware that few of them seemed to know what the Casa was. At last we drew up in a square that fairly shrieked "poverty." It was etched in the lines of the gaunt-faced women; it was written on the dirty children who played in the dust. It was lettered on the battered buildings, on the grimy washes that hung from them, and on the gnarled arthritic hands of the toothless old man who listlessly held out his newspapers as though he didn't expect that anyone would buy them.

This squalid square had a church. Its door was patched with miscellaneous bits of wood nailed at random over it until the original door was no longer visible. We went through the door and into a little room to find an old man seated at the telephone. Signorina explained that we had an appointment. While the old man shuffled off, a swarthy little fellow bustled in, dropped two sacks of potatoes on the floor, and left. Signorina whispered that here the people were so poor that often they made their donations in food rather than money.

A stout tall priest came in to meet us, shook hands with both of us, and began to speak English. Though his cassock was dusty and its edges were worn and ragged, he was a man with great dignity. He spoke with a heavy British accent. This is not uncommon in Italy; many Italians have learned their English from the British. But within a few minutes I was certain that this man was really British.

I spent some time as he talked to me trying to decide whether I liked him. In retrospect I found my answer. I liked him very much—but he didn't like me. He had great fluency and color. Though every sentence was packed with information that I needed, I could tell it was a canned speech. This tired busy man did not entirely conceal the fact that English-speaking visitors were a frequent duty and a horrible bore.

He told the story quickly . . . The scugnizzi—the word means "fast-spinning top"—are tough, aggressive poor boys of Naples who live by their wits. They are astonishing little boys, hard, courageous, and unsentimental. They are uniquely Neapolitan, and so is the Casa for them.

I failed to ask the date of the Casa's founding, but it seemed to be about ten years old. Its founder was Father Mario Borelli. Father Borelli was once a scugnizzo himself. Some years ago he had been assigned to this run-down, impoverished church in the heart of Naples slums. (The British priest, almost in spite of himself, warmed to the story of his beloved director.) Father Borelli knew these boys and the desperation of their plight. He had just one thing to offer them beyond love and acceptance: his dilapidated church to serve as a roof and shelter against the cold Neapolitan nights. He knew from his own childhood that his cassock would serve as a barrier to gaining their trust and so, with the permission of his imaginative superior, he was allowed to wear the apache-like rags of the scugnizzi and to live and sleep among them on the Naples water front. Only after he was well accepted by their gangs did he reveal his identity; then he tried to persuade the desperate, starving, liberty-loving boys to come with him to his church.

The first boys came only to sleep and to share the little food the priest could offer. Their reluctance to give up their liberty was strong. Very cautiously, little by little, in minutely increasing doses, he began to insert discipline and rules. To live in the Casa, a boy must stay there one day a week, then two, then four, then six, until finally he must agree to leave the Casa only to do errands, to go to school, or forage for work. Any boy who chose could leave forever at any time. But the majority stayed and word got around to other cold, hungry boys in other gangs, and at last young Father Borelli and his ragged crew of urchins had given birth to a desperate but truly vital institution.

As the British priest talked, he led us through the establishment. We saw first the dormitory that priests and scugnizzi had built together – of sticks and tar paper with the same patchwork boards on boards pattern that had marked the church door. The close-packed rows of neat, clean beds were pathetically covered with scraps of faded, torn – and, I was sure, much too thin – bedding.

Next the priest led us to the little chapel – like the dormitory so ramshackle that the afternoon sunshine crept through the cracks. He said, "It's very humble, but it is really theirs. You'd never believe how much they love it." The stations of the cross were little foot-square oil paintings done by one of the boys – no young Leonardo, this boy, but he got the idea across.

The priest opened a door and drew out his vestments and an unadorned silver chalice. He said, "I got these in England. They're very simple but quite lovely, I think." So they were. I thought how rare it was for the Catholic clergy to find beauty in simplicity of vestments. He showed us the top garment that a priest wears when he says Mass, and then said almost affectionately, "Those boys cannot learn to fold anything!" He refolded it, doing only slightly better than had the boys.

We went out into the inner square of the Casa. I find it hard in retrospect to recall how it went together. It seems that one side of the small square was formed by the back of the unused church through which we had entered, another by the fronts of the dormitory and the chapel. The other two sides, I believe, were formed by dilapidated tenements. Their families may have had back exits to the streets of Naples, but their front doors opened onto the court of the scugnizzi and perhaps they, like us, got out by going through the abandoned church.

The court was full of the fine dust that was a mark of the slums of Naples. Little boys were playing soccer, and as they kicked the ball a brown powder settled on them, so that I could not tell whether I was seeing the classical southern European coloring or whether it would wash off. The boys left their games spontaneously to greet the priest. One tiny urchin took a run and jump and landed squarely on his paunch, rocking him off balance for a moment. With great good nature and vigor he turned the little urchin over and gave him a mock spanking that delighted him. One boy was wearing handsome soccer clothes which he proudly displayed. As we walked away the priest said, almost to himself, "I'm worried about that one. He may be needing a special kind of care." (Had the equipment been stolen?)

The priest led us next to his dreary little office and apologized for its untidiness. He offered us cigarettes—the first time I had seen a priest do this in Italy. Just after we were seated a Negro boy ran up, hooked his arm around Father's neck, and whispered briefly in his ear. Father rumpled the boy's kinky hair affectionately. After the boy had left I asked, "Who would have been the father of that boy?"

"Who knows?" he asked dispassionately. "Who were the parents of most of these boys?" (American troops had been in Naples when this boy was born.)

He apologized for our having to sit with him while we awaited Father Borelli. I was reveling in the opportunity to get English answers to the questions buzzing in my head. "What happens to the sisters of these boys?" I asked.

"Ah, the sisters," he said. "That's another matter. Some families are rather more protective of their girls. Though the girls have their problems too . . . ghastly, terrible problems."

I asked how he, an Englishman, had found his way to this parish. He said, "I love Naples as only a foreigner can love it. It is a great city—wonderful people, wonderful boys."

I commented that in America I often worked with delinquent boys. "Oh," he said sympathetically, "that would be very hard. They're really hard to reach. Our boys respond to love, fairness, and our careful lack of sentimentality."

I asked whether the boys were troubled when they first came. (It's a boy's own decision to enter the Casa, and it seemed to me that it must feel a little like entering a monastery.) "Dreadful! dreadful!" he said. "Those first few weeks . . . nightmares . . . wet beds . . . sobbing in their sleep." He said that the first thing that happens to a boy is a hot bath, then a careful examination by a doctor. "They're in such awful shape when they come," he explained, "that we usually lose one or two a year." (My memory says that there were about a hundred and twenty boys living at the Casa at the time of my visit.) "The first three weeks we encourage a boy to eat all he can," he said. "After this, we all share alike what there is to eat."

Now it was time to join Father Borelli and we walked through the old church to reach his office. The church was piled high with the discarded furniture that was a major source of income. The boys repaired and resold it, the priest said—"but sometimes they have to use it for firewood in the winter."

I asked how long the boys stayed. "Until they're about twenty," he said. "We have to get pretty firm about it with some of them. It's the only security they have known and they hate to leave it. They go into the schools of Naples to learn trades. But," he said bitterly, "even as skilled workmen all they can earn is about $2.50 a week. I pray that they'll find decent work and be able to live in Naples, but I fear that they will have to go away. Perhaps to England. The English love Italians."

"But," I protested, "England is overcrowded and has an unemployment problem. Why not to America?"

He smiled somberly at me. "This makes you want to forget your quota system, eh?"

Father Borelli turned out to be a short man with curly sandy-red hair and a boyish face. He looked to be about twenty-seven, but as I thought of the history of the Casa I realized he must be much older than that. He shook hands, saying in perfect English, "How do you do, Mrs. Charnley?" But that was the end of his English and as he began to talk my weary ear registered a totally incomprehensible kind of Italian. This must be it—real Neapolitan Italian.

I sank into a chair, gratefully accepted the demitasse of strong

Italian coffee, and began the familiar struggle against overwhelming weariness. Father Borelli and Signorina Filadoro had a long, animated conversation, almost none of which I understood.

But some of it registered. The British priest had been a member of the nobility who had left England to accept the vows of poverty and was using his brilliant intelligence in the service of God and the scugnizzi. A third priest came in, a young man handsome enough to have been assured of immediate employment in Hollywood. He wore a different cassock and belonged, I finally figured out, to the order of St. Philip. He was trying to persuade Father Borelli, who like the British priest was a garden variety of parish priest, to join his order. "In three months I shall become a Filipino," said Father Borelli. I was so befuddled that for a desperate moment I thought he was going to go as a missionary to the Philippine Islands.

In response to a request from the signorina, Father Borelli showed me a collection of excellent pictures of himself and the scugnizzi during the period that he lived as one of them. They were so full of color, costume, flavor that I suspected they had been carefully posed. Father denied this vigorously, showing me ones in which the boys had covered their faces because they feared having the police get their pictures. In some of the night scenes flash bulbs must have been used. With a wry smile Father explained that one of the scugnizzi had taken most of the pictures with a stolen camera and that the boys felt safe when stolen goods were used.

There was a picture of a half-starved, filthy, angelically beautiful little boy sleeping on the sidewalk over an air vent from a building. The pathos of this picture, which was obviously genuine, moved me so deeply that I think I would be haunted by it had Father not told me the end of the story.

"I found him," he said, "just like that. I took his picture. Then I carried him in my arms to the Casa and we had months when we didn't know whether he would live."

"Was he about five years old?" I asked.

Father smiled gently. "The typical American mistake in guessing children's ages, signora. Nature gives us Neapolitans small frames. Starvation claims its inches. No, this boy was ten years old, we think. Now he is married and proudly brings his little daughters in lacy white dresses to visit me on the birthday of my name saint. He makes a good living. He is a good husband and father."

I learned that an Australian, Morris West, has written a book about the Casa — the British title is *Children in the Shadow,* the American edition *Children in the Sun.* Father said that the book was an accurate picture of the Casa dello Scugnizzo, but that he wished it had been written by a Neapolitan. "Only a Neapolitan," he said, "can tell without sentimentality the story of the beauty, the bravery, the ugliness, and the magnificence of Naples." (Signorina told me that I could buy the book at the Lion's Bookstore in Rome. Later I did so.)

The pictures lay in my hands because I was reluctant to give them back. They told a story in a way that words could never do. Father Borelli apparently read my mind, for he asked whether I would like them. I selected three and asked whether I might pay for them. He refused, saying, "These pictures will travel to America. I feel that they will bring us good fortune."

I was troubled that he wouldn't accept money. I had come to the Casa and smoked a cigarette given me by the British priest, I had drunk their coffee, and now I was taking away with me as a gift pictures that must be worth 800 lire. I was doing this in an institution where the boys didn't have enough to eat!

I asked about his financial problem. He said that it required about a hundred dollars a day to run the Casa. Almost any afternoon, he might look into the till to find it empty. But always, toward the end of each hard day, "something happened." "We have a little miracle almost every week," he explained casually. Sometime when I am in America, I thought, I must see that I take a part in "a little miracle."

He and the signorina talked on and on. Her eyes shone and she was obviously deeply moved as he told her of the months when he laid aside his cassock and donned the garb of the scugnizzo.

He spoke of the trials against which his cassock usually protected him . . . being approached by prostitutes and homosexuals, the need to eat stolen food, the horrors of being infested with vermin . . . I cannot say precisely what I heard. I fought weariness as I never remember fighting it before in my life, but I was losing the battle. Finally I said to the disappointed signorina that we must leave now. It seemed selfish to me. She was having such a fine time listening to this amazing young priest. I hated to break in with my personal emergency. But it really was an emergency.

We drove back through the streets of Naples in the dark. Charitably she asked no conversation from me. The car drew up in front of our hotel. I stumbled as I got out.

Her merry, gentle little laugh rang out. "Guarda alla povera signora," she said to the chauffeur. "È ubriaca con la stanchezza." (Look at the poor signora. She is drunk with fatigue.)

She was exactly right. Mitch and Debby were waiting in the hotel room, expecting that we'd all go out to dinner. "Too tired to eat," I muttered. "Fascinating day. Tell you tomorrow." In five minutes I was asleep.

About midnight I wakened tense, restless, and hungry. Quietly I dug around in the dark to find a chocolate bar, my coat, and a cigarette. I pulled a chair over to the window and looked out on the silent city. "Fair Naples sleeping, her vigil keeping . . ." I found myself remembering those lines from "Santa Lucia."

I was grateful to Signorina Filadoro not only for all the professional sights she had shown me but for giving me a new way of looking at Naples. I had felt on previous brief visits that it was an ugly city wearing its poverty brazenly, with beggars on every corner, and a press of hurrying, stony-faced people that made me think of Chicago. Somehow in the course of my day, without ever consciously looking at the scenery, the flowers, or the people, I had come to know that this city was one of the great and truly beautiful cities of the world. How could I let Signorina know my gratitude? (Next day, as we left, I sent her a big bouquet. I wonder how she translated it.)

In this story of the Casa, I have departed from the usual pattern of this book, and used a "real name" – Father Mario Borelli. His address is Casa dello Scugnizzo, Largo Gennaro à Materdei, 3, Naples, Italy. I give his name and address because I want his daily miracles to continue. Perhaps someone reading of his struggles to help the scugnizzi might have an impulse to put a dollar – or more – into an envelope in order to have a part in a miracle!

It is not that I think the Casa more deserving than many other remarkable Italian institutions I have visited, but that most other institutions can count on some help from church, state, or social agencies. Father Borelli's Casa has only its miracles.

April 28

THE BUSINESS of keeping a journal has its problems. No matter how long and detailed it becomes, important parts of the picture are always left out. For example, I have never even mentioned my new American friend, Janet Maher.

Janet and I met at one of those large, elegant cocktail parties which are given for Fulbrighters from time to time by prominent Italian families or sometimes by members of the American diplomatic colony.

Janet, a pretty Irish-faced woman with wonderful silver hair and a fine button nose, greeted me warmly with a Midwest American voice and the special kind of friendliness and lack of pretense to which I always respond. As she walked up to meet me I was aware that she carried a handsome and elegantly Italian cane, and that her limp was quite pronounced. After that, though I had many pleasant times with her, I was rarely aware of the limp. She ignored it, and so did her world.

But it was important to her. It had offered her a year in Italy and sometimes she said it was a low price. Janet was the kind of American who, having tasted life in Italy, becomes addicted to it. Her first visit had been on a research grant that had taken her all over Italy, and she had made many friends in and out of social work.

For five years she had dreamed of coming back—not to work but only to wallow in the beauty of Italy. Then it happened—the automobile accident, the months in the hospital, the repeated and not quite successful surgery. When it was over and she held in her hand a sizable insurance check she said that her first idea was, "All right, I'll limp—but not in this ugly shoe. What I need is an Italian artist-shoemaker." She said she had looked again at the amount of the check and gasped, "I can afford it!"

I often used her for the purpose that Father de la Roche had suggested that Signorina Sletto use me—to cry on her breast. I found her lusty humor and her solid notions about Italians and their social work both bracing and helpful. One problem was that she was so engrossed in moving about from one wonderful spot in Italy to another that she was often away from Rome. I couldn't lean on her as much as I would have liked to.

Did I say "lean on" Janet Maher? This would make her laugh. She was much too full of humor to have allowed that. Seeing her and being with her was tonic and refreshment.

On this day I had been wishing she was in Rome so that I could talk to her about this improbable seminar I was getting ready for. But it was no use. She wasn't there.

I got out my papers, some notes, and two dictionaries and began to shuffle through them unhappily. I started two or three sentences of outline only to pull them out of the typewriter. I was trying to begin an outline on casework with children based on the rich Giobbe case. "How in the world," I miserably asked myself, "do you give a lecture on casework to people who know the x-y-z's but not the a-b-c's, without offending them?"

I slid back into my old American resistance to case recording. "Isn't there a phone call I must make? Of course—it's unforgivable how long it's been since I've talked to Signorina Mannini! After all," I reminded myself, "I am working for ICS as well as SANC."

Calling Signorina Mannini was effective as an excuse to get

away from writing, but as a morale builder it was terrible. I explained to her that I was hoping that I could spend some time at her agency both before and after the June seminar. I told her that I had written several articles based on my observations of institutions, and I had also learned how to read and criticize case histories. I asked whether I might get together with her soon to work out some plan for how ICS might use me.

Splash! I got the ice water right in the face.

"It was nice of you to call," she said pleasantly, "but my staff and I are in a very busy period, and it doesn't seem likely that I could see you."

"Perhaps next month?" I asked.

"No," she said thoughtfully, as though consulting her calendar, "I'll be very busy at least until August."

"But we'll be leaving in mid-July," I said, finding it hard to believe the nice clear Italian that I was understanding all too well.

"What a shame," she said. "I do hope that I run into you before you leave. It was nice of you to call."

"Brrrr!" I said as I hung up. Maria looked at me puzzledly. "The signora would like me to bring her a sweater?"

I wondered unhappily what that call had meant. Was Signorina Mannini angry about the day that Mitch and I didn't go to "one more institution"? Had I accidentally ended a meeting with some unfortunate word? Had Father de la Roche, who I thought tended to undervalue her sharply, said some harsh thing that somehow got mixed up with my name?

I turned sadly back to the Giobbe case. How to do this? I remembered reading a novel in which a parachute jumper always said as he jumped, "Here goes nothing." I sat down to work on nothing. The phone rang.

"Hi . . . surprise!" said Janet. "How would the Charnleys like to feed me and a guest tonight?" I patted the telephone. After all, it could be kind. Janet had piqued my interest in her old friend Domenica di Montignacco, who had taught for years in an Italian school of social work.

"Wonderful!" I said. "Do you eat rabbit?"

"Of course we eat rabbit," she said. "What do you think we are — Minnesotans?"

Maria, who had been working near the telephone, nodded happily. Though she couldn't understand any English she seemed never to miss the mood of this language. "Now the signora doesn't need a sweater," she teased.

Happily I told her about the guests and all the wonderful things I wanted her to cook to go with the rabbit. Her mood soon matched mine. Nothing pleased her as much as guests for dinner. Almost before I had finished talking, she was reaching for her mesh shopping bag. She asked Debby to go along and I heard them giggling on the way down the stairs. Maria and Debby had achieved something close to a friendship almost from the first, even when Debby's Italian vocabulary wasn't twenty words.

The call did wonders in unlocking my thinking. What was wrong with the Giobbes as a family? Fernando at age eleven was a juvenile delinquent — though never so labeled in Italy, where the term seemed to suggest a dreadful and uniquely American disease. He had all the privileges of an adult son who was permitted to make his own rules. Who makes the juvenile delinquent start obeying? The father, the head of the family. And who needs to love the delinquent? The mother. But Mr. Giobbe is just a shadowy waiter in the case whom nobody consults and Mrs. Giobbe is so busy playing the father's role that she can't be mother; so first she slaps Fernando and then she kisses him. And who is supposed to plan for Fernando? His young married sister who should be playing the role of the pregnant young wife. Role playing! That would be a way to teach "the new American way."

It began to fall into shape for me. Never was there such a good case to show how mixed up a family could become when everyone played the wrong role. Rarely could you find a family readier to start functioning again if a good social worker would help Fernando, for example, to start being an eleven-year-old boy. This he could do if a social worker could help his father to start acting like the head of the family. The Giobbes were a family that should succeed rather quickly because its members loved each other.

My typewriter chattered through the day and by late afternoon I knew quite well what form my first two hours were going to take. It was a great relief. It meant that I could be really relaxed with Janet and Domenica.

This fine evening began with enough outdoor warmth so that we could have cocktails on the terrace and bring our guests in on our family preoccupation with the planes that flew over us toward Ciampino, the Rome airport. One of those planes, not too long hence, would be bringing Blair to us.

Domenica turned out to be as attractive as Janet had said. And she spoke excellent English! I found myself telling her and Janet about all my woes – how I had mysteriously offended Signorina Mannini, about the terrifying subjects that I was going to have to lecture on, about my puzzlement over the lack of discipline in the SANC office, and how I might bring this up in my lecture on supervision.

Pieces began to make patterns as we talked. The concept of role playing as an aid in diagnosis and treatment was completely new to Domenica. As Janet and I explained it she first looked puzzled and then said, "Oh yes. In Italy we say, 'Il padre è il capo della famiglia, ma la madre governa!' (The father is the head of the family but the mother governs.)" She laughed. I laughed too, remembering that shortly before I left America I had heard that there was little juvenile delinquency in Italy because the Italian family is headed by a strong, authoritarian father. Juvenile delinquency, I had now come to understand, is always low in a country in which the delinquent is neither labeled nor counted.

I asked Domenica about those authoritarian fathers. Case histories which I had read described dominant mothers. "You do find authoritarian fathers in Italy," she said, "but they are growing more and more rare. They are still common in the deep south."

The idea of helping various members of a family back into the appropriate roles from which they had strayed interested her greatly. She asked good questions about how a treatment plan could be based on the concept. In the end she said, "But this is perfect for what you need to do. It is unfamiliar and just complex enough that your audience will be very interested, and it will keep them away from the theoretical, psychoanalytical labeling in which they get so ensnarled."

Maria's dinner was excellent and the conversation was excellent. When the two women left long after midnight, I felt a little guilty. They had come as guests and I had used them as consultants. I felt as though I should have sent them a fee.

April 29

I BEGAN THE MORNING with a letter to Signorina Mannini in which I enclosed the two talks on institutional care of Italian children that had been used by SANC. I told her that I could not have written them without her cooperation in helping me see the institutions. I suggested that she use them in any way she liked. And then, timidly, I expressed the hope that the opportunity to meet with her before we left Rome would not be left to happenstance. I didn't now exactly what broken fence I was trying to mend, but I hoped that the letter might help with whatever had gone so wrong.

This was the day that I was to meet a new group of nuns at the School of Social Work for Religious Persons. I was far away from practice in reading my manuscript, so I sat on our terrace and read it aloud to myself. I was proud of my progress. The rhythm seemed good and I stumbled less.

At five thirty I arrived at the school, more serene than ever before about a talk. Italia Lombardo, to my surprise, greeted me. It turned out that she taught this class. As the new group of nuns assembled, I reached into my black portfolio and drew out—the wrong script! The subject was as suitable as the other for the purpose of the class but I had never once practiced reading it.

Should I offer to come back another day? I decided not to. I had an impulse to tell Italia about my mistake but I decided that this would mean that two instead of one of us would be suffering. And I might as well admit it honestly—I had been having such good luck with Italian that I was a little giddy and had begun to kid myself that I could give a lecture without studying for it.

I was a magnificent flop. I stumbled, sputtered, and my rhythm was that of a car trying to make up its mind to run on a subzero Minnesota morning. I sensed the polite tension in the group and the puzzlement in Italia. (She had never heard me read a manuscript before.)

As I floundered along, I'd keep looking at the page number. Four more pages to go. How terrible! I wished I knew how to faint convincingly. Finally and painfully it ended. Italia came to my rescue at the end and got a discussion going in which it was soon quite easy for me to participate.

I remember that parts of this discussion were really good. One nun said that the suggestions for change that I had made might work in America but they never could in Italy. I asked the group to list one by one the suggestions that couldn't work; and slowly, little by little, they began to see that perhaps after all, with the same kind of modification of attitude that they themselves were experiencing during our talk, those in high places in Italy could change their attitudes too.

When at long last the class was ended, Italia and I went to a nearby caffè for coffee. When I explained about the accidental switch in manuscripts she was most sympathetic. I mentioned my anxiety about the coming seminar. She was firm in saying that I really should work without a manuscript. "You are stubborn," she said, "about believing that you cannot really speak Italian. I tell you that you speak well. But it is dull to listen when you read."

She told me that the next day she was going by bus to an institution in one of the hill towns. There was a beautiful long ride and after it there would be a long walk. She would enjoy doing both with me. And during the ride we would have time to "talk of many things."

April 30

AT SEVEN THIRTY I stood at the appointed corner to meet Italia. The hours that many workers keep in Italy would have caused riots in America. Perhaps if you work a thirteen-hour day you have to waste some of the hours gossiping. Of course it really wasn't thirteen hours — there was that three-hour break at noon. But Americanly it seemed to me that if you began work at 8 A.M. and stopped at 9 P.M., you had worked thirteen hours. As we were riding out in the bus I explored this idea with Italia. I assured her that social workers in Italy must be near exhaustion all the time. She, on the other hand, couldn't understand how Americans could keep going in the afternoon with only an hour off at noon.

Our ride was slow and delightful as the big bus maneuvered along the twisting tiny roads through the centers of the villages. At the end of the trip we had a mile's walk down a country lane to reach the institution. Italia said this was a common problem. You used public transportation as far as it went and from there on you walked. No job for the weak of arches!

As we walked, I questioned Italia about the time wasted by my office mates. Why, I asked, did they turn to each other for answers to casework questions rather than going to her?

We were early for our appointment, and we sat on a big rock in the bright sunshine to talk. I remember thinking as she answered me, "She is like a client with years of pent-up anxiety that needs to be spilled."

Italia described the problems in her year-old job as supervisor at SANC. Her predecessor, an untrained social worker, had run the agency as though it were "a big party." This woman was a political appointee who, recognizing that social workers at SANC were among the most poorly paid in Italy, tried to make the job attractive by demanding very little of them. They had broken the habit of asking for help, for that supervisor would have understood much less about their problems than they did themselves.

A year ago she had died suddenly. Dr. Alberghi had seized the opportunity to hire a qualified supervisor. When Italia had arrived she found the workers openly defiant at her insistence that they change their patterns. Their resistance to supervision was very high. They pointed to an old rule that said that a worker with two years' employment had graduated from the need for supervision. (Domenica had said that resistance to supervision existed in almost every agency. Was it, I wondered, a manifestation of the Italian culture in which every Italian strove to be boss of his own tiny business instead of working for someone else?)

I described to her how agencies in America work—the statistical count each month to show just how many interviews a worker has achieved, the mutually enjoyed supervision that goes on for years, the insistence on good performance and a record of achievement when one is on the job. Was this possible for Italy?

Italia listened, questioned, and approved. There were a few agencies in Italy that functioned something like this, she said, and she firmly believed that this was what Italy needed.

I described my puzzlement at the fifteen-minute interviews I had observed and at the fact that when a client left a return appointment time was rarely given. It was as though only at moments of crisis was a client to come in, or only if after a week, a month, or a year he was "still hurting."

She said these things needed to be said to the entire group, but added that I had some distorted impressions because the workers in my office were "the worst loafers" in the agency, with the exception of Alta Quello. I responded that this raised my hopes, because I had seen in all of these workers moments when they wanted to serve their clients well.

She made the problem at SANC clearer for me. Between her and Dr. Alberghi, the national executive officer of SANC, was a woman who was Italia's direct superior. A political appointee, she was not lazy—in fact, she was energetic. But she directed all her efforts at saving the agency money. Whenever a caseworker made a plan for a family that involved spending money, this woman would trim it so drastically that it would be killed. Or she would question and argue the validity of the plan so bitterly that the worker, perhaps apathetic anyway, would "forget" the whole idea.

This woman was "very difficult but not impossible because she didn't mean to be destructive." When Italia argued a plan with her, she would almost always approve it.

"Isn't this, then, your most important job?" I asked.

She smiled wearily. "For one hundred new cases a month?"

"Then," I said tentatively, "can't you build up your workers' courage in your supervisory meetings?"

"You forget," she said, "they do not come to me for supervision."

"But they must," I protested. "They must come or be fired. Surely Dr. Alberghi can see that?"

"He does," she said. "He says, 'Fire them all and start over.'" She paused. "Quite a few have left voluntarily. They don't mind being fired because the pay is so low."

"But these are trained social workers," I protested. "They chose to be social workers and went two years to school to learn how. Now they must choose again. The salary situation is deplorable and something needs to be done. But neither you nor Dr. Alberghi can let them sit around being bad social workers."

How, I asked, did she ever hope to win? "I hope to win," she said, "by replacing each old worker who leaves with the Alta Quellos who are angry about salaries but will not take it out on their clients. I have chosen seven new good workers. They came young, dedicated, really wanting to serve clients. Five of them are still good workers. Two of them have become corrupted by the lazy old workers."

She glanced at her watch and got to her feet. We walked on in silence, she thinking, no doubt, of new examples to help me see the problem more accurately, and I still baffled about how you start a reformation movement in a situation like this.

Happily the institution we visited turned out to be one of those gems that always lifted my morale. This institution, San Stefano's, had many characteristics that America would do well to copy.

As we walked into the charming villa, Italia told me that years ago it had been the home of a wealthy Roman merchant who had just one son. At thirteen, the boy had died, and the parents could not bear to live at the villa with its memories. They had given the villa to an order of priests to form a "humane and happy institution" for boys who had special problems. It now housed thirty-five boys whose support came either from their own parents or from the patron in Rome.

The institution was administered by a sensitive, delicate young priest who, though wholly masculine, had an almost maternal gentleness when he spoke of his boys. He was assisted by two seminarians, four lay teachers from the village, a part-time social worker, and the village women who did the cleaning and cooking. There was also a wonderful old gardener to whom the boys often brought their troubling secrets and who responded to them like "a skilled psychologist."

Every boy at San Stefano's had the same problem — a reading block coupled with normal or better intelligence. Father Macci believed that the failure of a bright boy to learn to read always had its roots in emotional entanglements with parents or parent-substitutes. He thought that, if such a boy were brought to a congenial setting and allowed to choose to learn again to read from the very beginning with a sympathetic teacher, great progress could be made.

His rule for the conduct of his staff was simple. The boys must be treated with the same courtesy, kindness, and thoughtfulness that is shown to "a distinguished adult." Whatever they did about trying again to learn to read must be entirely voluntary.

The earmarks were those of a well-run, pleasant children's institution. There were four classrooms. Number One was set up to handle no more than six boys. Here I saw five tall, well-built, good-looking boys patiently learning to write the alphabet. Their teacher was a sweet-looking woman of about thirty. Father Macci explained to me how a boy came to enter Room Number One.

When a boy arrived at San Stefano's he was often frightened, defensive, and embarrassed. Father explained to the boy that he was welcome to stay at the institution as long as he liked, playing all day if that was what he wanted. But when and if he got curious about how other boys like himself had learned to read late in life (and a gentle explanation of why they had failed was given) he might wander into Room One and stay as little or as long as he chose.

Eventually the boredom of playing alone coupled with the deep wish that lies in all of these boys to read would overcome him and he would wander into Room One. He would find his new friends all unembarrassedly working hard at kindergarten problems. San Stefano's had found it wise to admit just one boy at a time and never to bring in a new boy until the last newcomer had firmly "joined" Room One.

Most of the boys in Room One learned the beginning of reading and writing at a dazzling speed. "These emotionally blocked learners," Father explained, "know a great deal. Actually they know many parts of reading and writing. Once they dare open the little sealing-off door in their brains they zoom ahead like geniuses for a while."

A boy moves exactly at his own pace from Room One to Room Two. There is no pressure to hurry or to achieve. Nobody is smart-alecky or superior toward slow learners, for they were all originally slow learners.

We moved from one learning room to another until we came to Room Four, the highest. "These boys," Father Macci explained, "are now performing at the level that is appropriate to their age and ability. They need a few months or even a year or two of performing at capacity before they feel safe enough about themselves to move out to the village school.

"Five of our boys now go to school in the village and three of our oldest have reached our ultimate goal. They go by bus to Rome each day, where they are learning trades. One, who will be leaving us soon, is a pre-medic in a college in Rome. They may leave to take jobs, to marry, or to go home while still quite young if they have homes to go to. Since we can care for only thirty-five, and since our waiting list is long, there is a terrible temptation to hurry them which we must guard against. These boys have been hurt by being hurried. To succeed, San Stefano's must be a 'take your time' school."

There was much to admire about San Stefano's. I was especially pleased to learn about allowances and bank accounts. Each boy is given 100 lire every Saturday. (The town movie costs 30 lire.) He can use his money for candy, movies, or whatever he likes. He is encouraged but not required to bank a little each month. And each boy has his own garden where he can raise any crop he wants to. He sells his crops to the cook at local market prices. One boy had that day collected 300 lire for salad greens. Boys select their own clothes. The only cost restriction is that though a boy may have whatever garment he chooses, he must pay one per cent of the cost of it.

Father Macci and Signorina Lombardo had some work on a referral to talk over. I suggested that Father Macci arrange for me to sit quietly in the back row of Room Four to watch the boys in school. After a bit I would wander out into the garden to wait for Italia.

Father introduced me to Professor Guido and I asked that he not interrupt his class but just allow me to observe. Unhappily for me, he refused, and stopped everything to show off for the Americana. He talked to me in a terrible baby-talk Italian, explaining what they were studying. They seemed to be doing geometry that morning. The boys, who were between eleven and thirteen, were attractive youngsters, but it seemed to me that Professor Guido was making them as uncomfortable as he was making me with his baby talk. We smiled at each other foolishly and sympathetically. At last, the professore hit on a good idea. "Would the boys like to show the Americana their workbooks?" They would indeed. Their workbooks impressed me greatly. One boy had drawn the entire electrical plan for the villa including lighting, doorbells, telephones, and all the rest. Another boy showed me an incredibly neat geometry workbook. "Is math hard?" I asked him.

He smiled. "No, signora, grammar is hard but mathematics is very easy."

Looking at these workbooks — music, geography, various kinds of mathematics, design (both artistic and mechanical) — I found my impression that children do more complicated projects at an earlier age in Italy than they do in America reinforced. Neither

Deb nor Blair had done written projects to rival these in their school in America.

One boy asked me to point out on a huge map of the world where I lived in America. I found myself giving a lesson in geography on "what it's like in Minnesota." Another boy raised his hand and explained that many of them would like to have international pen pals. Could I give them the names and addresses of boys their age in Minnesota to whom they could write? They liked to exchange letters, stamps, sports pictures, and comic books. I gave them the name of the principal at our children's school. I explained that the answers to their letters would be written in English and that they would need to find someone to translate them. They assured me that this would be easy. (It always is easy in Europe. I thought how hard it would be in Minneapolis to find someone to translate their Italian letters.)

The teacher learned from his pupils and stopped talking baby talk to me. When the class was dismissed I went out into the garden. I was hardly seated when a nice young man appeared with coffee and cigarettes. A student of the New Roman School of Social Work, he was on a work-study assignment at San Stefano. Each evening he returned from classes to have his evening meal and to sleep there. He earned board, room, and "a very tiny salary" for this work.

Our conversational goals were in direct conflict. I wanted to learn more about this excellent institution and he wanted to learn all about social work in America – especially how well "they" paid. We compromised by taking turns with our questions.

As we talked I idly watched a boy of about seven playing in the garden. Inside of five minutes I had him classified as emotionally disturbed. He was playing by himself in the garden, running about with a live salamander in a plastic bag. He seemed unaware of my observing him. Once he boxed vigorously with his shadow on the garden wall. Sometimes he talked and laughed to himself. Sometimes his face would be contorted by a sudden frown followed by a furtive looking about as though afraid of someone or something that might be coming up behind him.

"That is a mentally ill boy?" I asked the social worker.

"Yes," he agreed. "He's just been here three days. Your friend, Signorina Lombardo, brought him. He's in that beginning period when all children seem abnormal. This is something much stronger, though. We'll give him a month or so to see how he adjusts when the newness wears off and he begins to feel safer."

"And will he eventually join the others in Room One?" I asked.

"Very probably," the young man said.

"And if he cannot adjust here – if he is too ill?"

"There are institutions in Italy that specialize in helping this kind of child. Fortunately for him his parents are wealthy."

Our conversation was interrupted when a handsome and expensively dressed woman of about forty walked over to us. After asking permission she sat down to join us. She asked me about my accent. Was I American? Then she told me about relatives who had gone to America, and how she yearned to visit them.

I studied the size of the many diamonds in her rings and thought to myself, "You can afford to go tomorrow, signora." I remembered then something that my tutor, Signora Ugonio, had taught me. When I had remarked about the lavishness of the jewelry that wealthy Italian women wore she had said, "Many a Roman woman wears her husband's bank account. People who have been through wars and political revolutions often feel safer putting their money into diamonds than in banks. This is one reason why you rarely see an Italian woman wearing inexpensive costume jewelry. We make lots of it. I find it beautiful and enjoy wearing it myself; but mostly it is made to sell to you Americans."

The woman chatted on affably. I deduced that she had been to San Stefano's to visit her son and now she was waiting for a car to take her back to Rome. I explained my interest in San Stefano's. She said, "You will visit hundreds of institutions in Italy before you find one as wisely and humanely run."

A car driven by a chauffeur drove into the grounds. She shook hands warmly with both of us before she left. Several minutes later Italia came out the front door and we began our walk back down the country road. I felt a little selfish. Very easily I could have arranged for a ride back to Rome; but I had so enjoyed our bus ride out and our conversation that I was unwilling to cut it in halves.

I was right. Our conversation on the way back was as rich as it had been on the way out. I had had time to think. I asked her what would happen if she circulated an announcement that each worker in the agency must attend a weekly supervisory conference and Dr. Alberghi signed it. She said that the resistant workers would come once or twice and then would keep saying, "Sorry, I forgot." I said that it would seem at this point that Dr. Alberghi would need to call them in to say that they would lose their jobs if they continued to forget. She smiled. "This is what he believes I should do, but I don't like it. He is willing to fire everybody."

She said, "And can you, in a supervisory meeting, teach social workers who do not want to learn?" I said that I didn't believe that you could at first, but that you could use the hour to challenge their right to sit at their desks and keep suffering clients from getting service. Such a worker could choose to leave social work in an underpaid agency. But she had no right to choose to stay and be a bad social worker.

Italia talked on and on, pouring out her distress at the spot she found herself in. I said, "I think you are a very kind and gentle person. I think it distresses you to think of asking social workers to leave. You would rather reform them." She agreed sadly.

"I think you care even more what happens to the clients of SANC and you know and fear that SANC will stop hiring trained social workers and will replace them with untrained women who will work fast and get a lot done, whether it is good or bad."

We walked along in silence, each thinking of the job she faced. Finally she turned to me.

"I think the Fulbright program is a very wonderful thing."

May 1

THIS WAS as beautiful a day as any romanticist might ask May in Rome to offer. Mitch and Debby readily agreed that we use it to take all the little boys from Santa Euphemia's for a ride. Our Volkswagen Microbus was called "an eight-seater." We decided it should be possible to take as many as twelve little boys at a time, even with the three of us and a nun to act as chaperone. About three trips, we thought. Debby had said that we should ride into Rome, for the sights of the city would be more interesting to the boys than the familiar countryside.

As we drove our little bus up the winding lane edged by wonderful Roman umbrella pines, I spotted a nun out in the fields completely surrounded by running, dancing, prancing, wiggling, squirming little boys. "That looks like the first load," I suggested. Mitch stopped to let me go join them.

Most of the boys abandoned the nun and ran to meet me. They remembered me, the car, and my promise. "Is this the day of the ride, signora?" they demanded. I said that we must first ask the mother superior. This surprised them. "But of course she will say 'yes,'" they said.

One little boy, Antonio, seemed to be the spokesman. He chattered out the news since my visit. "We have a new boy!" I looked over the faces and saw a three-year-old who looked unfamiliar.

"Is it he?" I asked.

"Oh, no, signora," Antonio said, a little condescendingly. "He's vecchio (old)." I apologized to the vecchio three-year-old. Antonio jabbered on, pointing to a boy not much beyond two who held the sister's hand and toddled along as she came toward me. "That's the new one," he said. "He's very young. He's so young he's almost a baby." As we walked along several boys raised their arms to me to be picked up. As I lifted them I got quick soft little kisses on the cheek; then they were ready to be put down. They wanted to touch me as we walked. I had given one hand to each of two boys. Others clung to my arms and one solemn-faced boy walked behind holding onto the hem of my coat like a veil bearer for a bride. I was reminded of a statue of the goddess of fertility in the Borghese gardens in Rome that has a dozen breasts and is freckled with tiny foetuses.

Conversation with the boys was extremely funny. I still hadn't learned the "tu" form of address, so that when I addressed Antonio formally as "Lei" he caught his breath in surprise, gulped, and continued what he was saying, slower and much louder.

Antonio told me that the big kids (the five-year-olds) had gone on a camping trip to the sea. Next year he might be old enough if they did it again. The mother superior confirmed Antonio's report and said that because there were so few boys we could easily take them all in one trip.

She and another nun opened the car doors and began to load little boys in. The front door of the institution opened and out poured a dozen or so more. In fascinated and unbelieving amazement Mitch and I watched as she loaded two nuns and twenty-four little boys into the car. Debby, who was already in the back seat, gigglingly scooped a cross-eyed, retarded-appearing child onto her lap. "Dad," she teased in English, "did you forget how to say 'too many' in Italian?"

In the excitement of getting loaded into the car the new little boy was forgotten and he began to cry, fearing, I think, that he would be left behind. I sat in front and held him on my lap. Antonio stood right behind me and kept up his steady flow of loud, careful words.

As we started the ride, the two nuns led the little boys in a prayer for a safe journey. I accused Mitch afterwards of having been the most fervent prayer in the crowd. He was a bit unnerved by the responsibility of this crowd of tiny boys, and he drove at a sedate ten miles an hour into the country. As he drove he wondered what the strain of all this weight might be doing to the little German motor, but decided that there was nothing to do now but hope. My two-year-old seemed to feel that, now that he was being held, things were safe again. He sighed, cuddled up to me, relaxed, had a b.m. (fortunately the rubber pants were good), and then went to sleep for the entire ride.

Debby reported that her little boy was also deeply contented. On the whole trip he said just one word — "cow," as we passed a white ox. The boys were gay, talkative, and excited. They often burst into song — one on the order of "Old MacDonald Had a Farm." Debby loved its syncopated rhythm. "And all the little cats went meow, meow, meow." (It was interesting to notice how they accented the first syllable in "meow.") "Maybe," Debby observed, "Roman cats meow with an Italian accent."

I had wanted Mitch and Debby to see these children as I had seen them to test my impression of them. They agreed that these were happy, contented, outgoing children.

When we returned to the institution Mitch and Debby played with the children while I talked with the mother superior. They both noticed what I had noticed. These were children who did not mind well, and who felt secure about not minding. The nuns seemed to control them more by distraction than by firm voices or actions. The mother superior suggested that when we had time we should take our bus to call on other branches of her order in Rome and take other children riding. "Look at them," she said, pleased. "They are so contented!"

As we left, we patted the car affectionately and praised it for the monumental feat it had performed. Though this had been a charming experience and though Mitch and Debby had loved the boys as much as I had, we all agreed that we would not put our little bus again through such an ordeal.

May 12

I HAD SPENT these last ten days working on the outlines for the three lectures that I was to give in the fateful June seminar. Signorina Quinzi had asked that I write "a little brochure" describing the general content of the lectures. These and the translation of the Giobbe case would be mailed out to the social workers who were to be invited.

Yesterday I had left the outlines at the desk of the New Roman School of Social Work. Today Signorina phoned to say that she, Father, and Signora Sacco had all read them. They were delighted with them. "It is wonderful," she said, "the way you have managed to include in them all those little studies that Father asked you to make."

At a time like this the telephone is my favorite medium of communication. Signorina Quinzi couldn't see my mouth drop open. Nor could she see my wild-eyed look as I sought frantically to make sense out of this improbable reaction to my outline.

But breathless as her statement made me, I was not foolish enough to protest when the miracle for which I had hoped had suddenly arrived.

May 13

Now that my outlines were done, I remembered my promise to Dr. Alberghi and Italia Lombardo to do a paper on how SANC could begin a program of foster home care for children. I went to see Italia today so that through discussion I could begin to get a sense of how my American knowledge of this area of work could be sorted out and molded into a scheme useful to an Italian agency making its beginning. Our three-hour conversation was a golden experience, for comprehension for both of us seemed to be at about ninety-five per cent.

I had learned from her that SANC intended to begin in a small way — perhaps with about ten or fifteen homes — to offer foster home placement for the first time in Italy. All the agency was waiting for was my "how-to-do-it writing." I began by asking about Father de la Roche's objections — the law of penal responsibility for foster parents, the belief that the program should start after an intensive propaganda campaign and that Italy was too class conscious to accept this kind of program.

With infinite tact she explained that Father de la Roche's ideas were, of course, "characteristically brilliant and excellent." She and Dr. Alberghi hoped that eventually all of them could be taken into account. But, in the meanwhile, "We would like your help in starting the program immediately in a small, unpretentious way."

SANC had made a tiny beginning by several times giving the daily stipend that would usually go to an institution to a relative of a needy child so that he could be maintained in a home. These experiments had worked well enough that Italia and Dr. Alberghi thought that success might also be achieved in the homes of some who were not relatives.

We talked long about the philosophy of child placement and the techniques a worker uses to make it a helpful experience. I drew a little diagram to illustrate how the social worker stands in the center of a triangle of heightened feelings that inevitably exist among foster parents, real parents, and children. I tried to explain how a worker uses basic casework skills to help each to ventilate feelings about the others, how she applies her knowledge to help each find a workable relation to the others. I remember how, as she fully understood, her eyes shone.

We talked about the financial aspects of placement. SANC usually paid 300 lire (50 cents) a day to an institution. To exceptionally good ones, like San Stefano's, it was sometimes possible to pay twice that much. Italia said that she was afraid to go above the 300-lire fee because, though she could find a way to pay it to the first foster homes, she would then have established an economic precedent which her agency could not continue were the program to succeed and expand. I urged her to begin at 300 lire, frankly explaining to the foster parents that she did not think it adequate, and promising to do everything possible to get a higher stipend later.

"You wouldn't," I asked hesitantly, "ever pay 300 lire to a foster mother to care for a child if his own mother could support him at home with that same 300 lire?"

The olive-green eyes studied me worriedly, seemingly to ask, "How could you think this?" I explained that sometimes I worried because what Italy needed even more than foster homes was relief so that families need not be broken by poverty.

The eyes smiled. "But of course, signora, this is what we all worry most about and want most for Italy. But it is not something you and I can do. It will take a Garibaldi!"

I added, "A Garibaldi who can find a Dante to write his speeches!" We went back to work on the problem we could do something about. We talked about selection of staff. How many cases should a worker carry? How many people should begin the work? I urged her to begin with just two workers – a homefinder and a placement worker. Little by little as she, the placement worker, and the homefinder worked together on perhaps four or five cases they could begin to share what they were doing in their staff meetings, drawing others into discussions about the suitability of a specific home for a specific child, so that the whole group could be learning together. When her whole staff had got its feet vicariously wet, she would find other workers showing that they too were ready.

I said that I had thought a great deal about SANC's inability to pay an adequate salary to its workers. Was it possible that, if SANC become known as an agency where a social worker could learn this vital new kind of casework, this might compensate young workers in coming here for a few years? She laughed. "Dr. Alberghi and I are ahead of you. We have already talked of this," she said. "Now we are both looking to you for help in getting our program started." Then she asked hesitantly, "We are troubled that there is so little time left. I suppose there is no hope – but could you stay another year?"

I shook my head sadly. There was, as she had said, so little time. I yearned to be able to give her the books of Dorothy Hutchinson and Henrietta Gordon, and my own, to have her read and digest them so that we could talk about them before I left. I wished that I could send any of a half dozen American friends to Italy who could carry on our job.

I left that day tremendously elated. The hope of foster home placement that I had dreamed of for Italy had moved from "impossible in this culture" through "perhaps we could achieve it sometime but it will take decades" to today's "we shall start immediately with two caseworkers and four or five homes."

My sorrow was that my agency—SANC really felt like "my agency"—was to write "the beginning" to its program just as I was about to write "the end" to my experience with them.

May 14 to May 20

DURING THESE DAYS I worked on my final paper on starting a placement program. In planning my outlines for the June seminar I thought that I had done everything. But now I found that I must add a new ingredient. It was my deep wish to leave behind something so useful and practical that two workers from SANC who had never seen a foster home, who did not know the word "placement," could get an understanding that would help them begin doing this work without stumbling into all the pitfalls that plague beginners.

In Italy five years before I had been writing about child placement for American social workers, most of whom would have already done many placements and all of whom would have experienced supervisors. I remembered how hard it had been then to know where to begin. How much more challenging to do a short piece for totally inexperienced workers!

My first stumbling block was vocabulary. There are words used in the literature of child placement that require whole sentences in Italian. I had been aware that Italian social workers had picked up several terms like "casework" and "group worker" intact from English. After a good bit of pencil chewing, I wrote a preamble in the form of a little dictionary, with four English words to be used in placement: "la homefinder, il placement, la placement worker, and l'applicant." It delighted me to be in the grandiose position of declaring some words masculine, some feminine, and knowing that Italians would have to learn the gender of my four words as I had had to learn it for their thousands.

To answer my question on how to begin, I harked back to my first course in casework. Anne Fenlason had got us started with the principles of casework: "Imposed plans do not succeed . . . we tend to be what others consider us to be . . . similar experiences are never similar . . ." Dogmatic as this kind of approach may have been, it was a good beginning. Was it this memory of my own first casework course that made me decide to define a series of "Principles of Placement"? Or perhaps it happened because I was living in Rome where from time to time the pope rose up and spoke ex cathedra, thereby establishing some principles of his own.

This was the outline that I finally used:

Some Suggestions on How To Do Foster Home Placement

I. New vocabulary of four English words.

II. Introduction. (I explained my need to lay down dogmatic principles that must be tested and thrown out when they do not apply.)

III. Recruiting foster parents. (This was a dilly as a mental exercise. Almost no one in Italy even knew what foster parents were!)

IV. Selection among applicants. (On which of the hundred people who phone—the agency had just one line which was always answered by the undisciplined receptionist—or write, or come in person does "la homefinder" follow up?)

V. What goes into a foster home study?

VI. Some classical types of homes to eliminate. (This is where I became outrageously dogmatic. Examples: Number four, "People who are extremely religious"; number ten, "Applicants who believe there's nothing wrong with a child that a good spanking won't cure." I sighed over the good homes that a skilled homefinder could conceivably find in these two categories.)

VII. Some characteristics of good foster parents.

VIII. Types of children most likely to succeed in placement. (With so many Italian children living outside their own homes, it should be possible to select some who would be pretty sure to succeed. This seemed important to me while the program was seeking to commend itself to a dubious society.)

IX. Types of children least likely to succeed in placement. (This really hurt as I described the needful children in institutions. I prayed that they could survive there until Italy accepted this kind of child care.)

X. How to select a home for a specific child. (I drew the whole staff in on this, for I realized that this was a way of educating all at once.)

XI. How to make a placement – in twelve not-so-easy steps!

XII. Follow-up steps.

XIII. Concluding remarks. (This was an apologia for my dogmatism and the shortcuts I had used. My last paragraph was: "I offer this outline and plan of procedure with humility and with faith that the Italian social workers will have the artistry to twist, change, and alter it as need be. An Italian agency as it begins to do foster home placement may refer rather frequently to the Charnley Outline on How to Do Foster Home Placement. But within a few years, I hope, a structure of placement will grow from it that will have a fresh, original validity of its own.")

The outline finished, I was bursting to get it translated and into Italia's hands so that we could go to work on it. I brought it immediately to Giorgiana Ugonio, but she quite appropriately at this time was more actively engaged in playing her true role – that of mother to the beautiful Alessandra – than in doing translations for a visiting American social worker.

And so, while Signora Ugonio practiced what I preached for the Giobbe case by playing her appropriate role in life, I stewed for two weeks waiting for my translated manuscript.

May 17

Because of my own intense busyness with writing and reading cases, because the Italian language and I were getting along nicely together, and because Signora Ugonio was properly preoccupied with her baby, I had given up my tutoring sessions with her. I asked for an appointment today to do a kind of trial run on the still harrowing prospect of two hours of ad-lib lecturing.

We began by admiring the beautiful baby. I had the always delightful experience of holding her while she finished her bottle. I chuckled to myself about the bottle. Early in my acquaintance with her pretty young mother, when we talked of many things in order to help me learn conversational Italian, the signora and I had had a long discussion about whether she was to breast-feed her baby. I had learned that it was against the cultural mores for an upper-class Italian woman to do so. The educated woman in Italy either hires a wet nurse or puts her infant on a formula. Signora Ugonio had rationalized that she would use a formula because "it's more regular in its consistency and because I wouldn't have milk anyway because these things are hereditary and my own mother didn't have milk."

I had tried to fight for the unborn Alessandra's right to the important experience of breast nurture. I had been able fairly easily to take away the excuse that Signora Ugonio would not have milk by explaining that she would probably have it unless she expected not to. Signora Ugonio, an intelligent woman, understood this very well. She came also to accept my hypothesis that it really was a sounder emotional and physical experience for both mother and baby. But I had been guilty of poor social work in failing to heed the violation of cultural mores that I was asking of her. Despite the displeasure of the signora's mother and friends, and despite the surprised but basically tolerant attitude of the doctor, she had begun to nurse her baby from the first. After a week of breast feeding, she had developed a breast infection and the doctor immediately put Alessandra on a bottle; and of course all her friends warned her to be more careful in the future about so casually accepting theories from "that American social worker." "Breast feeding babies is all very well," they had said, "for a peasant. But surely not for you!" Try as I would to adjust my thinking to variations in mores, it was a lesson that I had to learn and re-learn.

Once Alessandra was bedded down, we turned back to business. When I explained that Father de la Roche was adamant that I must do six hours of lecturing without manuscripts she gave her delightful, "Spaventoso!" (Terrible!) She insisted that I call Father and get him to change his mind. I should explain to him, she said, that my tutor said that though I had made excellent progress in Italian, this was an outlandish request.

Patiently I described to her my stunning lack of success in getting Father de la Roche to change his mind about this or anything else. I told her that I had my notes in English in my hand. I wanted to try for the next two hours this quite impossible assignment of giving her a two-hour lecture. I suggested that she have a paper and pencil and when I didn't know a word or when my mistake was so gross as to make me incomprehensible, she should write down the English and the correct Italian.

"Va bene," she agreed (though the shadow on her girlish face suggested that going along with some of my ideas certainly required a good bit of flexibility).

The lecture on supervision was hard because it called for some fresh vocabulary — phrases like "the use of time," "statistical reporting," "basing supervision on case history recording." I worked long and hard and though I stumbled frequently it finally came to both of us that I really could do it. Once again in Italy I found myself achieving the impossible.

She and I were both delighted, I because I had learned this much Italian, and she because she had just learned how good a teacher she was. I left her apartment, I'm sure, slightly flushed with victory. Just outside her door I saw a street vendor selling fresh cherries, the first of the season. I went up to him and in my excellent Italian asked, "How much for a kilo of cherries?"

Quickly he took in my American accent and my American clothes. As though he were dealing with a feeble-minded child, he raised his hand and with exaggerated clearness counted his five fingers. He was trying to tell me that a kilo cost 500 lire. All Americans in Italy complain from time to time about this kind of experience. There are some Italians who, having decided we are foreigners, will never listen when we speak Italian. Usually I felt frustrated and annoyed when this happened. Today it seemed funny.

May 19

JANET HAD INVITED Mitch and me to be her guests at Il Piccolo Mondo (The Little World), a most charming Roman restaurant two blocks off the Via Veneto. Her other guest was to be Emilia Lazzareschi, a distinguished woman journalist who worked for an important liberal weekly, one that supported a political group active in social reforms.

Signorina Lazzareschi was tiny, spontaneous, and gray-haired, and she spoke flawless English. We spent more than two hours over canneloni and green salad; she not only talked journalism and politics with Mitch, but also gave me some new guidelines in my expanding understanding of Italian culture. I remember her unveiled irritation as she explained how, in this nation of very rich and very poor, the rich are identified with the Christian Democrats (Italy's leading political party), who, in turn, are closely linked with the *status quo* and the church.

The strength of the church politically is felt by the poor in such areas as the legal (in contrast to the moral) bans on artificial birth control and divorce, the high cost of getting married and of dying. The wealthy Italian can go to another European country to get a divorce. It may be a violation of his religion, but a "foreign-bought" divorce is legally acceptable in Italy. The poor man who makes an unfortunate marriage, however, cannot afford to leave Italy for a divorce. If he drifts away from his wife and establishes a family with another woman, as frequently happens, the children of the second union must undergo the embarrassment of using their mother's last name as long as their father's first wife lives.

Mitch asked why the rich of Italy were not taxed to help support the poor. He spoke of our distress that there were no government funds to hold impoverished families together. She laughed bitterly as she described the corruption in taxation. Many wealthy families in Italy have never paid any taxes, she said, nor is there any pressure put upon them to do so. She told of having gone to the tax office some years earlier to pay her taxes. She was treated with suspicion and distrust, and it was made quite clear to her that this kind of aggressive good citizenship was not welcome.

As she continued her description of the problem some of the pieces in my understanding began to fall into place. Though many of Italy's wealthy families do not pay taxes, they are concerned with preserving the *status quo*; and in order that there not be too widespread hunger and too gross poverty, they give large sums of money through the church to support institutions. Some of them are beginning to give money directly to social agencies and by skillful selection it is occasionally possible for an agency to give direct relief to a mother to hold her family together. But direct relief is regarded with suspicion, and agencies need to choose carefully the families to whom they give money. Should a mother "on relief" become involved in a scandal, the public would say, "See what happens when money is given to the poor? The children would have been better cared for in an institution!"

I was elated to find so bright and aggressive a woman fighting for the causes I believed to be so vital for Italy. But my joy was short-lived. As I pursued my ideal of adequate relief so that no family need ever be broken for reason of poverty alone, I discovered that "left-wing" Italy was still pretty "right-wing conservative" in social thinking. She thought it "totally impractical" for the government to engage in widespread relief to hold impoverished families together. She thought institutional care was better. She explained it this way: "An educated American woman like you, Signora Charnley, cannot even imagine the squalor, filth, and utter stupidity in which the parents of many of these children live. They are not fit to be parents of children." I reminded her that all these problems were born of poverty. She shrugged.

I was trying to see more clearly the position of the church. I thought of all the social workers I knew who were, of course,

Roman Catholic. I wondered what would be the problem for them in fighting for social justice and actively opposing the tenets of the Christian Democratic party. I had learned long ago that through the centuries Catholics have been free to fight for social reforms, even those not in tune with what the church seemed to stand for politically. I knew that the church taught that every member had the obligation to challenge social injustice and that a man was violating the principles of his religion only when he opposed those very rare stands of the church which had been officially declared through the centuries by the popes to be "matters of faith and morals."

I asked Signorina whether it would be possible for a Catholic to remain a Catholic in good standing and still fight the Christian Democrats politically. "Theoretically, yes," she said. "In some elections only a small percentage of Catholics have voted Christian Democrat. And this is all right, though various unfair pressures have been exerted.

"But," she continued, "you used the word 'fight.' Let me tell you a story — a very sad story — about my mother."

Signorina Lazzareschi described her mother as a devout woman, well enough educated so that she understood the intricacies of what she might and might not do as a good Catholic. The signorina's younger brother, about thirty, had completed a definitive history of church and state in Italy that was pointedly critical of certain political abuses of the church. It was a plea for reform. His mother had been proud of the book, proud of her son. When she went to confession, the priest told her that it was a wicked book and that it was her moral duty to use every possible form of maternal pressure to get her son to withdraw it from circulation. This she refused to do. She pointed out that St. Francis of Assisi and Catherine of Siena had criticized corruption in the church. For ten years, this good Italian woman, with a literal belief that she had jeopardized the security of her soul, went without absolution. Finally the old priest died and the new young man assigned to the parish began hearing her confessions and giving her absolution.

I thought of this episode and tried to apply it to people like Italia Lombardo, Teresa Quinzi, and Maria Mannini. What did they do in fighting for social justice? My guess was that they all used Father de la Roche or someone like him as a confessor.

I had a sudden comical mental picture of that wild-eyed priest in the confessional saying, "Why did you have this emotional need to steal?"

To be a social worker in Catholic Italy must require some very complicated mental gymnastics, I decided.

May 20

THOUGH Signora Ugonio hadn't completed the translation of my article on foster home placements, I stopped in to explain a confusing part. She had set the table for tea. Whenever we spoke Italian, I paid for an interview. When we spoke English, it was a social call. Today we spoke English.

I asked her to tell me about her own childhood and especially about her education in a school without boys. Did this lack of coeducational experience pose problems for a young girl?

At first she was puzzled; then she saw what I meant. "For me it was no problem," she said, "because I had such a wise mother. Though she had nothing but daughters — poor thing! — boys were always welcome at our house and we had many wonderful parties." She laughed at a memory. "When I was about twelve a very nervous sort of nun from my school called my mother, terribly agitated . . . or is it aggravated? It is impossible to tell those two English words apart! . . . Anyway, she indignantly said that I had ridden off on the handle bars of a boy's bicycle." She laughed again and her face was so young and gay that she looked about twelve.

"Do you know what my darling mother said?" She paused so that I should not miss the dramatic effect. "She said to that nun,

'How nice of you to let me know that Giorgiana is bringing home a guest. I shall start making hot chocolate at once!' "

Then she became more sober. "But I was lucky in having wise parents. Some of the girls in my class knew so little about boys they were afraid to say 'Buon giorno' to them. This makes very bad—how do you say it?—crushes. The girls fall in love with the pretty young nuns and write silly poetry to them and cry easily if the nuns look cross. Those poor nuns! They are wondering what they do wrong to cause such foolishness. They are innocent; but this way of bringing up girls is an important mistake. My Alessandra shall go to a school with both girls and boys!"

Before leaving I asked Signora Ugonio whether she would help me find some information that I badly needed. I would pay her for her time. Would she look up facts on what happens to the children from institutions after they became adults?

She answered solemnly, "I will gladly do it for nothing. Working with you has turned my thinking inside out. All those papers you write! Always before I knew just what Italian children needed and now I don't know anything any more." She made a face at me. "You see what you've done? Ruined my nice complacency. Yes, I shall call my friend who is a fine librarian and we shall see what we can find for you."

May 23

I WAS IN A STRANGE POSITION. It was too early to start cramming for the June seminar. I intended practically to live with Giorgiana during the week of the seminar and study for each speech intensively, then go to the seminar to spit it out, forget it at once, and take on the next one. It was the way I had crammed for college exams in courses like neuropsychiatry and history. I remembered once while walking to such an exam thinking that if I were to turn my ankle and fall half my knowledge would spill out.

Since Italia had been called out of town I had no assignment at SANC. Signorina Mannini had never responded to my letter to her at ICS. And so I found myself with a little island of time before the pressure would begin again.

I was unhappy about it. I had grown so deeply involved in my mission to help SANC get its placement program under way that I resented leisure.

There was another reason that I wanted to be busy. Blair was to arrive by plane on June 1, and as the time drew near our psychological clocks and calendars had come to a halt. Time refused to budge.

We all tried to pry it back into motion with busyness. Mitch was spending many days at Radiotelevisione Italiana studying the production of newscasts. Debby was whizzing through French novels at such a dizzy rate that her tutor told me that he thought she could be moved ahead an extra year in French when we returned to America.

And I was an unhappy lady of leisure!

May 24

THE TELEPHONE and Janet Maher rescued me from the time clot today. She had just had a call from three visiting American social workers, all teachers from eastern schools of social work. Could I make it for cocktails and dinner?

In a few hours I found myself sipping an excellent martini (Janet scorned "gin nazionale" and used only Gordon's) and having my favorite kind of conversation—shop talk with bright social workers. Janet had also invited Laura Vecek, an English-speaking social worker who had been displaced so many times during the war that I never did identify her native country. She had an American master's degree in social work and had spent the last five years in an agency established for Jewish displaced persons. This agency, now about thirty years old, had been set up after World War I. History had never quieted down enough to give the agency a breathing spell; it was kept busy helping the Jews of Europe and those who migrated from North Africa to Italy. All its workers were American educated, and they carried on much as they might have done in America.

I learned with interest that virtually any Jewish Italian could turn to her agency for relief when it was needed. There was almost no Jewish family in Europe, she said, that could not show genuine dislocation and acute financial loss due to religious persecution. It seemed ironical that today in Rome only the Jews had somewhere to go to get relief when they needed it. "The ghetto can work both ways," I thought.

The visiting social workers were outstanding women in the field of social work. The book of one had been required reading for all students in social work when I was in school. I had read articles in various journals by another. Their questions and observations were lively ones, and we all had a fine time.

They were most interested in my observations about children in institutional care. The conversation started when I mentioned to the Jewish worker that I had been trying ever since I arrived in Rome to meet a balia – the special kind of wet nurse used by both social agencies and wealthy Italians to nurse newborn babies.

I told the Americans what Father de la Roche had told me about how a doctor arbitrarily decides that one child should go to a balia, another to an institution. I described how babies sent off to balias in rural poverty-stricken homes were often forgotten there for periods as long as five years.

The feminine blonde woman whose book I had been required to read, and who looked younger than I, was deeply moved by my story. "But," she asked, "isn't this really better than being sent to an institution where the baby may die of murasmus or where he will, if he survives, probably become schizophrenic?"

This was the conversation I had been yearning for. I spilled out the picture of my own confusion. I had been firmly educated by the experts in both social work and psychiatry that this was the probable fate of the institutionalized child; yet in the institutions I had visited I had rarely seen the marks of childhood schizophrenia that almost anyone who works with disturbed children in America could recognize. And in the institutions for infants I had seen no signs of murasmus, that "wasting-away disease" which claims the lives of institutionalized babies. The death rate had been exceedingly low in infant institutions, and the deaths that were listed seemed often to follow surgery to correct congenital deformities.

The three Americans looked at me with puzzlement. "There are," one of them said, "many writers and speakers in America who are not going to believe you."

"I know," I responded serenely. "If I had stayed in America and some social worker came to Minneapolis and had said in a lecture what I am telling you now, I would not have believed her."

I talked on, describing impressions from the twenty-five institutions I had visited. I felt their critical eyes on me. The struggle on the face of the blonde was almost violent. It was easy for me to empathize with her. I knew just how I would have felt in her position. Undoubtedly in her school of social work she had been teaching the opposite of what I was saying. She had been quoting the most respectable sources. There is nothing more uncomfortable than to start to question what you have always been sure is true. Didn't I know this? Hadn't I just been through it?

I said that I had made several efforts to learn statistically what happens to these children when they leave the institutions. It would seem almost inevitable from what we know of personality development that the methodical severing of ties every four years, the living of a whole lifetime without a mother-figure, would at the very least create sociopaths. Incipient sociopathy is not something easily picked up in group observation. I would not deny that I might have been spending my time watching children who were sociopaths in the making.

"But," I said, "if this is so, why is the crime and delinquency rate relatively low in a country where so many children have this kind of experience?" I turned to Janet. "Janet," I asked, "do you or Domenica di Montignacco have theories about what happens to these children?"

Janet shook her head. "Domenica and I have often talked about this. We're sure you're right about the low incidence of schizophrenia. I described to Domenica the withdrawn ones, the dreamers, and the ones who rock rhythmically in their beds and their chairs — the classic types we know in America — and she had never seen or heard of one in seven years of teaching social work!"

"And what about the hypothesis that they may be sociopaths in the making?" I asked.

She nodded. "I think that's nearer right. But that's just a guess. I'd bet a thousand lire that you won't find any reliable statistical answers. This country has a whimsical approach to social statistics, you know." She paused, choosing her words thoughtfully. "Domenica always has a class discussion about what happens to the graduates of these institutions. The students seem to think that there is a high incidence of unmarried mothers. The boys may or may not get into delinquency. It appears that they make harsh, authoritarian fathers."

"A reasonable if unscientific answer. It's what you'd expect, wouldn't you?" one of the social workers asked.

I explained that all I had to offer from five months in Italy were observations by myself — an American with a good deal of experience and some skill in spotting outward signs of serious inner turmoil in children. Except for the institution in Florence (which was set up to care for mentally ill and retarded children) and except for a very small scattering of children — perhaps one to an institution — I had seen no evidence of dangerously withdrawn children. And the children in Florence were referred directly from their own homes, so their disturbances were not institution-created. I said that Italian social workers believed that there was damage traceable to broken homes, broken ties, and the regular movement of children from one setting to another, a deeply tragic failure to prepare children for sound adjustment later in family life. They knew, too, that these children were suffering as an adult would suffer were he moved about involuntarily like this. But though the social workers opposed institutional care, they were not talking to me about the total personality disorganization that leads to a lifetime in institutions for the mentally or criminally maladjusted.

I knew that my brief observations had not proved anything. But I said I believed that they pointed to a solid question that needed to be carefully studied, not only for the benefit of Italian children but also for children all over the world.

"We really must know," Janet agreed. "In these days when we live under the threat of the atomic bomb, we may, if we survive, be planning substitute care for millions of children. They may be American, Italian, Asian, or African."

We dreamed up a study, happy as social workers always are when they are spending some imaginary millionaire's money. We saw teams of social workers, psychologists, and social statisticians visiting countries all over the world where children live in institutions. We decided that two years of full-time work would be minimal for each study. It might take five.

I wanted the team to work backwards, too. If I had had another six months, I would have been visiting institutions for the mentally ill and for criminals to look back into what their childhoods had been. What percentage of these misfits had been institution-reared?

"Is there a cultural factor involved that we are missing?" one of the teachers asked.

"I'm sure," Janet said, "that there are many. We begin with parents who believe that they are doing a noble thing when they hand their children over to the priests and nuns to educate."

"And we continue," I added, "with people who take care of the children believing not that institutional life is a tragedy for children but rather that it is the most normal thing in the world."

We were certain that such factors had an important part in our answer and so we added cultural anthropologists to our teams. We wondered too about the low incidence of mental illness in the Italian population.

I amused them by describing the answer I had received to this question. An executive in social work had said, "We Italians aren't the type for mental illness. We're more likely to get tuberculosis."

The lovely blonde woman said that an American psychiatrist who had worked and studied in Europe had told her that northern Europeans are more subject to the depressive kinds of mental illness, whereas southern Europeans, and especially Italians, are more likely to have the manic types.

As we affectionately recalled our delight at the explosive emotions of Italians, their outpourings of joy and disgust, their vivid gestures, we speculated that perhaps many of our favorites were slightly manic.

On into the night we planned the international study that seemed so important to us; we continued to puzzle hard over the quality in American children that produces such negative responses to institutional care.

This was a deeply satisfying evening. It revealed to me how lonesome I had been for this kind of chatter. And I recognized that this was one of my steps toward a coming readiness to say, "Arrivederci, Roma!"

May 29

ITALIA had phoned me several days ahead to ask me to spend this morning at SANC. She said, "We have been busy reacting to your paper and now I have planned a series of conferences about it."

My first meeting was with a Signorina Silvana Nino. In vain I tried to tuck her into the administrative structure of SANC. She was somewhere below Dr. Alberghi and somewhat above Italia; she was not the difficult untrained supervisor who slashed the budgets and the hopes from the caseworkers' plans for their clients. She told me that, as a graduate of the League School of Social Work, she was sorry she had missed so much of my time in Rome, but she had been on special assignment in Sicily. She was warm in her liking for my articles and spoke eagerly about how excited Italia and Dr. Alberghi had become at the thought of the new program for SANC.

Italia sat beaming, with a look I suspect I show at times like this – when my boss is being especially receptive to a plan I want to see move ahead. Signorina Nino told me that she and Italia had selected the two workers who were to begin the program. "Signorina Alta Quello will be 'la homefinder' and Signorina Maria Constanino will be 'la placement worker,' " she said.

I looked down at my arm to find it covered with goose pimples. I was that excited. Alta, my special pet, was to have that all-important job. I couldn't remember Maria Constanino, but I trusted Italia's judgment. It was fun to hear the words "la homefinder" and "la placement worker" on Italian lips for the first time. Italia went to bring the workers to the meeting. I felt as though I were to take part in a historic occasion. "I should have brought pink champagne," I thought.

We settled down, the five of us, for a hard morning's work. I had no problem with frivolity in this meeting. Four hours later I realized we hadn't even paused for the mid-morning coffee ritual.

We went over my paper inch by inch. Signorina Nino began by asking whether the publicity drive from which one might expect to get perhaps five good homes from one hundred applicants could be eliminated. She said, "I'm sure you recognize, signora, our wish to do this little experiment with a handful of homes very quietly."

They had, it developed, some friends in the clergy, and some other resources, through which they hoped to find homes without drawing the attention of "all of Rome" to what they were doing. I approved, though I cautioned them that often when a social worker goes to a family that has all the proper qualifications for foster parenthood there may be a lack of motivation that preordains the home to failure. They listened, and they asked intelligent questions. Italia said that Signorina Constanino had a case that had "sort of a foster mother in it." They would like me to read it.

I wish I had taken careful notes on the fine understanding that their questions reflected. Signorina Constanino asked, I remember, "On matters of importance who is the boss? The real mother, the foster mother, or the agency?" She led us into a revealing lesson in casework.

I said that, inasmuch as the real parents retained custody, they ought to have final authority in controversial situations. I added that if a mother held to her right to make either grave omissions or commissions, the agency could exert pressure by refusing to continue to care for the child outside his own home. "Give us an example?" Alta asked.

"Let us say," I began slowly, choosing my words like beads to string in a necklace, "that a child needs surgery to save his life If the mother were to refuse to allow the operation, the agency would need to refuse to continue the care of the child."

"But suppose," asked Italia, "that the mother withholds some privilege that does not endanger the life of the child but that might cause emotional scarring?"

I explained that this is the typical core of the difficult placement case. The worker needs first to establish a relationship with the mother so that she can understand the mother's choice. When the caseworker understands what is blocking the mother, she can work toward freeing her to give to her child what he needs.

All through the morning we worked, scrutinizing and questioning each statement I had made. Over and over, I was able to show them what I meant by saying that the principles I had set up were to be tested, changed, altered.

These two supervisors and two caseworkers made me work hard, but it was satisfying work. The language barrier wasn't great because of Italia's wonderful skill in putting on my tongue the words that I sought. I couldn't always understand Signorina Nino as clearly as I did Italia, but I came quickly to respect a fine analytical mind at work.

Near the end of the morning Alta asked whether I had brought with me from America a foster home study. I had. But its thirty single-spaced pages presented problems so typically American and so deeply un-Italian that it would confuse her more than it would help. So I said that I would write one — a fictitious one. I couldn't have it translated for them because I had used up my Fulbright fund for this purpose. But Signorina Nino said that they would find a way; and they began to buzz about cousins and sisters-in-law who were "clever at English."

We parted by shaking hands, of course . . . first, my dearest Italian friend Italia, next her fine capable supervisor, and finally Italy's first placement worker and Italy's first homefinder.

June 1

DEBBY, MITCH, AND I arrived at Rome's funny little airport, Ciampino, a full hour early. We knew we were far ahead of the clock, but we were powerless to stay away.

It was a hot, dusty day. The place was crowded, so crowded that it was necessary to keep a sharp eye out to find a seat. It was just as well — we were too excited to sit still.

Through a long afternoon we watched one plane after another land. To my amazement — for the first time in my life — I was anxious about their safe landing.

Finally it came. A little speck in the sky . . . and then the announcement, "Flight number 303 from Paris."

Debby said, "Eeeh!" à la Lucille Ball.

Mitch tightened his hold on my arm.

We watched the plane curve into a glide and come down. "Oh, Mr. Pilot," I begged silently, "set that boy down gently and smoothly."

He did. Perfectly. The plane landed far from the observation platform so that all we could make out debarking were anonymous people. No one specific boy. They started at indecent leisure, following a maliciously dawdling stewardess, across the hot concrete. At last — could that be Blair?

Yes, it was Blair. He was wearing a real man's suit and carrying a little blue bag. He was talking to a man beside him who was shorter than he was! (Blair's foster father had written that he was "growing like Iowa corn.") I assumed that we would run up and hug him but forgot about the customs barrier. For fifteen minutes we waved at each other foolishly through a glass partition. Blair was trying in vain to tell a customs man by gestures that his parents were out there and would give him a ride back to Rome. The customs man was trying to get him into line to take the airport bus.

Afterwards Blair said he never understood just how he did it. It was like somebody else talking when he said, "Ma signore, mio babbo è qui con una macchina." (But, sir, my dad is here with an auto.)

The magic Italian words worked and Blair was allowed to escape from customs. All four of us were talking at once during the dusty walk to the "macchina." It felt wonderful to be a family again.

As we sat in the car Blair said, "I'm starved! What's for dinner?" We all laughed delightedly. What a clever boy!

June 3, 4, and 5

MORE TIME during these early June days was spent admiring my son than seemed entirely reasonable. Having waited so long to get to Rome, Blair now wanted to see it all at once. I could understand his impulse. He was in Rome on a sightseeing vacation. The rest of us lived and worked there. After breakfast, after lunch, even after dinner he'd say, "What'll we go see now?"

Our feet and our energy soon gave out from accompanying such an insatiable sightseer, and finally we began to take turns. Between my turns I moved confidently to my typewriter to write in English the foster home "study" that I had promised Alta and

Italia. It had sounded an easy assignment, one I expected to enjoy. After all, I had done dozens of foster home studies. They were easy. As for fiction, I had written it by the pound in high school and college.

It was an attractive idea, all right, and as I write about it now it still seems as though it should be fun. But I couldn't do it. I invented the fictitious foster family. I located it in a house. I then tried to dream up a major line of motivation, several minor ones, three or four positive features, and some negatives — all designed to have meaning and validity in the Italian culture.

I began with the applicant coming to the agency and asking the homefinder whether she might apply to board a child. That was clumsy, so I tried having her phone in. No go. I'd write the middle interview first — the home visit. That idea went, too, and another and another. To my dismay, I realized after three days that this pleasant little exercise was beyond me. I had to settle with embarrassment for explaining to Alta by phone that in place of a fictitious home study, I would mail her a real one from America.

June 9, 10, and 11

I SPENT THESE DAYS at SANC reading records and having conferences, sometimes alone with the workers and more often with Italia and "la placement worker." At last I achieved one of the roles that Father and I had planned from the first — that of case consultant at SANC.

It was a rewarding experience. I came to realize that, at least in spurts, some very good casework was being done at SANC. I saw some relationship therapy with children that I think any American social worker would have been proud to claim. The work with parents was less strong than that with children, but here too I saw occasional flashes of excellence.

It was tantalizing that with so much done so well, the lack of some vital basic step would negate it. It was as though a cook had taken every step exactly right in making an angel food cake—except that she hadn't bothered to regulate the oven.

The Grecco case was a fine example. Tomaso Grecco was a boy in his late teens who had spent most of his life being an industrious and generally promising young citizen in an institution for boys. The major threat to his success in graduating with a diploma in mechanical drawing was his neurotic tie to his mother. The mother, a prostitute, had had five illegitimate children, and was destructive in her relationships with all of them. As Tomaso approached manhood she seemed to realize his potential as a wage earner, and she began in a most seductive way to urge him to leave school and come to the village of his childhood to live with her. Maria Constanino (la placement worker) had been his caseworker. She had done an admirable job in helping Tomaso in his torturous ambivalence toward his mother. She helped him to understand that, like every boy deprived of mothering, he was reaching out for it now, but that he had extended his hand to a woman incapable of responding. His turning to her for what she could not give could only result in pain. Maria rode the waves of his ambivalence skillfully; she didn't falter when he ran away from school and presented himself hungry and penniless at her office at SANC. She understood that he had had to escape from the place where each day he must re-answer for himself the question, "Will I do what my mother asks in this letter?" In Rome, he could live like a man and lose himself in the big city.

Maria helped him find an apprenticeship in a rug-cleaning or rug-making shop—I was unsure of my translation. She arranged housing and meals in an institution. His salary was 2,000 lire ($3.42) a week! It took every lira he earned for board and room so that he was left without carfare or money for cigarettes.

Maria sustained him during this period of deprivation and intense loneliness. It appeared for a while that he might either run to his mother or move into a serious depression.

Fortunately one day he ran into a middle-aged woman whom he had known in his childhood. She took him home to dinner with her and her husband. Tomaso, with his lonely need for mothering, found himself in the home of a warmhearted woman who too was lonesome, now that her youngest son had married and moved out.

He visited his old friends frequently and one day he brought the woman to SANC with him to meet his caseworker. Tomaso had found himself a foster mother! Together they explained the plan to Signorina Constanino. The family could not afford to take Tomaso in and feed him. But with the 2,000 lire a week, they could manage. This was what they all wanted. Signorina gave her blessing and a foster home was born.

Tomaso had been living in the home for eleven months. He had had an increase in salary and the woman was helping him to save money so that he could go to school in Rome and earn the diploma which he had abandoned a year before—the diploma that was vital for his future.

The social worker visited the home each month. While the woman and Tomaso seemed pleased to see her, they wanted the call to be purely social and they were now resisting her efforts to do casework. "What had gone wrong?" Signorina asked.

I discussed the Grecco case with Maria and Italia in conference. Tomaso was now twenty years old. He was happily located in his foster home. He had broken his tie with his mother quite successfully. "What more," I asked, "did the signorina wish to accomplish?"

Both women were silent. Finally Italia spoke. "Perhaps in time he and his foster mother may quarrel. Or perhaps his tie to his mother may sometime become reactivated."

I said that both of these things were possible, but my guess was that they would not happen for a long time. Could it not be that Tomaso and his foster mother were not reaching out for help from Signorina Constanino because her job was done? All that remained was to convince them that there might be times ahead when they might need to turn back to her, and that she would always want to help them. But for now her job was simply to say, "Arrivederci!"

Both Italia and Maria were surprised and pleased. I was

puzzled. It seemed odd to me that a social worker who had been able to do so expert a job had no realization when she had accomplished her goal.

I saw a chance to take another step. "I predict," I said, "that you will reopen the case before Tomaso asks your help."

They stared.

"In a few months when you have a child who is ready for foster home placement, you will approach this good woman to see whether she would do this job for a second child. She could be your first 'regular' foster mother."

I asked whether they would like to talk with me about how they might do a foster home study on this home and prepare it for receiving a child of SANC. Italia and Maria were very eager to hear. Italia said, "But wait. We must not do this without la homefinder."

In a few minutes she was back with Alta. Maria and Italia talked Italian-fast, summarizing the case for Alta. Her eyes shone. When they had finished, I began to talk about how she would go about doing her home study and how Maria would reopen her relationship with Tomaso to see how he would feel about sharing his new home with another child.

I turned to Maria. "You will want a child who will not threaten Tomaso. How about a girl under ten? You must ask Tomaso whether he would rather have a little sister or a little brother and begin to help him want to help another child succeed. It will be a very good home for a little child, I think, and helping a little child will be therapeutic for Tomaso. You must not be dismayed if he shows jealousy. You must help him to express it, and to see that this little child in no way diminishes the mother he found for himself."

Three pencils raced across the pages. I hadn't wanted to give a lecture. I had wanted to have a case discussion. I frowned at the pencils. "If you put your pencils away," I said, "I think you will find that you will remember most of what we say. And if you don't we can talk about it again tomorrow."

Rather reluctantly they put their pencils down. We kept talking about preparing Tomaso's foster home for another foster child until the office closed for lunch. After lunch, I came back and we talked much of the afternoon, using this proposed home study as a launching platform for ideas about other homes that Alta would be studying.

How much better this was, I thought, than the fictitious case history I had tried in vain to write!

June 12

I HAD CONTINUED reporting to SANC almost every day, reading and discussing cases, until today when I had an appointment to meet a member of the supervisory staff.

My knowledge of Italian had zoomed, as had my knowledge of social, emotional, and economic problems in Italy. One night at home a visiting American journalist – a former student of Mitch's – had asked me a question about "the poor people of Rome." Five months ago I could have felt very expert in giving a sharp clear answer. Now I realized sadly that I had stayed long enough and learned enough that I would never again feel like an expert who knew the answers.

The supervisor to whom I was introduced was Signora Annalisa Alberghetti, a sour-faced, gray-haired, moustached woman with masculine hands and a masculine voice. This was the political appointee Italia had told me about, the woman who slashed budgets and casework plans with a ruthless red pencil. Signora Alberghetti was a widow who had worked at SANC since its beginning.

Italia said that she had been asking repeatedly to meet "that Americana with all those American ideas for my agency." Italia had said no more; but her unspoken words were, "Watch out. Be diplomatic. I may suffer for what you say."

At first I felt smothered by the extraordinary bigness and masculinity of the signora. But I soon learned that she used the gruff voice in a hearty, jovial way. We got on well enough together.

I opened our conversation by expressing the idea that as I learned more about life in Italy, I had come to realize how little I knew. This seemed to please her. I asked her opinion about many things. This also pleased her. I was not quite as manipulative as this sounds. I really wanted to understand the attitudes of someone who typified conservative thinking in social work in Italy.

I quizzed her and Italia about the question that haunted me as our stay in Italy approached its end. Did either of them know of any valid studies that would show what kind of adjustment the child who is institution-reared makes in adult life? Genuinely puzzled, they could think of none. (Signora Ugonio and her librarian friend had been unable to find any statistical answers for me.)

I asked whether they would speak from their experience. In America, I said, we believed that institutional life for normal children causes deep-etched scars to the personality. Our experts taught that this kind of living might produce an adult so ill that he would have to live a good bit of his life in a mental hospital. Or, if not this, he might become a criminal spending much of his time in prison.

It seemed to me, I said, that this was not the way it worked in Italy. I would be grateful to the signora if she would explain to me what she thought happened to graduates of Italian institutions.

Signora Alberghetti seemed to make a genuine effort to give me correct answers; she turned often to Italia for help and corroboration. The two women were firmly agreed that institutional care was not good for children. They thought that many of the girls were so inexperienced in meeting boys, so unprepared for life when they were released, that they reached out sexually to the first young men they met. The result was many illegitimate children . . . and many babies for the institutions. Those who were fortunate enough to marry before becoming pregnant were often poor mothers because they didn't know how to run families.

"Nor," said Italia, "do they know how to give love, never having been loved." Even the married girls, I learned, often gave their babies up to institutions, as though they could not recognize how bad the institutions had been for them.

"And the boys?" I asked.

They became poor fathers. They were brutish and authoritarian – the kind of fathers who want to beat and bully but not to earn respect or affection. I asked whether the men also sent their children off to institutions.

The two women conferred a bit. "Only the illegitimate ones." They went on to say that the primary cause of institutionalization was poverty. If the parents had any sense of failure in turning their children over to institutions, it was a sense of economic failure. But the man who grew up in an institution would often starve his children before he would yield to his wife's pleas to "let them go where they can at least eat." The two women agreed that the father who had grown up in institutional care was more opposed to using it for his children than his wife was. They were unsure when I asked whether this was because of protective feelings toward the children or a determination not to give this evidence of economic failure.

I said that an Italian woman had told me that many institutionalized children became nuns and priests. The two women shook their heads in unison. "This lady has misinformed you," the signora said. "It is a rare occurrence. Nuns and priests come from normal homes where they receive a call from God."

I asked about the chain reaction that operates alike in Italy and America. Inadequate, unhappy parents rear damaged children who in turn become inadequate parents. "It is social work's first job to break these chains of generations of unhappy living," I said. Then, remembering the slashed budgets, I added, "I believe that social workers are justified in spending a great deal of time and money in reaching out to a single family to get it going right so that the children in it may eventually become adequate parents."

Both women nodded their approval. "So many things," the

signora said, "are possible in social work in America that are not possible in Italy."

I agreed that we have special advantages in America, but said that Italian social workers too could use their skills and their limited financial resources for similar causes – working to hold families together, fighting for the rights of abandoned babies, working for the use of foster homes instead of institutions.

The signora talked at length about Catholicism as a force that slowed progress in Italy – always without displeasure or passion, much as she might complain about the weather. I said that also in America it was the strong religious groups – Catholic and Protestant – that tended, with the best possible intentions, to maintain institutions for children who could live more wholesomely elsewhere.

I said that I thought the problem for social workers in Italy was to enlist the aid of propagandists – writers, educators, journalists, and others – to educate Italy in the truth about institutional care. Too many Italians now believed that the child in institutional care was a lucky child. The special tragedy was that so many parents believed that they were doing a wise and noble act when they turned their children over to the nuns and priests.

The signora smiled and shook her head. "It is possible that our propagandists might convince the people. But who is skillful enough to convince the church?"

It seemed to me, I said, that Italy had already made a beginning. Propaganda, as I saw it, was not selling false ideas, but rather educating toward the acceptance of truth. In the Roman School of Social Work for Religious Persons, an important beginning was being made in educating nuns from many orders.

"True," she said, "but who is to educate the priests?"

"Perhaps some twentieth-century saint has already begun," I suggested.

She and Italia laughed spontaneously. "This would cause such an uproar that we surely would have noticed it!" she said.

We had a long talk. The signora seemed to me bright and personable after I broke through my first prejudice. My chief problem with her was that I thought her too fatalistic in accepting defeat. Italia, Primavera, Alta, Father de la Roche, and Father Vincelli did not feel the cause was lost because of the conservatism of the church. (Though perhaps Father de la Roche was a little more doubtful than the others.) Was the church Signora Alberghetti's personal scapegoat? "Because the church is so powerful, there is no use spending agency time and money to save a few children from institutional care" — was this her view?

Yes, this probably was what caused her to wield her pencil against the caseworkers' plans. It interested me that she could express the same goal for Italy's children that Italia and I had defined. And I remembered also that if Italia went and fought for any child or any case, she always won.

"Her defeatism is not strong enough to withstand enthusiasm," I thought.

June 13

THIS MORNING I was settling down at SANC to read the umpteenth case that Italia had brought to me for consultation when Signorina Silvana Nino, Italia's handsome brunette supervisor, asked whether I would have a few minutes to come to her office for coffee and "an informal discussion."

After reading just so many case histories, whether in English or Italian, it is a relief to find an excuse for escape. Signorina Nino led me into a kind of sitting room, ornate with ugly gilt and red-plush furniture, where Dr. Alberghi and Italia were waiting.

We sipped coffee and ate little cakes. We exchanged polite but, I thought, genuine remarks about their satisfaction and mine at my stay at SANC.

Signorina Nino told me that she and Italia were excited and pleased at invitations to attend the seminar I would be giving at the New Roman School. Dr. Alberghi asked whether I didn't think that it would be a good idea if "la homefinder" and "la placement worker" could attend too. They had not received invitations.

I said that I would be pleased to have anyone who wished to attend do so. I thought as a matter of courtesy it would be wise to call Signorina Quinzi at the school to ask her permission. They agreed, but their faces told me they didn't believe she would allow the additions. (When the seminar took place my good friends Alta and Maria weren't present.)

Signorina Nino had the invitation in her hand. I asked to see it. There it was all spelled out in Italian, including the Giobbe case. (It amazed me a little, and seemed typical of the school, that I alone had not received the announcement.)

There was another question they wished to discuss. They were agreed that foster home placement offered a wonderful new direction for SANC; my help had been useful; but they wished I could stay longer. What might be the possibility of one of their workers going to America on a Fulbright grant to enroll in the University of Minnesota School of Social Work and to be placed as a student in my agency, to learn "everything you know about placement"?

It was an entrancing idea. I urged them to consult Signorina Scalzo at the Fulbright Commission. I was vague about how Fulbright grants work in reverse. Fulbright lire could be used for transportation, I thought; but some other source had to be dug up for living money.

I suggested that a social worker who applied should speak English well, and that she should be prepared to spend at least two years in America. I explained the American belief that social work is generic, and that one must understand as much as possible about human behavior before he can begin to acquire the specific skills needed in foster home placement work.

There was no way that I could say whether either the University of Minnesota or my agency would be the ideal place for a Roman grantee. I personally would love to have Italia, or Maria, or Alta. But I knew too that there were many other academic settings in America where a student could learn what she needed to know to do the placement job in Rome.

For Dr. Alberghi, this was our farewell, and he dignified it by gracefully kissing my hand. I was sufficiently Italianized now so that I was pleased rather than embarrassed by the gesture.

June 16

THIS MORNING I arrived at nine at the New Roman School; finding all my friends occupied, I explained my problem to the secretary. Could she give me a copy of the letter written by Father de la Roche describing the lecture I was to give next week? She gave me careful scrutiny and said that the letters included confidential case history material. "I know," I said, "I wrote it."

"But," she protested, "you are asking me for Father de la Roche's letter! How could *you* have written it?" It was good to see so much care in protecting confidential material. But I felt annoyed at the silly trap into which it had led me.

Finally the girl disappeared, and returned with the mimeographed sheets. I took them to a sidewalk caffè, ordered my cup of espresso, and settled back to read and simultaneously enjoy the delight of being outdoors in Italy in June.

Letter from Father F. Xavier de la Roche from the New Roman School of Social Work, May 24, 1958

I have the information to give you that Signora Charnley, who has had many years of experience in supervision and casework and is at present on the staff of an agency that focuses on services to children in the USA, the author of a volume called *The Art of Child Placement*, writer and lecturer on various aspects of social work, at present a Fulbright grantee placed under the auspices of the New Roman School, will on June 24, 25, and 27 from the hours of 6:00 to 8:00 P.M. give three brief discussions which have been selected by herself.

The conference is based on and held at the conclusion of her observations of children's institutions in Italy and her work with the agencies ICS and SANC and her professional activity with the records and workers of these agencies.

The results of her observations and her suggestions of ways to better the situation whether it be in the agencies or in the schools and suggestions for preparing social workers for their work will be stressed in these brief seminars.

In the name of the Coordination Committee for Social Work Information of Rome which has approved the suggestion, and with confidence that the results will be useful and will result in improving the teaching of casework and the supervision of students in the four schools of social work, and also will be of use to the various supervisors in the various agencies, I have the pleasure to invite you to take part in these seminars and to ask you to confirm your intention of so doing.

Cordially,

FATHER F. XAVIER DE LA ROCHE

The second page went on:

Seminar To Be Given by Jean Charnley on Three Aspects of Social Work

June 24 — Subject: "Casework with Children." Members of the group are requested to read the enclosed summary of *The Giobbe Case* — a record selected from an Italian agency. This lecture will often be related to the case. Signora Charnley will deal with the academic preparation of the child welfare specialist; personality traits of the worker who chooses this specialization; an analysis of the Giobbe case, stressing principles of casework with children in diagnostic and treatment aspects of the case. She will offer a description of role playing within the family as a shortcut to understanding the diagnosis and treatment plan for the Giobbe family; and will analyze the strengths and weaknesses of the social worker as shown by her recording.

June 25 — Subject: "The Supervision of Social Workers in the Area of Their Use of Time." Signora Charnley sees the misuse of time by caseworkers as a problem with which supervisors must help. She will discuss the emotional implications in the use of time; a suggested pattern for statistical reporting of a caseworker's activity per day, per week, per month, and per year. Signora Charnley will stress the need of regular supervisory meetings for every worker and recommend relating at least one supervisory period per month to a frank analysis with a worker of his own statistical report of his activities. She will suggest that shortcuts in time could be achieved by appointments established weeks in advance, by a regular pattern of "days in the field," and by the use of summarized recording. Signora Charnley will recommend that agencies be held open one evening a week for the use of working parents; formal recognition of the "coffee break"; and establishment of a sharp predetermined period of time for the typical interview. Signora Charnley sees excessive misuse of time as a group morale problem when it is widespread in an agency and as an emotional problem of the individual when it occurs infrequently. In either case, it is a first order of business for the supervisor to face directly with the worker, and the supervisor should believe that the worker's use of time is one of the most important aspects of the supervisory job.

June 27 — Subject: "The Selection of Foster Homes and Some Suggestions for Continued Work with Them." Signora Charnley has prepared this paper to show how Italy might begin to find, select, and use foster homes. She will describe a possible demonstration project that might begin with a small number of children in foster placement and will suggest ways to choose foster homes and the kinds of children who are most likely to succeed in placement. She will describe how to screen applicants and some outstanding characteristics of workable and unworkable foster homes. She will include a detailed picture of how a home study is done in America. She will also describe in a detailed fashion the steps in preparing a foster family and a child for placement, as well as follow-up steps that should be taken by the caseworker to ensure the success of the placement.

I was charmed by the elegant flavor that my words took on in this beautiful language. For one golden, dreamy moment I thought, "How fascinating this sounds! I wish I could attend." The spell was broken as I remembered that I'd be there . . . I'd be there!

June 17 through June 24

When Giorgiana and I had concluded on the basis of my trial run that it was just faintly possible that with infinite effort I might manage six hours of ad-lib lecturing, I circled the calendar from June 17 through June 29 in heavy black.

Giorgiana agreed to give me two hours of tutoring each day and generously offered to attend each lecture with me. (Italians were always pleased and impressed by the Fulbright gift of experts to Italy; but Giorgiana and Italia had especial warmth about them. "What a stupendous thing for one country to do for another! And then, when an American comes to do a job, she half kills herself at it!")

I've never worked as hard in my life as I did just then. Mitch and the kids sympathetically left me alone day after day. When they were home Debby and Blair cheerfully forewent as basic an adolescent right as listening to jazz on the radio. Even Maria, the world's prize interrupter, tiptoed around the house muttering about "la povera signora!"

I talked Italian to myself from morning till night. Mitch did the perfect thing. He and the kids went out and bargained furiously with an Italian sculptor for an exquisite little bronze nude which we had seen together and agreed that we couldn't afford. The second day of my studying, he brought her home and set her up in the dining room. I stopped talking to myself and began to lecture to her. She was a lovely attentive listener.

I really made gains in vocabulary and sentence structure with the material I wanted to present; but time and again my overstretched brain would rebel and I would be unable to ask Maria for a glass of water.

Among other aberrations, I apparently forgot how to tell time. I arrived at Giorgiana's house about forty-five minutes early on the afternoon of my first lecture. She was in her bath, and the maid suggested I might like to see the baby. I picked up the lovely Alessandra, who was wearing the yellow Carter's baby dress I had ordered from America, and I had a fine time giving her her first lesson in English. Playing with her was the perfect relaxation for that tense moment.

Giorgiana joined us and approved of my speaking English. "We must train her ear to your lovely language," she said approvingly. She took Alessandra from me for a few minutes of farewell play. My ear began sorting out what the Italian mother says to her baby. At one point Alessandra made one of those delicious, comical, strangely quizzical faces that so often flit across a small face. "Now," said Giorgiana laughingly, "you look just like Father de la Roche . . . Non voglio un prete! Voglio solamente una bella bimba!" (I don't want a priest! All I want is a beautiful baby girl!)

On our drive to the school, Giorgiana amused me with a variety of stories. We passed an unbelievably ornate mansion with vast grounds — we could barely glimpse it from the street behind its walls, trees, and shrubbery. I said that I had often wished I might get inside.

She said, "But we may not go inside. That was the residence of Mussolini. Now it has become a huge institution for children. When Mussolini lived we could not see it. And now we cannot because the nuns and the government keep the public out." She thought a minute. "But I'll bet you could get in," she exclaimed delightedly. "It is absolutely unthinkable that you should return to America now. We could pretend that you are not a master of the Italian language and I would go along as your translator. And this time, I would pay you a fee!"

Alessandra and Giorgiana each had done her bit for me, and I arrived at the school almost relaxed. But as I began to mount the stairs, my anxiety seemed to rise ten degrees with each step. It was five fifty-seven. The lecture was to start at six.

When, oh, when would I learn about the Italian attitude toward time? At six ten, we went into the library where the school librarian showed me a copy of SANC's national magazine and the article "How America Succeeded in Thinning Out the Number of Children in Institutional Placement" by Signora Charnley. She suggested that I might like to sit down and read it.

I reminded myself again to stop fighting this culture and yield to it. So, ten minutes after my lecture was scheduled, I sat down to read my article (published several weeks before — no one had thought to show it to me). After five minutes or so, Signorina Quinzi, looking even more the flawless, glacial Vogue model than usual, came in and said that perhaps I would like to come to the lecture room?

We sat in the room, Signorina Quinzi on my right, Giorgiana on my left; they thoughtfully spoke to me in English. The room began to fill up and when about thirty people were assembled, Signorina Quinzi introduced me in her musical Italian. Before she had quite finished, Father de la Roche came bustling into the room and took a place at the far end. I found myself thinking that if he wore beads, like the nuns, they would be in a constant dance. His muscles seemed always to be hurrying somewhere even when he was sitting down.

I had talked no more than three minutes when I knew that everything was going to be all right. This was an audience that nourishes a speaker. Their faces spoke of sympathy, warmth, a willingness to work at understanding me, and an expectation that what I had to tell them they wanted to know.

Georgiana's hand which held a cigarette gave up the tremor that I had noticed while Signorina Quinzi was introducing me. "Brava!" she whispered. I wanted to stop and hug her. There is no word in English that says as much as this—and I knew that Giorgiana didn't use it lightly.

I was saying some bold things and treading consciously on a number of toes. For example, I knew that most of the faculty people from the four schools of social work represented at the meeting had not been practicing social workers before they began teaching casework. (To an American this is astonishing; but it is necessary to remember how young social work was in Italy.) As I talked about the curriculum for students who were to do casework with children, I said that I believed it essential that teachers have had experience in this field. I felt a stir on my right from Signorina Quinzi; I was aware of one raised eyebrow on Father de la Roche's face; and I didn't miss the almost ear-to-ear grin of approval from Signorina Mannini of ICS. (Yes, she was there despite our last chilly phone call. I hoped that I had knocked down some of that invisible barrier.)

I also struck out at the timidity of caseworkers and their tendency to help their child clients gloss over, deny, and push back pain. My audience began to talk back when I said, "The child who strikes out in anger is always a frightened child. The children's social worker must ask herself, 'Of what is he afraid?' rather than start with, 'How do I stop this badness?'"

One after another they picked up the idea, questioned it, and struggled with it before they took it in. As they talked, often two at a time, Giorgiana kept up a machine-gun sputter of whispered English in my ear.

The school had furnished everybody a tablet and two well-sharpened pencils. They took notes furiously and I observed that Italian social workers could, when necessary, talk without using their hands.

The effect of my effort to teach role playing in the Giobbe case was electric. Not a word about the oedipal situation, but rather talk about basing a case on restoring a father who had abdicated his job as head of the family. These workers fought against this new style of case analysis from which the treatment plan emerged. I found an unexpected partisan in Father de la Roche who said good-naturedly, "Mrs. Charnley, I wish you all the luck in the world in trying to teach this bunch of suffragettes to let a man run his family. I shudder to think what they might do to you if you were a man teaching such heresy."

The concept of role playing as a tool in diagnosis was new to them and they fought with a healthy resistance. They pleaded a different cultural pattern—an argument I was able to take away from them. They spoke of "fine healthy families in which the women wore the 'pantaloni.'" I agreed that mother-dominated families could run smoothly. But I said that if we merely understood and accepted distorted family roles, the result would be very little movement in our clients. I asked them to think of chronic cases and to ask themselves how much their clients had improved with the approach of understanding and acceptance of people as they were. Little smiles of agreement began to appear.

I began to distinguish among the representatives of the four schools. The three young men from the School of the Holy Spirit looked passive, baffled, and withdrawn, but workers of the other schools bit in deep. A brilliant, handsome young teacher from the League School of Social Work argued passionately against my plan for the Giobbe family. She and Father locked horns firmly, and she became so angry that she had to turn away from him. For many minutes she directed her sputtering frustration at me. In the end, almost angrily, she said, "You convince me. This is uniquely the social worker's tool—not just something we borrow in a diluted form from psychiatry. I am going to start teaching it!"

The group argued, agreed and disagreed, but never for a moment took my place as leader away from me. At eight twenty, Signorina called time and asked whether we could continue tomorrow night with our discussion of the Giobbe case. I felt that to have to continue to think about the Giobbes as I prepared for the lecture on supervision would be impossible and I said firmly that I would need the full two hours for tomorrow's subject. If the group wanted to, they could talk with me about the Giobbes tomorrow night at the conclusion of the lecture.

I was keyed up and exuberant. I congratulated my overworked brain on a new-found elasticity. I should never have let it know. It balked. As the members of the audience came up to talk to me, it froze. Not one word I spoke was intelligible. I turned in complete dependency to Giorgiana, who immediately diagnosed and met my problem.

Only after the group had dispersed and we started out of the building did I see Father de la Roche.

"I never knew," he said in nice, clear English, "what a provocative speaker you were going to be. Just because I'm willing to translate for you and see that you get to say your say, don't get the idea that I'm agreeing." He turned on his heel and went chuckling down the hall. I never have known whether he was teasing. I do know that the kind of support and direction he gave from the sidelines, while he seemed no more active than any other member of the audience, had a great deal to do with the success of that first lecture.

June 25

The vocabulary of the lecture on supervision was almost catastrophically hard, for I began by teaching how an agency should make a statistical count of interviews with clients. From the first Italian numerals were hard for me, and in spite of having resorted to counting every flight of stairs I climbed, like a compulsive neurotic, I still had achieved only a nodding acquaintance with figures.

In order to say, "From nine o'clock until ten o'clock," I also had to face some balky prepositions. I finally got the prepositions somewhat under control by waving my left hand to reinforce the "from" and my right hand to support the "until." The little bronze girl seemed to smile benevolently as the Americana became Italian enough to get shoulders, elbows, and wrists into speech.

Six o'clock Tuesday evening arrived with a minimum of trauma. By six fifteen the same audience was assembled, except those three young men. When I asked Father whether we should wait for them, he said, "You would wait forever. Couldn't you tell? You scared them away last night." He smiled approvingly and took his seat at the back of the room.

I began my lecture with the flat, uningratiating, and undiplomatic statement that I was quite certain that, though Italian social workers worked much longer hours than Americans, they gave less help to fewer clients.

I paused to look for defensiveness or anger in the faces — those volatile Italian faces that communicate as clearly as though their attitudes were labeled. What I read was agreement and acceptance.

I said that I was concerned for the welfare of the clients and for the future of the field of social work in Italy. Nodding acceptance again. I said that I did not intend to discuss the why of it but only to make a suggestion or two that might help to bring about change.

Using the blackboard I described the system of statistical counting common in American agencies. I drew graphs and charts to show norms of activity and to explain how in my own agency our attempt to bring our workloads up to national levels resulted in doubling the number of clients we interviewed.

As I sketched out the technique of counting services to clients, note-writing hands around the table flew. Father did not take notes but shot one clear question after another. He looked beatifically happy. (Of course! This was the man who in February talked so enchantedly about his "excellent statistician" and who dreamed of the day that social work would become a measurable science.)

When I began to talk of the emotional complications in relating to a time schedule, the group seemed even more alert and Father a little less. I spoke of the social worker's resistance to the supervisor in relation to her own individual reaction to authority. I pointed out that most humans work out their hostile feelings toward people in authority step by step—first the parents, then the bossy older siblings, then teachers, policemen, priests, and tax collectors.

Something in my words puzzled the group and I turned to Father for help in translation. As I listened, I realized he left out "the priest."

With a nice twinkle, Signorina Quinzi came in quickly. "Now, Father! Translate honestly!" He made a wry face.

Among the time wasters that I questioned was the plethora of detail in their hand-written case histories. I said that no agency could afford to have social workers keeping laborious case histories that showed all steps in the process while unattended clients sat and waited. Wham! I split the group noisily in two. Though Giorgiana worked furiously, she couldn't keep up. Wearily she said, "All I can tell you is that the practicing workers support you violently and the teachers think you are pazza (crazy)."

Signorina Quinzi quieted the group long enough for me to explain what Giorgiana, the only non-social worker in the group, had discovered. This fact had the answer in it. The supervisors faced the practical problem of getting the job done for the clients. The school wanted records for teaching purposes. I brought up the name Giobbe again. I had condensed twenty-four pages of case history into four pages containing more than enough material to keep all of us occupied for two hours. In my rewriting of the Giobbe case, they had seen how a brief summary could tell the whole story.

I went after the worker who refuses criticism for wasting time. I tried with a private grin to teach them about the scheduled coffee break as formal recognition of the impulse to gossip during working hours but also a way to catch this gossiping in a time limit. "Coffee break" I translated literally as "fifteen minutes for descending the stairs to go to the caffè" and it seemed to me that maybe this unwieldy phrase in itself would make a scheduled coffee break seem silly.

Because I had observed hours spent in trying to reach clients to set up appointments, I tried to teach the American system that each interview should end with the setting of an appointment for the next. In explaining the general failure to do this, Signorina Quinzi said that she thought it was due to social workers' insecurity about the services they had to offer. It was as though the clients were doing the social workers a favor by coming to keep the appointments.

I responded with genuine surprise – partly at the validity of a point I had missed in my observations. I found words spilling out of me about my deep conviction of the contribution that social work makes. "Social work is young in Italy, so you are unsure. But in a few years you will see irrefutable evidence that your people value it." I told them many things they didn't know about America – the clients who spend six weeks on a waiting list to see a social worker . . . the fees that wealthier people gladly pay for services. I amazed them by describing social workers in private practice who, like doctors, work alone in offices and charge ten and twenty dollars an hour. I quoted what a woman who had had help from a private practitioner had told me. "Of course it is expensive. But it costs no more than a car or a trip to Europe – things that wear out or fade – whereas the help I get is forever. It is as though the worker taught me to walk when I always believed I could only crawl."

Many American concepts that I gave were helpful, I know. But I gave them nothing as valuable as a hope for pride in their profession and, I believe, a beginning of faith. I suggested that it was the job of the schools to teach not only clearly but also with real conviction. (The faculty members looked a little uncomfortable.) "And then," I said, "when the faculty has done its job and sent out graduates full of eagerness to practice their new profession, it is the job of the supervisors to keep the faith and wish to succeed alive." (Now the supervisors looked uneasy.) I commented on what Giorgiana had noticed and pointed out—the separateness of the two groups. I said that though I had not been introduced I could go around the room pointing out which person belonged to each group because of their facial responses. They quickly understood my point and I had only to say that if I could come back to Italy and lecture to them again in five years I hoped for the sake of the field of social work in Italy I would know only that I was lecturing to social workers.

The two hours flew. I remember only one interruption. Just as I had been struggling hardest with the unwieldy intertwining of numbers and prepositions, an uproar of hammering came from the corridor. Father de la Roche scowled and said to me in clear English, "What the hell are those damn fools trying to do?" Signorina Quinzi, Giorgiana, and I choked.

June 27

GIORGIANA AND I approached our last lecture in quite a lighthearted fashion. I had become so serene that I had canceled yesterday's cram session and our family had taken the afternoon off for a swim at Fregene.

I had been planning to base tonight's lecture on the material I had prepared for SANC on foster home placement. Signorina Quinzi spotted my manuscript and suggested that Giorgiana read it. She explained that she was being scolded by the group for having scheduled only six hours. If the meat of the material were read, there would be more time for discussion. The group paid me Italy's ultimate compliment. By five minutes after six we were all assembled and ready to begin. I explained that Giorgiana was to read the manuscript and give the group a vocabulary lesson, introducing them to "la homefinder" and "il placement."

Giorgiana read so rapidly, I could see, that they couldn't take notes. I interrupted to ask whether the school could have the material mimeographed.

Tonight the audience was my largest. I learned the reason. The heads of the three Roman child care agencies had pleaded for permission to bring other staff members specially interested in foster placement. A few weeks ago I had been thrilled that SANC was to begin a foster care service. Tonight I learned that the other three agencies had the same plan. As one executive explained it, "For years our clients have been hiring foster homes on their own — badly and inexpertly — but we are as often surprised by the successes as by the failures. As agencies we have arranged foster care with grandmothers and aunts. In our agency we want to try this program the way Signora Charnley describes it."

There were murmurs of assent around the room. At one point in the lecture, Giorgiana held up a little orange and black booklet which many American agencies use in recruiting foster homes. It began, "Once upon a time there were some children who needed homes. There were fat children, thin children, good children and some rather naughty children . . ." The illustrations had been done by a foster father for a private agency in Ohio. The simple English sounded beautiful in Italian.

At eight fifteen the group showed no impulse to break up. After Signorina Quinzi had made a warm closing speech of thanks, they got to their feet, but did not leave. They continued with their questions. Several asked for appointments. They would come to our home. I explained that I had promised SANC that I would work there every morning that remained of our stay in Italy. Eagerly they filled up my afternoons.

Father de la Roche had been absent. Signorina Quinzi explained that he had received an urgent request to fly to Milan. He had been wonderfully helpful and supportive in my first two lectures, but I was glad that he wasn't present tonight. He had been more than deft in supporting me even when he was in disagreement. But I wondered whether the rush to begin placement programs without his pet statistical study might not have been more than he could take.

A few weeks ago I had been present at the birth of foster home care at SANC. Tonight, it had another beginning in three more agencies. And inasmuch as these were home offices in Rome for national agencies, it was really the beginning for the whole nation.

I regretted that I had had so little concrete help to give them. I wished that they might have had translations of some American books and articles on placement. Though they were written for use in the American culture, I would have trusted this group to select what was applicable.

On our ride home in the taxi, Giorgiana and I relaxed in the sense of "mission accomplished." I tried to put into words the enormous debt I felt to her, and she responded in trite English, "Don't mention it." Then, seeming to feel the coldness of the stereotyped response, she switched to Italian, hugged me, and said, "I am going to miss you. You are my very favorite pupil. You and my adorable Dr. Salk! But social work is so much more interesting than poliomyelitis."

At home I found Mitch and Janet waiting with pink Italian champagne to celebrate. My toast was to "the last lecture in Italian I will ever give in my whole entire life." We drank to that, but it turned out to be no guarantee of the future.

June 28 to July 4

I HAD TO BREAK my promise to SANC to visit the agency every morning.

All through the black week I had been dimly aware of ominous throbs in a molar; I think I must have effectively begged, "Not now!" But the morning after my job was done it claimed its right for attention through a swollen jaw and a not-to-be-denied pounding. I reached for the list of dentists supplied by the Fulbright office and chose one on the basis of his handy address and the fact that – said the list – his languages were "English, French, Italian, and German." The typist must have made a mistake, for he spoke three of them, plus Spanish – but no English.

My guess was that I had lost a filling. He looked at the tooth and said gravely that I had "una grande cavità." My problem: In Italian is a "cavità" just a hole, or is it a diseased hole? Whatever it was, he went to work on it, and dismayed me by scheduling a series of appointments. To my amusement he assured me that I was lucky to have had this trouble in Italy because "American dentists are quick to pull teeth that have any little thing wrong with them." Just before we left home, American dentists had warned us to fight off Italian dentists who wanted to pull teeth.

Complicated by the demands of my tooth, the last days in Rome were frantically busy. There was the beginning of farewells, all of which involved visits. There was a trunk to be bought, packed, and shipped; papers and reports to be filled out; and a steady stream of appointments with social workers who wanted to know more about placement, more about supervision, and – almost without exception – more about how someone from their schools or agencies might get a Fulbright grant to study and experience foster home work in America.

Though I short-changed SANC a little on my promise, I more than made it up by agreeing to a second six-hour seminar on July 8, 9, and 10 for the entire SANC staff and any other workers who could find a way to come into Rome from the provinces. Italia wanted me to use the materials I had used at the school, but with some changes. For example, would there be some way I could make my use-of-time point more diplomatically to this group of expert time wasters? And the casework with children . . . it was wonderful, but what they needed even more was help in casework with families. I agreed—the response I was receiving made it impossible to say "No." I wonder now whether any circumstance would make me agree in America on July 1 to give a seminar in less than a week with new and revised materials. It was to be a week with no preparation time built into it, and I was almost light-hearted about the fact that Giorgiana was to be away.

A new problem that week was that Maria, our maid, moved into what I could only describe as a serious depression. On the slightest provocation she would burst into tears; her explanation was always that our family was abandoning her. "You will go away to America and forget all about me." And Signora Charnley, who lectured so confidently on helping children and parents deal with separation, was a total flop in helping Maria prepare to say good-by.

July 4

MITCH, DEBBY, BLAIR, AND I were having our own separation problems. All of us except Blair had been away long enough to have felt some homesickness; but life in Rome had been so full and exciting that we were by no means ready to leave.

On July 4, we went to the American Embassy for the celebration. American flags were flying. A nice brassy band was playing Sousa marches. And children dressed in their Sunday best ran noisily and happily through the crowd licking pink ice cream cones and drinking lemonade. The ambassador made a speech we couldn't hear. After the ceremony, we went to sit for a few minutes at a Via Veneto caffè and were soon joined by an acquaintance who introduced us to several friends. As we listened to them we realized disapprovingly that these Americans were so seduced by the charms of European living that they had given up all but technical rights to their own country. We found ourselves suddenly with a fine Fourth of July yearning for home.

Janet came to a farewell lunch with us. She had ten months more in Italy. It was a lunch in which we all were conscious of our American roots, and Janet confessed to envy that we were going home when she wouldn't see New York again for almost a year. It was a satisfying meeting. Despite Maria's red eyes, we were at last beginning to be psychologically ready to say good-by to Rome.

This July 4 afternoon, like all those July afternoons, brought its social worker to our apartment. And she seemed the most interesting of all.

Signora Stefania Vicenza was a dark, handsome Italian woman who wore a high-fashion "sack" dress. She spoke the kind of Italian that was easy for me. She had spent a number of years in the Rome Child Guidance Clinic and had been hired recently by the Association of Roman Schools of Social Work to set up a training program for forty students for the next academic year. There were to be five supervisors for the students, and their clinical experience was to take place in two of Rome's largest "houses of maternity." She said that she had many problems and already in my lectures I had answered some of them. But could I help with her particular assignment?

I told her honestly that her assignment sounded Herculean. It seemed to me that it might be possible to handle forty students from one school—but from four! She said soberly that this was true, but she was face to face with a system that could not be changed. Did I not think that there would be a healthful stimulation as the students mingled and learned from the differences in their preparation? Would not these differences filter back to the schools and give impetus to the casework teaching?

I could agree that she was right, but I warned that the assignment called for both courage and assurance. I feared that her time might be swallowed up keeping peace among warring schools. She said with a smile that it might be that it would be hard, but "not so hard as in America where thinking is more solidified."

I asked her to tell me about the houses of maternity. She described them excellently. I remembered that Father de la Roche had mentioned them in our first conference. "In every district in Rome, ICS has established houses of maternity with specialized services. Each has a 'nest' where working mothers, sick mothers, and 'just too busy mothers' may leave their children for day care and two good meals. At six o'clock the mothers take their children home for the night.

"The houses were established by law during the Fascist period. The Fascists' orderly minds were much concerned with the health and strength of babies. Many of the Fascist-written laws remain excellent. The greatest weakness in the program is that it is geared more to the physical well-being of children than to their emotional needs."

Signora Vicenza said that one of the hard jobs for enlightened social workers at the houses of maternity in keeping families together is to oppose the deep cultural notion that institutionalization is good. Heroic mothers with tears streaming down their faces give up babies so that children can be educated and cared for by the nuns and priests. The mothers believe that only through such sacrifice can children achieve the opportunity to earn a decent living. The uneducated "medical social workers" accept this belief at face value. Signora Vicenza and her student supervisors hoped to teach the students how to persuade parents that a child's place in his own home has values far greater than the security of institutional care. And she had become, she said, "so much excited" at the alternative of temporary foster care.

As I had talked at the seminar she had had a "shining idea." "Many of the poor mothers who use the nest for day care are fine, solid citizens – good mothers who accept day care only for the food it gives their young. If the agencies could select the best of these mothers and give them the small stipend that an agency usually pays an institution, perhaps they could become foster mothers. I agree with your warning of the inadvisability of using a next-door neighbor as a foster home parent. But what if we found foster mothers through the houses of maternity in north Rome for the babies from the houses of maternity in south Rome?"

It seemed a most ingenious and workable idea. Parents could visit by bus, but they would have neither the money nor the energy for the daily visit that tends to tear a foster child in two. Signora Vicenza's lively intelligence answered its own questions almost before they were stated. But her humility meant that she wanted me to hear her plan in every detail.

She had thought of having the little orange and black pamphlet which I had shown issued in Italian. The teacher at the nest would draw it to the attention of women whom she thought of as good mothers. The pamphlet would urge such women to talk with the students who would be arriving in September.

It was an excellent plan. She had done what my imagination had failed to do for the workers at SANC. She had discovered a potential group of foster mothers and had found a way to get her message to them.

At this point Maria, red-eyed and sniffling, brought us coffee and stopped to tell the somewhat surprised Signora Vicenza that the whole Charnley family was going to abandon her soon. When she left the room, I explained that I found this excessive grief a minor burden. Signora Vicenza laughed. "Oh, she's just being Italian," she said, and then added teasingly, "but this is what you were teaching us. It's healthy to display feelings, not to swallow them."

I turned to a fresh aspect of casework in the houses of maternity. I had learned that babies frequently were sent from them into the countryside to live with the wet nurses called balias. Could she tell me more about the balias? They seemed the closest I had come to foster mothers in Italy.

Her eyes flashed with scorn. The balia system, she said, was a disgrace. When the doctors first set up the program for the houses of maternity there was a belief that frail babies would profit from mother's milk. At first only prematures or children of tuberculous or syphilitic parents were sent. Now, she said, it depended on the attitude of the doctor. "Some doctors think that if the baby has a mouth and the balia has nipples on left and right, bringing them together constitutes 'a casework plan.'"

But, I asked, wasn't it better than institutional care? She said it was only with exceptional luck. Most balias have thrust aside their own babies to give milk to agency babies. They are harsh, stupid women who have commercialized their maternity. Some balias who are unsupervised will secretly nurse two babies when they do not have enough milk for one. Sometimes agencies bring babies to balias and fail to reclaim them for ten or twelve years. The check for care goes out month after month and the child, knowing only that he is not really one of the brood in which he is growing up, lives in puzzlement until one day a medical social worker comes and—she made a gesture showing something being torn apart—the child is snatched up and carried off to an institution.

I told her that I had asked to see the balia system, but that it seemed to me I was met with embarrassment. I was reluctant to leave Italy without the experience. She said, "Tonight I shall telephone you and I shall arrange to have someone take you to see a balia."

We returned to her students. How many students could a supervisor carry? How many cases could a student carry? I taught her about the cooperative case in placement with one student being "la homefinder" and another one doing "il placement."

She asked many very sophisticated questions. For example, "Do you know the kind of mother neurotically attached to her child who needs to live with him in order to hurt him a little every day?"

Indeed I did!

She continued, "What I cannot understand is how a social worker could persuade such a mother to let a child live away from her. The child would need it badly, but if the mother let a foster mother be good to her child she would be giving up her daily emotional satisfaction."

I said that she had described the most painful question in child protection today. It is so hard, I explained, that only a few social workers have solved it.

A few do so by confronting the mother with the thing she is doing and holding her to the need of change if she is to find happiness. I explained that this is a dangerous approach because such mothers often "just disappear."

I described the rare cases in which I had seen mature social workers succeed by offering sympathy instead of anger to the sick woman who had known only rejection. Some gifted social workers could offer such a mother so nourishing a relationship that the woman could release her harsh clutch on her child to find satisfaction in the accepting relationship with a social worker.

She nodded. "The social worker would become the loving mother that the woman never had?"

I felt again the wrench at leaving Italy, felt the bitterness of having discovered Signora Vicenza only when I had one foot out the door.

We talked for three hours. At the end, I told my new friend that she was the first social worker I had met in Italy who seemed ready to go to work in America's best agencies. I asked her where she had received her education. She said that she was a graduate of the League School but that she had learned most of what she found useful from a beautiful mother, a loving father, and a young grandfather, a doctor, who was wise in his understanding of human behavior.

As we parted she was lamenting that I would not be here the next fall when her problems would be real instead of theoretical. I suggested that she might write me. We discovered then that we had an excellent marital linguistic arrangement. Her husband knew English. She would write me in Italian and Mitch would read her letter to me. I would respond in English and her husband would translate for her.

She said that it was wonderful having a gifted husband like hers. "I have borrowed your book from the library and I am going to say to my husband, 'Please, would you be so kind . . .?'"

July 6

Signora Vicenza kept her promise that I should see a balia. On this second-to-last Sunday in Rome Mitch and I had an early afternoon appointment at the Piazza Buenos Aires with Signorina Elena Minoso. To my surprise we were met by two women – Signorina explained to me that the mousy, silent little woman was the mother of one of the children whom we would visit. Signorina Minoso drew me aside to explain that the woman was an unmarried mother who worked as a maid in her home. I was glad to give her a ride to see her baby, but felt a little disappointed because I wanted to ask questions about the balias and the babies that might be threatening to this young mother.

Signorina startled me by saying, "That is a matter of no importance."

Mitch had a nice practical solution. "Put her in the back seat of the bus. You two sit in the second seat. Don't forget how bad the acoustics are!" He was right. We could talk in absolute privacy.

We drove about two hours out of Rome to Alatri, a mountain village in a most beautiful but most impoverished area. The little town perches high on a mountain top, and the farms around it cling desperately to the hard dry mountain soil. Women wear graceful peasant costumes – low-cut blouses, great full black skirts drawn tight at the waist – and walk about bare of head and foot. The more prosperous families near the valley, where crops find a little more nourishment, have donkeys, but the poorer families use their women as beasts of burden. The young girls and women seemed exceptionally beautiful, with strong facial structure and high coloring that reminded Mitch of the beautiful descendants of the Celts along the coast of Brittany.

Mitch shouted this comment to Signorina Minoso and she called back above the rumble of the bus that it was apt. The young women of Alatri had the reputation of being the most beautiful women in Italy. "But life here is so harsh," she added soberly, "that they grow old years before their time. They fade early."

The men of Alatri, most of whom seemed to be sitting in clusters in the shade playing cards or sharing newspapers, were dressed in conservative city clothes much like the men of Rome. I asked Signorina whether they were relaxed like this because it was Sunday. (My feminine instincts rebelled at seeing women erect under their heavy copper pitchers of water, or bowed down by bundles of fagots strapped to their backs. I shall always remember one Millet-like woman who walked along barefooted with a scythe in one hand, her head and shoulders buried in the load of hay she carried.)

"No," Signorina said, "there is a real unemployment problem here. Perhaps these men will have a few weeks of work repairing roads for the government if they are lucky, but that is all. Each family grows its own food on its little plot of land, and there is a little bartering. But there is rarely cash."

I knew the answer, but I had to ask. "Why don't they help the women with all that carrying?"

She shrugged her shoulders. "It is not the custom."

Alatri is a village unique in Italy. It is a village of balias. (The dictionary lists "La balia, feminine singular: wet nurse; il balio, masculine singular: husband of a wet nurse.") When I mentioned il balio to Signorina, she explained, "It is a very vulgar term and it is not polite to use it."

Signorina was not certain how this unusual occupation had its beginning, but she "guessed" that it had been flourishing for hundreds of years. Originally, the balias nursed the babies of the rich women of Rome. Some of this still goes on; but more and more in recent years it has been the social agencies that bring the babies to Alatri. Alatri is known as a place where you can always find a woman with milk to spare.

Alatri has its own information system—an old woman who makes a slim living by keeping agencies informed of mothers ready to wean their own babies. She is a simple, uneducated old woman who tours the countryside constantly keeping track of dates of birth and supplies of breast milk. She goes always on foot, and covers many miles a week. She is a great telephoner. Each cluster of homes has one telephone and she phones each area regularly.

She also telephones balia news periodically to the agencies in Rome.

It took a dozen questions to learn about this Alatrian with the unusual job. Signorina Minoso, a woman of few and short words, made me work much harder than usual to learn what I wanted to know. Finally, somewhat wearily, she said, "In America you must have women that will tell you where there is an empty house to rent? This woman can tell you where there is a balia with a good milk supply."

Signorina Minoso had on her case load about twenty-five children with balias. These babies would usually be placed for adoption when they were about one year old. (Send up a flag! Adoptions in Italy!) Signorina was the only adoption worker in her agency. She averaged about twenty-five to thirty a year. The other workers in her agency struggled with problems of long-time care, sometimes keeping the children with the balias until they were eight or ten years old, sometimes transferring them to institutions soon after the babies were weaned.

Her agency also had institutions in Rome where an unmarried mother could live with her child and nurse it herself. When her milk supply gave out, she must choose either to take her baby home with her or to send it off to an institution. Signorina was convinced that it was much better for babies to be with balias than in institutions.

I returned to the subject of adoptions. Her babies were sometimes placed in Italian homes but were more often given to foreigners—people from Asia, North Africa, South America, and the United States. Any foreign family was eligible to apply for a baby so long as it was "a good Catholic family with a letter from its parish priest" and as long as the family seemed to be a kind one with "the proper motivation."

I asked about the Italian families that adopt children through her. She said that the parents must be older than forty. I said that I had heard that they needed to be over fifty. Stolidly she explained that at forty an Italian family may make "an affiliation" with a child, but that the child may not inherit from its new family or use its name until the adoptive parents have both had their fiftieth birthdays.

How many adoptions by Italian and foreign families took place each year in Italy? She had no idea. Would it be as many as five hundred? After careful thinking, she said she thought that it would come to more than five hundred and less than a thousand. I was somewhat cheered by this. Seven hundred children a year are not many to salvage from the half million who grow up in institutions, but it did help a little.

If one starts with acceptance of the use of balias, the practices of the signorina's agency seemed quite good. A social worker with a baby in a balia's home was required to visit once a month; in addition to the social worker's visit, a doctor called once a month; and the funny old agent-woman checked in once a month. Extra visits from the doctors were arranged for by the balia-finder if a child was ill.

Signorina Minoso's agency paid its balias 12,000 lire ($20) for every month a child was in care, even after he was weaned. This sum would be a great deal to a family that lives entirely from the soil. I wondered what effect it would have on a marriage to have the woman of the family be the only wage earner — and this on the basis of her milk supply!

I told the signorina that I had heard that other agencies paid lower fees — 6,000 to 8,000 lire — and that visits from social workers might be as infrequent as five years apart. There was a tightening of the lips of this ungarrulous woman, and the simple statement, "I wouldn't know anything about that."

"A woman of Alatri usually weans her baby at about five months, then takes on an agency baby and nurses him for another five months." With a vague memory of cultures in which women were said to nurse their last born for many years, I asked whether the milk supply was always exhausted at ten months. Signorina said that the milk supply tended to become poor and unnourishing after ten months.

Weary of questioning, I told Signorina about the American customs in adoption — helping a mother decide before her baby is born that she will give it up, putting the baby on a bottle from the first, and often achieving an adoption by the time a baby is one or two weeks old. Signorina said that this was an attractive plan but that European families seemed to feel that it was too risky. They wanted to be sure that the baby was "turning out all right" before they chose him.

Signorina Minoso said that balias were common in all of southern Italy, Sicily, and Sardinia, but she knew of no other community that made it a business as did Alatri. She said that balias are used a great deal in Rome but rarely in northern Italy. Rome she included with southern Italy, she said, because of the constant influx of southerners.

Asked why balias were not used in northern Italy, she said, "The northern Italians are better educated. They do not regard illegitimacy as such a disgrace. The unmarried mother often brings her baby home to her parents where he is reared with her brothers and sisters." I commented on the contrast with America. The more educated and prosperous a family in the United States, the less likely that a daughter could bring her illegitimate baby home.

Mitch, who sat alone in the front seat of the car, said to me in English, "This gal sure makes you work. Is she taciturn or angry?"

"Taciturn, I think."

"Keep on telling her about American customs," he suggested. "I think it loosens her up."

It did seem to work better when I got a little give-and-take into the conversation. Presently we left the main highway to travel several miles on steep, rutty little roads until we reached the farm of the balia where our passenger's baby, Roberto, was staying. The young mother became excited as we drove into the farm. Signorina called out, "Ciao, balia!" (Hi, wet nurse!)

The mother hopped out of the car and kissed the balia and all the balia's children on the mouth. (It was the first time I had seen this in this nation of cheek kissers.) The children, neighbors, and relatives swarmed into the yard to examine us and our remarkable car. Nobody explained my presence or Mitch's, but we were warmly greeted nevertheless.

One of the balia's children, a little boy who looked to be about seven, was specially greeted by the social worker and offered "many happy returns of the day." It was his twelfth birthday. (I continued to be fooled whenever I was judging the age of poor Italian children.)

The balia was a slim woman with a fading prettiness. She seemed warm and sweet in her manner toward us and the children. The mother, the social worker, and I were led into the crude little stone house that nestled so close to the earth as to seem to be a part of it. We went directly through some dank dark rooms to a small stone staircase that led up to a single bedroom. The rest of the family must have slept downstairs on the floor. The upstairs room was very dark; until the balia pulled the curtains back I had the sensation of being in a cave. When the light entered, I found myself in an immaculate small room furnished only with a huge double bed (named "a matrimonial" by Italians), a small chest of drawers, and a small crib crudely made from crossed branches with bark on them. Three huge pillows had been used instead of a mattress, and the bedding of the crib was dazzlingly white. Except for the dankness of the little stone room there was an air of immaculate, almost unnatural cleanliness about it.

With a small cry the mother hurried to the crib and looked down at her sleeping baby. Tears coursed down her face. "Roberto, oh Roberto!" she whispered softly, "your mama has come."

The balia worried to Signorina Minoso, "The baby sleeps."

Signorina said curtly, "He can sleep another day. Waken him to greet his mama!"

The baby wakened smilingly and when the balia gently lifted him from his crib I understood something Signorina Minoso had been trying to tell me. This was a crippled baby. Roberto wore an elaborate, beautifully made orthopedic harness which held his two little legs straight and spread apart. The doctor came every two weeks, the balia said, to adjust the harness to tiny changes in growth. (What a fantastically expensive process in this setting of poverty!) The balia not only was loving with Roberto, but also sensitive to his tremulous, teary young mother. As she changed his diaper, she showed the mother the clean, fresh skin on his buttocks — no diaper rash in this home! The balia announced that she had wonderful news. The last time the doctor had visited he said that Roberto's legs were developing nicely and that someday the boy would walk without a limp. Again tears flowed down the mother's face and she made a quick sign of the cross.

When Roberto was dressed we all went downstairs into the sunshine. More children had appeared and were giving the Microbus careful scrutiny. When I looked around the yard for the baby who had been displaced by Roberto, I found him in the arms of a young brother. The baby seemed half as big as the little boy who carried him. It was a common sight in Italy — this assignment of a newly weaned baby to an older sibling for almost complete care. In every poor village of Italy I saw them — boys and girls alike — playing their games, sitting in the sun, sometimes running with big, too-heavy babies bouncing along on one hip. It always shocked me, but I never saw an older child anything but kind and responsive to his young charge.

It was decided that we would leave the mother at the balia's to enjoy Roberto while we made other calls. Signorina Minoso told Mitch that the next stop was not far away. It seemed to us that we must have driven ten miles and I began to wonder whether the signorina really managed a monthly visit, because she seemed thoroughly lost; we stopped several times so that she could ask directions from the men who took their ease in the shade. When we found the home, a small stone house much like the last, it showed us an even more pervading and more terrible poverty. The man of the family wore shoes, a shirt, and a tie, but his barefoot wife was worn, bent, and misshapen. When she saw Signorina and me she gave a cry of alarm and asked whether we had come to take her baby away. Only after Signorina had repeatedly assured her did she go inside and emerge with a most beautiful five-month-old boy with sandy hair and a sunny smile. It was a hot day and she brought the baby from the house wearing nothing but a little undershirt. He was a fat, dimpled, healthy-looking boy — except for his poor buttocks, which were covered with angry diaper rash. We played with him, talked with the balia's husband, and accepted glasses of cold water. I asked about the diaper sores. What did the doctor say? The doctor said that it was good to expose the buttocks to the sun without a diaper. I said that American doctors believed this too. (This pleased her.) I added that American doctors suggest that when a baby has such sores it is a good idea to boil the diapers for three minutes after they have been washed. (This displeased her. She probably carried her dirty linen half a mile to a public trough to wash it; and she must balance on her head every drop of water used in her house.)

I asked many questions as we drove to the next home. The woman we had just seen had four older children and was "a very good balia." Her own last baby had died at birth, and she had been given an agency baby at once. The problem was that she didn't want to give this one up. Signorina said calmly that the separation, when it came, would be terrible for her. I suggested that it might be better to use only balias who had living babies. Signorina said dispassionately, "It is not my job to worry about the balias—just about the babies."

I became a preacher-teacher for a moment. "In America social workers believe it is their job to worry about the feelings of the women who care for babies, too. Every kind of human suffering becomes the social worker's responsibility."

Signorina was silent for a few minutes, and then, seeming to soften a little, said, "Perhaps I will give her another baby quite quickly. She is very 'brava' with babies—and besides she has lots of good milk."

As we rode along toward the next balia, I remarked that that last baby had been extraordinarily beautiful. Did she have a good adoptive home for him? Yes, she had a very good one. I asked about his parentage. His mother, a very pretty woman, had had a number of illegitimate children but she never wanted to keep them. When I asked about paternity, Signorina said, "Who knows?"

My last question had to do with the age of the balia. She had looked fifteen years older than her husband. The social worker shook her head. "She is younger, signora. You remember I said, 'The life is hard for women here'?"

For a little while as we drove toward the third balia's home the roads had been the same narrow rutty ones. But now, though they were equally rough and narrow, they seemed to have been designed by a roller-coaster engineer. We climbed the mountain on hairpin curls that ended in such sharp sudden drops that it seemed that our bus would somersault. Signorina saw my nervousness and teased me about it. "I go over these alone in the rain without anxiety," she said grandly. Finally at a crossroad, she suggested that we park and go on foot the rest of the way. We walked up a steep mountain path that led into a small farmyard full of people, children, dogs, and cats. With a casual "good evening," we walked through two more dry, dusty backyards until we came to the last little farm. It seemed to me that in American slums people lived no closer together than here.

The balia, another prematurely old-young woman whose sagging breasts and bulging abdomen showed clearly through her light cotton dress, greeted us pleasantly and took us in to see her baby. Again the dank, immaculate room with the cleanly shining crib. This one had an ingenious mosquito netting draped over it. In the crib slept a lovely dark-haired three-month-old girl who looked as tiny as a newborn. Signorina assured me that her size was "about average for three months."

The balia's own children were out visiting. At the three balias' homes I had seen only one of the three dispossessed babies. I found that it was toward them that my sympathies were moving. What I had seen of Signorina's caseload made me believe that most of the agency babies received excellent care. It would be natural that it should be so. With the frequent visits of social workers, doctors, and the balia-finder, a family's income could go quickly if the baby looked dirty, hungry, or neglected. Besides, all three of the balias had acted spontaneously fond of the foster children.

We stayed only a little while. When we returned to the car the sky was beginning to take on evening hues. I discovered unhappily that signorina had three more stops in mind. I tried as tactfully as I could to extricate us from her vigorous schedule. The balias, their homes, the cribs of the children, the beaten-down-by-life look on the balias' faces had a depressing sameness about them. Not only was I exhausted but a kind of emotional malaise was creeping into me. Signorina was disappointed and, I thought, somewhat disapproving. But she accepted my firm decision to see no more balias that day. She directed us back down the mountain on a less hair-raising route and soon we found ourselves at a crossroad where two women and a baby waited for us — the first balia, the unmarried mother, and the little Roberto who stood so stiffly in his harness in his mother's arms.

The mother kissed the balia and Roberto and climbed sadly into the back seat of the bus. The balia held Roberto up and guided his tiny hand into the Italian farewell gesture, fingers curling inward toward the face. As we took off Roberto gave a regular sunburst grin, and his mother began to sob noisily.

Signorina knelt backward on the seat and spoke with her gently for a few minutes. "It is always hard on the mothers," she explained, "to see how the babies come to prefer the balias."

Our ride through the lovely long Italian dusk all the way back to Rome was punctuated by my involved questions about preplacement studies of the homes of balias (there were virtually none), about introducing the baby to his adoptive mother and father (accomplished in the most casual fashion possible), and about differences in casework teaching in the League School, of which Signorina was a graduate, and the New Roman School, to which I was assigned.

Signorina continued to give her short, direct answers. There wasn't an ounce of conversational flow in her. My questions began to come farther and farther apart.

By the time we reached Rome it was dark. In the dark and the silence I sat trying to figure out whether I had offended my guide in some way. This Vermont-like style was so un-Italian that I was genuinely puzzled by it. Somehow, though, I didn't think she was angry.

It turned out that I was right. As we drove back into Piazza Buenos Aires to let her off, she made quite a long speech. She had had a most delightful day and some of my questions had been "very stimulating." There were two very interesting institutions in Rome for unmarried mothers that she would like me to visit this week. She would also like me to talk with her supervisor about how adoptions are done in America.

Next Sunday, she would like to have the professore, the signora, la signorina, and il signorino have dinner with her at her parents' home.

Trying to keep the surprise out of my voice, I thanked her quickly, but explained that we had only six more days in Rome and they were full of many, many things . . .

She accepted the refusal most gracefully and after warm handshakes with Mitch and me, she hurried off.

As we drove away, Mitch started to laugh. What? I asked. "Sc many things," he said. "Your diagnostic thinking was lousy! Right up to the last minute, you thought she was mad at you." He chuckled again.

"And what else?" I asked.

"I'm laughing at what an absolutely indomitable interviewer you are."

We drove along in silence for a while until he said, "And I guess I'm laughing to blot out some of the pain and suffering I saw in women's faces today."

July 6, 7, and 8

THESE THREE DAYS were the days of my last assignment in Rome — my little seminar for the members of SANC. The first day I found myself facing some thirty social workers. My best friends from SANC all were there — Italia, Maria, Alta, Sofia, Signorina Nino — my noisy roommates and the other workers who had been at that unsuccessful talk on institutionalized children that I had given months ago. The dozen or so new faces belonged to workers who had driven in from the provinces that afternoon to attend the lecture of l'Americana.

I followed my outlines for the seminar I had given last month. My first lecture on casework with families was based on the invaluable Giobbe case. But what a difference in response! The worker for the disguised Giobbe case was a member of the group. (I never did know which one she was, but Italia had talked with her and assured me that it was "all right.") These members of SANC came together as a group to defend their co-worker and incidentally themselves for the Giobbe casework. My first problem, therefore, was to fight my way through the group hostility. No one spoke English. I was really hard put to find the words to let them know that this was not an attack on their casework but rather an exceptionally clear illustration to show a new way of thinking about clients. I remember especially their demanding how I could know from reading a case that the worker was resisting institutional care for Fernando Giobbe.

First I tried to explain that a supervisor who has read hundreds of cases learns to see between the lines and to sense unrecorded feelings. A roomful of stony faces assured me that they weren't buying this. "After all," said one, "didn't the worker try to telephone a dozen or more institutions looking for a place?"

I tried a number of descriptions of clues to show that, though the worker went through the motions, she made them without wanting to succeed. More stony faces.

I *had* to help them to see what a supervisor can deduce about feeling tones subconsciously portrayed in a recording. Fumblingly, I found a new approach. I invented a psycho-drama to show how a supervisor could tell that a worker did not want to give money to a client even though she eventually did so. Acting out the two parts with all the technique of a twelve-year-old giving an elocution recital, I played the role of the client asking for money to feed her family and of the social worker agreeing that she was eligible. But before giving her the money, I had the social worker argue with trite assurances that money is the root of all evil . . . you can't buy happiness with money . . . God loves the poor people. I had no idea whether these were also trite expressions in Italian. But they caused the group to laugh and, after laughing, to accept my hypothesis that in an evaluation of casework words sometimes speak louder than actions.

After the psycho-drama the group moved along smoothly for a while. But not so smoothly that I didn't repeatedly have to prove my points to this roomful of doubting Thomases.

Mostly the language behaved well for me. When it didn't, I sought Italia's eyes across the room to get her help. I discovered that she was unwilling to give it. I studied her averted face, the others in the room, and finally Signorina Nino on my right. That was it! Signorina Nino, Italia's boss, was chairman of the seminar. Italia was not going to take her role away from her. Poor me! Signorina's Italian was not as clear as Italia's.

This was a good group to work with. I contrasted them to the group at the New Roman School and found the difference quickly. These were practicing social workers who were going to try some of my ideas tomorrow and the next day. Their questions were "How do you make it work?" "What do you do next?"—the practical questions that social work asks so well. Last month's group had been supervisors and teachers who wanted theoretical concepts: "How do you explain role playing in relation to the Freudian concept of emotional development?" Social workers need both kinds of answers and I enjoy trying both kinds, but my heart is always closer to the social worker's questions than to the educator's.

We had run fifteen minutes past the end of the hour that first day when Signorina Nino raised her hand and said, "We must not be fooled by Signora Charnley's apparent ease and comfort with our language. She gives these lectures with great mental exertion so that her problem of fatigue is a serious one. Now she must rest for tomorrow."

Fatigued? I skimmed down the steps from the agency to Mitch and the kids waiting in the car as lighthearted and pleased as a teen-ager going to a date with her favorite boy. It was as though

I had been lecturing in America to a group of friends who, if they had challenged me, had also left me with assurance of accomplishment at the end.

The next day's lecture, which was to correspond to the one I had given to the other group on "use of time," needed extensive changes. After some thought, I rewrote it completely. I had to present convincingly a lot of important concepts: how to schedule interviews, how to time them, how to regulate a week's activity so that a social worker could see clients in their homes, see doctors and teachers, and still manage to get recording done. Also important was planning for at least an hour of supervision a week. This was the idea that more than any other I wanted this group to accept. How to do it? I had not forgotten their defensiveness yesterday about the Giobbe case.

So I began my lecture like this: "Today I am going to tell you as much as I possibly can about what it's like to work in an American agency." I described my own agency, Family and Children's Service in Minneapolis. I told them what the building and our offices looked like, how we used our secretaries, our telephones, our dictaphones. I told them about our hours, our salaries, our coffee breaks, our use of supervision. I described the client who comes to the office for the first time and the client who is coming for his thirty-third weekly interview. I talked about our concern with doing a good job, how fast we worked, how we kept a statistical count of what we were achieving. I described our problem of three years before when we discovered that we were below national norms in monthly client interviews completed and how each caseworker worked with her supervisor to find a way to become more efficient. I told of the deep satisfaction of the workers in finding their contributions to clients twice as great after they had altered work patterns. By presenting some of my audience's shortcomings as problems that my American agency had met and solved, I was able to let these Italian social workers look at themselves and discover that, just as much as American social workers, they wanted to do their jobs well and efficiently.

Some aspects of American social work practice seemed unbelievable to them. They were fascinated that a worker could welcome a weekly hour of supervision after years of work in an agency. And they were amazed and delighted at the way social work is valued by clients in America as illustrated by long waiting lists and — wonder of wonders! — their willingness to pay fees week after week for the privilege of receiving counseling.

I liked the looks I read on the faces around the room. These workers were daring to look realistically at their work and compare it honestly with that of their SANC colleagues in Milan, Turin, and Naples. They were getting ready to trust themselves in a supervisory relationship that I had said could help a worker to make such strides. They were psychologically ready to start. I wanted to seek out the expression in the lovely olive eyes of Italia, but I didn't dare.

At the end of this day Italia and I walked out together and she said, "Today you made a little platform under the agency. It is something we can all stand on. We can start to build from it. Like a house in Venice. Before today we were all standing with our feet in the water."

On Wednesday, I gave my last lecture. I used it to talk about how to begin to find foster homes and how to help parents, children, and their communities to accept this new approach. La homefinder and la placement worker fairly pummeled me with sharp, clear questions. Others took up their mood and manner and I felt as though I had gone from Minnesota to talk with placement workers in a neighboring state.

Italia asked the best question of all. "Do you know the community of Alatri?" I was happy to be able to say that I had visited it last Sunday.

"What would you think, signora, of developing another community near Rome like this — but instead of having balias, let it become known as 'the village of foster parents'?"

My mind spun backwards. In the *Saturday Evening Post* I had read of a city that was full of "halfway houses" for the convalescent mentally ill who needed a protected environment as they moved back to the reality of homes, families, and jobs. I remembered my first years in social work, when our homefinder, in a charming bit of a town — Nowthen, Minnesota, with a population of about twenty-five families — persuaded five of them to act as foster families.

I thought of the Roman social workers' problem: how to educate all of Rome in this new approach to child care.

"Oh, yes," I responded eagerly. "It is a miraculous idea. And when you have it in working order, always remember that this was your idea, not mine. This is how it must be with child placement at SANC. Just at first you may say, 'I remember, Signora Charnley said . . .' But after a bit you must forget all this and find your own ideas and create your own foster placement program. It will be really right because it will spring from what you have thought and felt, and will not be a mere copy of something an American once talked about."

My last lecture was ended. These social workers — my social workers, from my own agency — got to their feet and clapped and made pretty speeches and put into my arms a bunch of coral gladioli so large that I staggered under it. Then, seeing that I couldn't manage the flowers and my other things too, they carried the glads down the stairs and helped me into the car with many warm messages of farewell and thanks, and much urging that I hurry back to Rome. Maria, Sofia, Alta, Signorina Nino, and dear Italia were the last to whom I said good-by. When it came to Italia, we both found tears in our eyes. I wanted very much to embrace her, but my well-bred American reticence prevented me. She had some similar impulse, I know. Couldn't I always understand her unspoken words? I think I did then — that she decided I was still a little too American for demonstrativeness.

I climbed into the car half covered with flowers and off we drove through the Roman sunset. The pain of farewell was struggling against a happy triumph: "I really did it. I really gave those wonderful people some tools to help Italian children!"

Then I had a shocking thought. These were the workers I had only three months ago rejected as lazy and unmotivated.

"Oh, forgive me," I prayed.

INDEX

Index

Many of the names of places and people in this index, consistent with the plan of the book, are disguised.